The Smart Marketer's Toolbox

Eric Schulz

Copyright © 2012 Eric D Schulz

All rights reserved.

★★★★★★★

THE SMART MARKETER'S TOOLBOX

DEDICATION

This book is dedicated to those students who show up every day for class with a desire to learn and make the most of their college experience. It is a pleasure sharing my experience with you, and I hope the insights and knowledge I am able to offer will help you in your life and career.

CONTENTS

Section One: MARKETING STRATEGY

1. Marketing Overview — Page 8
2. Consumer & Marketplace Insight — Page 22
3. Mission Statements & Operating Charters — Page 38

Section Two: PRODUCT STRATEGY

4. Developing A Brand — Page 52
5. Brand Positioning — Page 60
6. Product Innovation — Page 74

Section Three: PRICING STRATEGY

7: Pricing Strategies — Page 104
8: Life Currencies — Page 124

Section Four: PLACEMENT STRATEGY

9. Powerful Packaging — Page 136
10. Distribution & Merchandising — Page 152
11. Product Mix — Page 166

Section Five: PROMOTION STRATEGY

12. Advertising   Page 182

13. Website and Search Engine Optimization   Page 206

14. Social Media   Page 220

15. Trade Promotions   Page 230

16. Consumer Promotions   Page 248

17. Public Relations   Page 270

18. Partnerships & Alliances   Page 282

19. Sports Sponsorships & Special Events   Page 296

20. Licensing   Page 322

BONUS CHAPTER

21. Effective Job Interviewing Skills   Page 336

Section 1:

Marketing Strategy

Eric D Schulz

Chapter One

<u>Marketing Overview</u>

Imagine for a moment that you are at a friends' home for a party, and to your amazement, in walks Elton John. After some brief introductions, he meanders over to the piano, sits down and starts playing a medley of his hits – an impromptu private concert. He doesn't sing. He just plays the piano. Classics like *Your Song, Rocket Man, Tiny Dancer, Bennie & the Jets, Goodbye Yellow Brick Road, Can You Feel the Love Tonight*, and many, many more. You listen, absolutely amazed at the pureness of the sound coming from the instrument, the crispness of the notes, the flawless execution as he strokes the keys in just the right way, at just the right times, making the piano sing like an angel's voice from heaven. You realize just what a unique and special talent Elton possesses in his ability at playing the piano and creating unique and memorable songs that stand the test of time.

Now, imagine this party in a very different way. Instead of Elton John taking to the keyboard, it is the hosts' 3 year-old son. He sits down and starts banging the keys, creating nothing but noise and utter annoyance -- this coming from this very same instrument that in the hands of Elton was made to sing like an angel. It is the same instrument, in different hands, with complete opposite outcomes. *Please, make him stop!*

Effective marketing campaigns are the handiwork of skilled and trained marketing professionals, not unlike Elton John playing the piano. Created in the hands of marketing pro, campaigns can be joyous and wondrous – they engage the customer, showcase products and services in relevant yet unexpected ways, and communicate how different, better, and special they are versus the competition. They delight and drive the customer to purchase their products.

The strategies and skills used to develop these marketing plans – created in just the right way, and executed at just the right times -- are learned through the training received from a skilled marketing teacher and mentor, then built upon by individual practice that can only be gained over time and through experience.

Many business professionals and small business owners – despite having no formal marketing education - believe they possess the skills to build and execute their own marketing programs. They underestimate the knowledge required to develop effective marketing plans. And, just like the 3 year-old on the piano, they end up making nothing but noise, annoying and potentially driving away potential customers, creating nothing of value and in fact, wasting both time and resources.

Created By A Working Marketing Professional

This book is designed to give you the tools and knowledge to effectively brand, build and execute marketing plans for businesses, products and services. The skills and strategies you will learn are applicable across the spectrum of businesses – from large consumer product brands to small mom-and-pops; from insurance agents to dentists; and from home designers to web-based businesses. It has been developed by Eric D. Schulz, a 25-year marketing professional who has spent a career leading marketing efforts for some of the world's best marketing companies – Procter & Gamble, Disney, Coca-Cola, and others.

At Coca-Cola, I developed and executed the world's most expansive and expensive marketing program, the company's sponsorship of the 1996 Summer Olympic Games in Atlanta, Georgia. The plan was executed in 152 countries around the world, at a cost exceeding $450 million dollars. Despite the hefty price tag, the campaign increased global sales volume by 9%, global profits by 22%, and Coke's stock price jumped 32% over the nine-month period leading up to the Games when my plans were being executed.

Many of the products you have in your home have had my hands guiding their success. I was the inventor of the spout on your orange juice carton; at Disney I created the "Direct-to-Video" movie category that generates almost a half-billion dollars annually for my beloved *Mouseketeers*. I have marketed household beverage staples including Folgers coffee, Hawaiian Punch, Coca-Cola, Sprite, PowerAde, and Minute Maid. I've consulted for eBay & PayPal, and marketed businesses across the spectrum of entertainment, including Ringling Bros. & Barnum and Bailey Circus, Disney On Ice, the Utah Jazz of the NBA, local television & radio stations, and a movie theatre chain. I worked with NBC and World Wrestling Entertainment to launch the XFL Football League, and have experience in the non-profit space with Special Olympics and the Utah Governor's Committee for the Employment of People with Disabilities. I've consulted with businesses large and small from Time-Warner and On-Demand to InCharge Debt Solutions, Perfetti Van Melle confectionary brands, and even Islandz Caribbytes, a small startup in the Bahamas selling unique tourist memorabilia. I even created and launched a prototype preschool for franchising, and developed the introductory marketing plans for a unique kitchen gadget called "The Shrimp Butler".

Through this wide and varied pool of experiences, I have brought together for this book the best practices and strategies that have been proven over time to be the most effective at generating customer interest and sales. The objective of this book is simple: to provide you with the tools and expertise to effectively brand your products and services, then build and execute marketing plans, tilting the table in your favor to sell more products using less time, money and effort.

Tactics Change – Strategies Do Not

While the *tactics* used to execute marketing plans constantly evolve – for example, the emerging opportunities with social media and mobile Smartphone marketing are new marketing tools still evolving – the *strategies* that lead to successful marketing plans have remained surprisingly consistent over time. This book will teach you the strategies that have been proven effective at generating customer excitement and sales, using contemporary tactics as vehicles for successful delivery – knowing that these will certainly change as time goes by and more effective tactics and new opportunities emerge.

Futurists say that as a rule of thumb, 60% of the jobs that will be available 10 years from now haven't been invented yet. With that in mind, it becomes all the more important for future marketers to steep themselves in knowing effective strategies, as the evolution of business and technology and the unseen and unknown opportunities of the future will certainly affect how we market our products and services.

The tool box that marketers use is fairly easy to compartmentalize:

Branding & Strategy

- Message Development
- Research Primary / Secondary
- Brand Strategy
- Brand Positioning
- Brand Personality

Marketing & Communications

- Communication Strategy
- Integrated Marketing Plans
- Traditional Offline / Online Advertising & Promotions
- Web Design and Development
- Environmental Consciousness
- Packaging

Social Media

- Campaigns - Promotions/Contests
- Tracking

Web Marketing

- Search Engine Optimization (SEO)
- Search Engine Marketing (PPC, Banners, Linking)
- Blog Marketing Optimization
- Social Media Optimization

Think about each of these as keys of the piano. Great marketers need training to learn which keys to push, at just the right moment, to maximize their effectiveness and how to blend them together to act in synergy with the other keys to create harmonious marketing programs that are all singing together from the same hymnal.

What Marketer's Do

Great marketers perform four essential tasks for their business:

1) They create a strategic, actionable plan to guide the branding, marketing and communications of their products and services;

2) They identify the essence of their brand story – and how to tell it with passion;

3) They develop and foster interaction with their customers wherever they are;

4) They use creative ideas to build marketing plans to grow long-term profits.

A few timeless principles guide them on this quest:

Know where you are going.

You can't tell your story without a solid plan. And you can't get somewhere new without knowing where to go. Strategy is like a map for marketing - without it, you'll most likely end up lost (or even worse, losing out on business.) Marketers take the time to understand their company and business objectives and identify clear marketing goals. They align those goals with a strategic plan that takes their business exactly where they want it to go, without getting lost along the way.

Tell your brand story with passion.

Your brand isn't your packaging or a tagline. It's more than just delivering a message from company to consumer; your brand is a story told by one human being to another. An enduring, consistent story can build an on-going relationship—and pull people to you like nothing else can. These people become advocates for your brand. And as they share your story with others, they also become your most powerful marketing tool.

Interact with people wherever they are.

Now that you have a story, how will you get people to listen to it? Your story needs to follow people wherever they go—from train stations to Twitter, from cell phones to Facebook, from billboards to blogs. In today's world, technology is the force around which all marketing orbits. Marketers use all these tools to talk <u>with</u> people (never at them) on every possible level. And they use metrics to measure those conversations, so that we can discover exactly what kind of impact they're having.

Make creativity profitable.

Can creative thinking really boost a company's bottom line? Can captivating storytelling actually move products off shelves? Absolutely. In fact, it can create a lifelong relationship with your brand. With formulaic marketing, you might boost short-term revenue. But with creative thinking and a truly relevant product, you build long-term profitability. That's why top marketers know that every dollar spent must tie to the strategy, story and technology that grows their brand—and helps their company thrive.

Telling Your Brand Story

Simply put, a brand is a story. It places images, thoughts and emotions within the mind and heart of employees, partners, current and potential customers.

Inspiring and memorable stories are comprised of words and images placed in a profound and sometimes complex order, yet still conveying a simple message.

The words, images and elements of a compelling brand story attach themselves to an individual's psyche and a culture's mores. Two contemporary branding campaigns that have effectively done this are Corona Beer's "Find Your Beach", and Dos-Equios 'The World's Most Interesting Man". They have effectively created "hall-talk" about their campaigns, while crafting sustainable competitive advantage through storytelling that defines their brands as different, better, and special in the minds of consumers, carving out niches completely unique from other beers.

A brand transcends beyond the product or service that it offers. **A brand is not what you make – it's what you make possible.**

The Brand Development Process

Brands are developed through careful planning and strategy. A successful brand requires years to develop and must be managed with consistent execution. This text uses the blueprints of the proven brand management process developed and perfected by the Procter & Gamble Company brands over the past fifty years, which has set the standard in the industry for branding and marketing excellence.

Brand Components Overview

A brand story is a platform from which recognition, loyalty and revenue is driven. A brand is comprised of two core components: message structure and visual attributes. These two components must have a symbiotic and consistent relationship to maximize marketing expenditures. Great marketers will translate their brand into an integrated communications program by utilizing this approach.

Brand strategies are not created overnight. In fact, it usually takes months of research and strategy discussion in order to define the foundational brand strategy. The process starts with research among consumers and the marketplace, which leads to developing a differentiated brand positioning strategy. This leads to developing the brand voice, visual identity, marketing strategies and plans, and ultimately, the execution of your marketing plans:

The Technology Revolution

Marketing Truth

The strategies proven over time to convince consumers to buy your products have not changed. The tools and tactics we can use as marketers to most effectively and efficiently reach consumers <u>have</u> changed dramatically and will continue to change over time.

It wasn't that long ago that "social network" was the term that described a group of ladies who get together at church to knit quilts on Saturday mornings. Senior marketers remember when there were only three television networks, and "appointment viewing" was Thursday nights at 8 p.m. to watch *"The Cosby Show"* on NBC. The most technologically advanced piece of home electronics was a VCR, with a flashing "12:00" on the face because most adults were too intimidated to program it.

Now social networks mean Facebook, Google+, LinkedIn, Twitter and countless affinity groups. Cable and satellite providers have diluted the effectiveness of TV advertising, bringing up to 200 channels into homes, specialized into everything from sports to history to home improvement, which can be of help in some cases if you're selling to a very specific audience, but a detriment to reaching consumers far and wide. Mobile phones are now complete entertainment devices, with the ability to stream TV, hold your music library, access your email, and give you turn-by-turn driving directions. DVR's have replaced VCR's, and appointment viewing is a thing of the past. Consumers record their favorite shows on their DVR's and watch them later, so they can skip through all the commercials (a very bad thing for marketers). About the only television programs being watched when they are being broadcast live are news and sports. Miss your favorite program or accidentally erase it? No problem. Just watch it at your convenience on your computer via streaming video on the web or your cell phone.

Advertising to youth has changed the most radically. Kids use the TV more to play games on their *PlayStation, Xbox* and *Wii* than to watch programs. They don't listen to the radio; they get their music from an iPod. They don't read the newspaper or magazines; they browse the Internet, use widgets or subscribe to RSS feeds for the things that interest them. The traditional media channels that have been used for decades to advertise to youth are becoming less and less effective.

Marketing Truth

A wise man once told me "it's not what you CAN do, it's what you SHOULD do". The question you need to ask is "Does this FIT with my brand strategy and drive the sales needle?"

Can vs. Should

Three or four times each week, a salesman comes into my office to show me his latest and greatest marketing tool. Most are technology driven, such as location based Bluetooth or GPS texting; "smart" database systems; and innovative Internet technologies. One gentleman came in to show me how I could upload a scanned photo of myself to his website, and his company could insert my face over the top of the actor's face in any commercial, and my eyes, mouth movements, and expressions would all look exactly like I was in the commercial. Cool, but what do I do with it? How will it help me sell my products?

Marketing today isn't just about initiating an email blast to your database, texting them, "tweeting" them, or creating a really cool mobile app. While those are tactics that CAN be used, they need to fit within a strategic plan that drives product sales. Just creating a great looking website the ad agency has convinced you to make "sticky" so that consumers come and linger doesn't necessarily translate into improved product sales or even increased brand affinity.

In 2008 Taco Bell created the most incredible website I've ever seen in conjunction with Sports Illustrated annual swimsuit edition. It allowed you to be a virtual Sports Illustrated swimsuit photographer with supermodel Daniella Sarahyba. You could virtually move around with a camera and click photos of Daniella, then print them out on your home printer. All the while, Daniella was chatting with you, just as if you were there. Awesome! Fun! Sticky? Absolutely. I played virtual photographer about twenty times. But did it make me go to Taco Bell to buy my lunch? No it didn't. Did it positively affect my brand image of Taco Bell? No again.

SMS Texting

American Idol made SMS text-voting the vogue, and it makes perfect sense for that program to use texting as their platform. But does it make sense for *Ford Motor Company* to send you text messages to try and sell you a car? No. Does it make sense for Ford to rip off the Daniella technology to create virtual test drives on the web? Absolutely! Should a sports team offer real-time score and team news / injury updates via SMS text to their fans? Yes. Do you want your local grocery store sending you text messages promoting their sale this week on *Fruit Loops*? Probably not. But would you like to go to your grocer's website and note the products you would like to get text alerts for if they come on sale? You might!

Barack Obama embraced SMS texting in his successful 2008 campaign for U.S. President, having voters register their cell phone numbers in order to get the first word on his selection for Vice President. Over 10 million Americans signed up – primarily young voters, who historically have been hard-to-reach for politicians through traditional media channels -- which gave Barack a platform of 10 million young, tech-savvy voters with whom he could then communicate directly in the two months leading up to the election. Here are just a few examples of things the Obama campaign did with these phone numbers:

- Raised funds by asking for donations.
- Conducted surveys (e.g. are you registered to vote yet? what zip code are you in?)
- On a state-by-state basis, sent reminder messages about the cutoff dates for voter registration and link to registration forms
- On a state-by-state basis, told people to mail in their ballots to vote absentee
- Invited people to campaign events in their area code
- Reminded people to get out and vote on Election Day
- Promoted other Democratic party candidates on a zip code-by-zip code basis

Barack is still embracing text messaging in his presidency, soliciting new sign ups on the White House home page, building an ever-growing network of voters with whom he can directly communicate. He's also embracing YouTube as a means of posting his weekly "chat" with Americans, a great way to give unfiltered information to the public, and a very smart way to use the tools of the technology revolution effectively. Several times during his presidency, he has sent email messages direct to his database urging supporters to contact their Congressmen to help push through a piece of important legislation, creating a ground-swell of support that couldn't be ignored by the partisan Republican Congress.

What you CAN do, and what you SHOULD do in a marketing campaign, is very different. Too often young marketing managers get caught up in the CAN do – what CAN we do with Twitter, Facebook, Google+, SMS Texting, Plaxo, LinkedIn, email marketing; mobile apps, widgets, RSS feeds or building micro-sites -- because it seems more exciting, cutting edge, and innovative to hurl themselves into this world of evolving technology.

Doing the SHOULD do's – brand positioning, websites, packaging, traditional advertising, point-of-sale materials -- seem old school and boring. The truth lies in between. Successful marketers need to keep a keen eye on all the possibilities presented by things they CAN do with new revolutions in technology, media and hardware, and integrate it if it makes sense into the plan of what they SHOULD do. The fundamental strategies of marketing...the SHOULD Do's haven't changed. The ways we CAN execute them have.

Learn From Successful Companies

The best way to learn is to keep an eye on how successful companies execute their marketing. I have been fortunate in my career to work for three of the top consumer marketing companies in the world: *Procter & Gamble*, *The Walt Disney Company*, and *The Coca-Cola Company*. These titans have all stood the test of time in proving how to effectively build a strategic plan for effectively marketing their wares to consumers. Having lived in all three environments, I've been able to assimilate the similarities and strengths each created in its brand management and marketing to share with you the best practices. But we also need to keep a keen eye out for the new. What's Google up to? What's Apple doing next? What are the movie studios doing differently in their marketing? We need to keep an eye on the innovators to see what possibilities are opening up that we can leverage as marketers.

Only one thing is assured: Everything changes. The world is not static. Stand still, and you'll get run-over. We have to keep moving, maintain a healthy dissatisfaction for the status quo, and always seek better avenues and methods for effectively communicating with consumers and generating sales. In this text, I'll share with you ideas on how to effectively combine the innovations of the technological revolution with the fundamental marketing truths of the world's best consumer product companies to build your marketing acumen and effectiveness.

The work is executed in five areas:

1) **Strategy**

Before you can enter the race, you have to design your racer. This section will address the mindset you must first have in order to be an effective marketer, and things you must do in order to effectively build a marketing plan --- understand your customer and the market through research and insights; defining your mission; and creating your operating charter. Defining your brand and your brand strategy.

2) **Products**

Once you understand your consumer, how do you effectively create a brand that becomes preferred by customers, and stands out from the crowd as being different, better, and special? How do you craft a brand positioning, and how do you create new products or services?

3) **Pricing**

There are dozens of strategies for pricing. How do you choose the right one for you? Sometimes it's not about money at all. In this section, we'll discuss traditional pricing and loss leaders to premium pricing. We'll also discuss different currencies that consumer use to make purchases – life currencies.

4) **Placement**

Your packaging, how you display the product, where it is sold – all have profound effects on sales. This section will cover powerful packaging ideas, merchandising and distribution strategies, and how to create the perfect product mix.

5) **Promotion**

The most vital piece of marketing is promoting your product. It can take place in many forms, from social media to advertising to special events and sampling. We'll walk through all the possibilities and give you some great ideas for cheaply and effectively creating long-term effects from short-term promotions.

One last thing and we'll get on with it. These principles, strategies and tactics are a lot like my favorite song by *The Eagles* -- *"Hotel California"*. The lyrics say:

> *"You can check out any time you like, but you can never leave."*

Once you enter the marketing world through these doors, I believe you will find the way you think about marketing and your own personal shopping experiences will be changed forever. Enjoy the journey.

Eric D Schulz

Chapter Two

Consumer and Marketplace Insight

I wish I had a dime for every time someone called me up, bursting with excitement over some brilliant new product idea they just had. Inspiration strikes in some strange and wonderful places; washing the dog, looking for car keys, flipping the remote. The thought emerges, "Gee, I wish someone would invent something to make my dog smell better, or find my keys, or keep my remote handy." Presto, the idea is hatched, and the product begins to take shape.

Sometimes the ideas are pretty good, and often the inventor has already dreamed up a catchy name, like "Smooch Your Pooch Sweet Smelling Shampoo." But marketing a successful product should never begin with a focus group of one. The problem with many of these homegrown inventions is the inventor becomes so intoxicated with his idea that he starts building momentum before he tests the concept. He violates the most important rule of the marketing game: Honor Thy Consumer.

Everything in marketing begins and ends with the consumer. Before you can sell your product -- before you even develop a product -- you must understand what the consumer wants and design your offering to meet his or her needs. *You* may want a dog that smells like the Rose Queen, but do other consumers share your desire -- and will they pay for it? If your product concept is on the mark, then your job is simply finding the best way to communicate that you've got the goods consumers want. It's a basic concept: <u>you can't create a need that isn't there, and you can't argue consumers out of what they want.</u>

Standard Research Methods

Marketing research is the systematic gathering, recording, and analysis of data about issues relating to marketing products and services. The task of market research is to provide management with relevant, accurate, reliable, valid, and current information. The ever-changing competitive environment and the ever-increasing costs attributed to poor decision making require that market research provide sound information. Sound decisions are not based on gut feeling, intuition, or even pure judgment.

Market research is:

Systematic: Systematic planning is required at all the stages of the marketing research process. The procedures followed at each stage are methodologically sound, well documented, and, as much as possible, planned in advance. Marketing research uses the scientific method in that data are collected and analyzed to test prior notions or hypotheses.

Objective: It attempts to provide accurate information that reflects a true state of affairs. It should be conducted impartially. The objective nature of marketing research underscores the importance of ethical considerations.

Marketing research techniques come in many forms, including:

- **Ad Tracking**: periodic or continuous in-market research to monitor a brand's performance using measures such as brand awareness, brand preference, and product usage.

- **Advertising Research** - used to predict copy testing or track the efficacy of advertisements for any medium, measured by the ad's ability to get attention (measured with Attention Tracking), communicate the message, build the brand's image, and motivate the consumer to purchase the product or service.

- **Copy testing** - predicts in-market performance of an ad before it airs by analyzing audience levels of attention, brand linkage, motivation, entertainment, and communication, as well as breaking down the ad's flow of attention and flow of emotion.

- **Brand equity research** - how favorably do consumers view the brand?

- **Brand association research** - what do consumers associate with the brand?

- **Brand attribute research** - what are the key traits that describe the brand promise?

- **Brand name testing** - what do consumers feel about the names of the products?

- **Commercial eye tracking research** - examine advertisements, package designs, websites, etc. by analyzing visual behavior of the consumer.

- **Concept testing** - to test the acceptance of a new idea by target consumers.

- **Trend-Hunting** - to make observations and predictions in changes of new or existing cultural trends in areas such as fashion, music, films, television, youth culture and lifestyle.

- **Buyer decision processes research** - to determine what motivates people to buy and what decision-making process they use.

- **Customer satisfaction research** - quantitative or qualitative studies that yields an understanding of a customer's satisfaction with a transaction or interaction with that brand.

- **Demand estimation** – used to determine the approximate level of demand for the product.

- **Distribution channel audits** - to assess distributors' and retailers' attitudes toward a product, brand, or company.

- **Focus Groups** – which gather together a group of customers in a room and discuss marketing / marketplace issues.

- **In-home testing** – going into customer's homes to eavesdrop on their usage of a product.

- **Internet strategic intelligence** - searching for customer opinions in the Internet: chats, forums, web pages, blogs... where people express freely about their experiences with products, becoming strong opinion formers.

- **Mall Intercept research** – many malls are equipped with small testing facilities to catch customers during shopping experiences for a few moments and test new products or concepts on them.

- **Marketing effectiveness and analytics** - Building models and measuring results to determine the effectiveness of individual marketing activities.

- **Mystery shopping / mystery consumer** - An employee or representative of the market research firm anonymously contacts a salesperson and indicates he or she is shopping for a product. The shopper then records the entire experience. This method is often used for quality control or for researching competitors' products.

- **Brand positioning research** - how does the target market perceive the brand relative to competitors? - What does the brand stand for?

- **Price elasticity testing** - to determine how sensitive customers are to price changes.

- **Sales forecasting** - to determine the expected level of sales given the level of demand. With respect to other factors like advertising expenditure, sales promotion etc.

- **Segmentation research** - to determine the demographic, psychographic, and behavioral characteristics of potential buyers.

- **Surveys** – phone, Internet, or in-person surveys are designed to develop quantitative, projectable data.

- **Online panel** - a group of individual who accepted to respond to marketing research online.

- **Store audit** - to measure the sales of a product or product line at a statistically selected store sample in order to determine market share, or to determine whether a retail store provides adequate service.

- **Test marketing** - a small-scale product launch used to determine the likely acceptance of the product when it is introduced into a wider market.

- **Viral marketing research** - refers to marketing research designed to estimate the probability that specific communications will be transmitted throughout an individual's social network.

All of these forms of marketing research can be classified as either problem-identification research or as problem-solving research.

There are two main sources of data - primary and secondary. Primary research is conducted from scratch. It is original and collected to solve the problem in hand. Secondary research already exists since it has been collected for other purposes. It is conducted on data published previously and usually by someone else. Secondary research costs far less than primary research, but seldom comes in a form that exactly meets the needs of the researcher.

A similar distinction exists between exploratory research and conclusive research. Exploratory research provides insights into and comprehension of an issue or situation. It should draw definitive conclusions only with extreme caution. Conclusive research draws conclusions: the results of the study can be generalized to the whole population.

Marketing research uses the following types of design:

- **Qualitative research** - generally used for exploratory purposes - small number of respondents - not generalizable to the whole population - statistical significance and confidence not calculated - examples include focus groups, in-depth interviews.

- **Quantitative research** - generally used to draw conclusions - tests a specific idea - uses random sampling techniques so as to infer from the sample to the population - involves a large number of respondents - examples include surveys and questionnaires.

Consumer is Key

Knowing that the consumer is at the heart of every marketing decision, researchers have invented ingenious techniques to get in tune with the consumer. Consumers have been ambushed, bar coded, spied upon and even hypnotized in the quest for information. Companies pour millions of dollars into research every year to help them understand what consumers are thinking and how the marketplace is changing.

But here is the big question: if you are looking at the same studies and doing the same types of research as your key competition, how is it possible that you will gain insights different – and better – than theirs? The answer: you can't.

Creating Intellectual Competitive Advantage

Top companies understand this fact, and force their marketing personnel to go farther than standard research methodologies to gain broader and deeper consumer understanding. This is where they create competitive advantage. They teach their marketers how to beat competition at the consumer learning game, where all good marketing begins.

So how do the top companies get better information than the competition? By spending millions, right? Wrong.

Marketing Truth

Top marketing companies teach their marketing personnel to gain strategic consumer insight through everyday life...watching TV commercials, browsing in stores, and talking with friends and family.

It sounds too ordinary to be true, doesn't it? Paying attention in everyday life is nowhere near as exciting as launching a half-million dollar research project, complete with one-way mirrors and hidden video. But don't be fooled by the trappings of research. Top companies know the best way to gain real world experience is in the real world, and they've made a science of it.

The Discipline of Observational Learning

At Procter & Gamble, the company rule is if you travel to another city, for business or pleasure, you are required to visit at least three stores that carry your brands and competitive brands. You walk in, look around, analyze the situation, and submit a report of those visits upon your return. Why? One reason is to try to pick up any competitive activities or test-market products that may have been slipped into a market, but the primary purpose is to teach the discipline of in-store walk-around learning. There isn't much to inspire new thinking in the typical office cubicle, but a store is filled with a wealth of stimulation to help you develop wonderful new ideas.

P&G isn't the only company that thinks this way. Coca-Cola regularly hosts a marketing summit that gathers all 2,000 of the worldwide Coke marketing personnel. The summit is three days of workshops, discussions and lectures designed to teach the marketing team how to be better marketers. How much of the meeting is spent talking about Coca–Cola and soft drinks? None. The entire three days are dedicated to analyzing other industries and other product categories!

At one summit, David Stern, the Commissioner of the NBA, gave a talk about the transformation of the league from the 1970's to the present. James Carville and Mary Matalin discussed presidential political campaign strategy. A rocket-propulsion engineer gave a speech on the evolution of the jet engine. The group then broke into teams and developed a marketing plan for the city of West Palm Beach, Florida.

Not one minute was spent talking about Coca-Cola or any other soft drinks. Why? Because you need to stimulate your mind with information and marketing strategies from other walks of life if you are going to develop breakthrough ideas. You will not develop revolutionary thoughts sitting around conference tables staring at your peers and your own products. You must vigorously pursue new stimulation and learning from sources far and wide, and then relate the learning's and make connections back to your business.

Idea Cross-Pollination From Other Product Categories

When I worked at Walt Disney Home Video, I taught the real-world observation habit to my brand team. Every Friday for lunch I would pile them into my car and we'd drive to several stores to look around -- not to shop, but to learn. We'd drop by the video departments and investigate new products, wander over into the toy and book areas and then to other parts of the store to see how different companies were marketing their wares.

We'd pick a different product category every week and go study it -- detergents, deodorants, soup, motor oil, frozen foods -- it didn't matter what the category was. We'd talk about the brand offerings, hypothesizing about the strategic insights that might have led to product development, their packaging, and different line extensions. We'd analyze which brands were doing it right and which were lagging. By performing this exercise on a weekly basis, we were forced to think strategically and stay alert about what was happening in a variety of different businesses. This information cross-pollinated our thinking and helped us recognize opportunities we otherwise would have missed.

For example, one Friday afternoon we found ourselves in the toy department at a Kmart store during a huge sale of Disney plush toys. Consumers were buying the toys by the armful. We noticed that no Winnie the Pooh characters were available. Several consumers were asking the store clerks if the Pooh's were sold out. When we returned to the office we made a few calls to our friends in Disney Consumer Products and discovered that there was no Winnie the Pooh plush toys available to the Kmart store, because Sears held an exclusive 25-year license on Pooh merchandise. We also discovered that this license was expiring in just a few months and would not be renewed.

That afternoon we began dreaming up an idea for our Winnie the Pooh videos. On the day that the Sears license expired, we launched a nationwide Pooh video and plush promotion, packaging the videos and Pooh plush characters together. They sold like hotcakes. All four sku's turned up on the Top 10 Video Bestseller list. In just three weeks, we sold 20 times more Winnie the Pooh videos than we had in the previous 12 months. By being aware of an unmet consumer need in a completely different product category (plush toys), we were able to produce huge profits for our video division.

Insight Requires Correct Interpretation

An important thing to remember is that consumer insight is only as good as its interpretation. How many times have you walked out of a meeting with a group of people and then had an argument over what was said? Everyone heard the same conversation, yet many came away with a different point of view; "I thought so and so said this" or "I thought so and so said that".

The same dynamic is true in the art of interpreting consumer insight. Your research probably won't produce a clear, single message, shining like a beacon from the heavens to guide your way. Much of what you learn will be open to interpretation, and many different interpretations may be legitimate. Your challenge is to resist the "Eureka!" impulse of latching on to one message (usually the one you *want* to believe) and ignoring the other, possibly contradictory, bits of information. It is important to keep an open mind and consider the information from many different viewpoints to try and understand the full spectrum of what you have heard or seen. The more open you are, the better you will be at making connections between your observations and your business.

I remember a story about a coffee category study at Procter & Gamble that revealed a new trend of sit-down coffeehouses developing in the Seattle area. That "trend" is now a huge global chain called Starbucks. The Folgers brand people looking at the information concluded that Folgers business was selling coffee in grocery stores, so they dismissed these boutique coffee houses as non-competitive. What do you suppose that "non-competitive threat" has done to Folgers volume over the last twenty years now that the Starbucks chain has over 17,000 stores in 55 countries and which spawned a new line of grocery store coffee?

And the Humble Shall Inherit the Knowledge

Many marketers have a tremendous arrogance about themselves and their brands. They somehow believe that they are smarter than everybody else and that the people working for their competition are bozos. They mistakenly think that analyzing competition can offer very little insight about how they can be better marketers.

To the contrary, the smartest thing you can do is to learn everything you can about competition and the product category in which you compete. You need to know what product benefits are driving consumers. And if you *are* a genius, your research will only confirm that fact.

Marketing Truth

> *Top marketing companies have adopted a new mental model about consumer understanding to breakthrough the status quo and advance to a higher plane of consumer insight. This new mental model is called "Knowledge Mining".*

Knowledge Mining is an in-store learning exercise to develop profound understanding about what steers consumer purchase decisions within a product category. It analyzes the different product attributes and consumer benefits offered throughout the category and helps marketers define the qualities that lead to purchase. Just as important, it reveals which product benefits are least associated with product purchase in the category.

Through the Knowledge Mining exercise, this in-store learning becomes a strategic road map that paints a clear picture of the consumer's psychological landscape. What is he or she responding to? What benefits or attributes tempt a consumer to pick up the product and put it in their shopping cart? Why are so many products in the same category ignored?

Naturally, if you understand the benefits and product attributes that drive purchase within your category, you've taken a quantum leap in understanding your consumer. Unfortunately, very few marketers have this depth of insight. Most just jump into the fray and start concocting as many marketing efforts as the budget will bear -- coupons, price reductions, advertising, promotions. They perform what I call random acts of marketing, trying this, trying that, never really learning much along the bumpy way. They have no clear strategic knowledge or vision to guide them, because they don't really know <u>for sure</u> why consumers buy their product or competing products.

How To Do A Knowledge Mining In-Store Exercise

Doing an in-store knowledge mining exercise is easy. Pick a product CATEGORY (i.e. toothpaste, energy drinks, deodorant, shampoo, motor oil, pain relievers...it doesn't matter which product category) that you want to analyze. Make sure it has at least 20 competitive items in the category.

Determine which product BENEFITS are "Gotta Do's" -- the things that ALL products in the category MUST DO in order to compete (i.e. for toothpaste: clean teeth, prevent cavities, freshen breath).

Then figure out the "Smart to Do's" -- the benefits that market leaders offer that set them apart and give them a distinctive competitive advantage. Again, for example in toothpaste "Total Protection" that Colgate Total and Crest Complete offer.

Then identify the "Dumb-to Do's" -- the things some products are offering as benefits that aren't valued benefits and do nothing to increase consumer appeal. Like "organic" toothpaste.

Once you have done just this…identified the "Gotta-Do's, Smart-To-Do's, and Dumb-to-Do's", you are way ahead of your competition in understanding consumer needs within the category and now have a roadmap for identifying opportunities for growth.

The Assumption Trap

Even the world's most successful marketing companies periodically fall into the "assumption trap," confident that they know enough to sell their product without pursuing new information to challenge their assumptions. I was snagged in the trap only a few months into my first brand management job at Procter & Gamble, working on the fledgling Citrus Hill Orange Juice brand. The brand was struggling, a distant third in the race against Tropicana and Minute Maid. P&G held leadership in about 90% of the product categories in which it did business. The third-place status of Citrus Hill had put the brand directly in the cross hairs of senior management. They wanted Citrus Hill to ascend to the top of the orange juice heap -- FAST.

The brand group and research team at the Winton Hill lab were frantically working on what they do best -- product upgrades. They developed and improved Citrus Hill until the juice won blind taste tests against all competitors -- particularly Tropicana and Minute Maid. "Aha!" we crowed. "Now we can beat the competition. We have the best tasting orange juice in the world."

We invested more than two million dollars in a new advertising campaign to tell consumers that Citrus Hill tasted better than any other orange juice and to declare the victory. Management was giddy with anticipation, and expectations ballooned. The new advertising aired. Everyone was ready with tall glasses of juice in hand, awaiting the next Nielsen Research reports to toast our triumph. The day approached, the envelope was opened and the mood suddenly darkened. Nothing had happened to sales. Consumers not only hadn't stampeded the juice aisles to pick up this new super juice; they hadn't even taken a sip.

The knee jerk response from management was that the advertising must have not been delivering the message effectively. As often happens, the blame fell on the advertising agency. Copy testing of advertising became a self-fulfilling prophecy, and so the brand invested another million dollars to create new advertising to tell consumers that Citrus Hill tasted great. Again with much hoopla, the new ads began airing.

One month later, the same result. No consumer response. "How could this be?" the brand group kept asking. "All of our consumer research tells us that 'good taste' is the most important thing to consumers in choosing their orange juice." This cycle of trying to reposition Citrus Hill based on taste preference continued for several more years, until finally P&G surrendered and pulled the brand from the marketplace.

What Consumers Say Versus What They Mean

Why did Citrus Hill fail? If you reviewed all of the traditional research, the positioning of Citrus Hill lined up precisely with what consumer were telling the brand group -- "good taste" was the most important thing; "freshness", "good nutrition for the family" and "orange juice helps brighten the morning" were secondary benefits. All these promises were built into the Citrus Hill positioning and expressed in the advertising copy and on the packaging. The brand group had used every logical and methodical tool in the P&G arsenal to understand why consumers should prefer Citrus Hill, yet came up empty.

What the brand group finally came to recognize is that purchase decisions aren't always based on the rational criteria consumers offer in focus groups and other research. Among competitive products, there is often very little difference in quality and product performance. This parity is especially true in categories in which the product is a commodity -- such as orange juice or coffee.

In this instance, while "good taste" was very important, most consumers didn't think their current orange juice tasted bad, or needed to taste better. Consumers believed "100% orange juice" is "100% orange juice" -- so how could there be a difference in taste between the brands? The Citrus Hill "better taste" positioning didn't make sense. Most consumers felt the brand they were currently buying tasted great. So consumers weren't lying --

taste was the most important thing to them. Nevertheless, that wasn't the differentiating criteria upon which their purchase decision rested.

Ignoring the segment of buyer who based their purchase decision only on low price (not a profitable segment in which to be a player), "freshness" was the product benefit upon which consumers made their purchase decision. Many consumers believed that fresh juice was better juice -- and they didn't believe that "made from concentrate" juices like Citrus Hill could be as healthy or fresh tasting.

The competitive "fresh" juices knew they had a consumer advantage and played it up -- even though, in reality, the processing and freezing methods of Citrus Hill made it more nutritious than many "fresh picked" brands. Category leader Tropicana's advertising featured an anonymous hand plucking a ripe orange from a tree and inserting a straw, a pair of lips sucking on the straw with obvious pleasure, and the tag line "You just can't pick a better juice -- for just picked freshness, pick Tropicana Pure Premium." Game over. Citrus Hill did not have a "fresh picked" product offering, and Tropicana had the perfect product and advertising – a straw in an orange -- aligned to the consumers' desire for "fresh" orange juice.

Had the Knowledge Mining methodology been developed at that time, Citrus Hill might have had a fighting chance to figure out the real consumer purchase drivers before millions had been wasted on research, product development and advertising on the losing promise of "great taste".

The benefits on Knowledge Mining are many. The insight gained can be used to ensure that you optimize your product positioning and that advertising messages are focused on the product attributes and benefits that drive purchase. It can tell you the best way to communicate with consumers, guide new product development and steer promotion planning. Best of all, Knowledge Mining is FREE. You can do it yourself in a couple of hours of just wandering around stores.

Being a better marketer means you have to be smarter and work harder than everybody else. Consumer insight is tough. You have to dig to find it. But it pays off in the end with better marketing plans that can truly make your products different, better and more special to consumers.

Give it a shot. Start looking at the world more strategically and analytically. I know for a fact you'll have fun. It's a great way to keep your mind sharp. If you start doing Knowledge Mining on a regular basis, it will change the way you shop, and it will probably change your brand preferences within some of your favorite product categories. A young lady in one of my classes at BYU informed me at the end of our semester that she hated me because of Knowledge Mining – telling me that she had switched brands in several categories because she couldn't support purchasing products that didn't truly understand their consumers, and that now, as she shops, she analyzes everything. She was grateful!

Chapter Three

Mission Statements, Operating Charters & Personal Charters

It is always surprising to me that so many corporations keep most of their employees in the dark about the company's overall business objective or the CEO's vision for growth. Everyone shows up for work and does what he or she was hired to do in his or her own corner of the building, picks up a paycheck, and goes home. Very few people outside top senior management really know the big picture or understand how any one particular job or initiative affects the company objectives as a whole.

It's true of any group effort that if you don't all know where you are going, you have a slim chance of arriving anywhere at all. Management consultants recognized this fact in the mid 1990's and began suggesting that companies develop corporate mission statements to help their employees and shareholders understand their ultimate goal. The results are often long, flowery, well written prose. For example, here is the published corporate mission statement of Hallmark:

> *This is Hallmark.*
>
> *We believe that our products and services must enrich people's lives and enhance their relationships.*
>
> *That creativity and quality in our concepts, products and services are essential to our success.*
>
> *That the people of Hallmark are our Company's most valuable resource.*
>
> *That distinguished financial performance is a must, not as an end unto itself, but as a means to accomplish our broader mission.*
>
> *That our private ownership must be preserved.*

Pretty as a Hallmark card, isn't it? I'm sure the senior management and a gaggle of consultants invested a lot of time and thought into developing this corporate mission. It sounds nice and it makes you feel all warm and fuzzy about the company.

Now, step back for a moment and think. If you were the senior management at Hallmark or any other company, would you publish your company marching orders for the entire world to see? Do you think that Hallmark's competitors at Gibson Greeting Cards or American Greetings might read Hallmark's annual report?

Corporate mission statements are a smoke screen! They're simply feel-good mottos developed for public consumption. Inside the company walls, employees often operate with a very different agenda and a very different mission.

Marketing Truth

> *The world's best marketing companies all have secret internal missions developed that are called "Working Mission Statements".*

Working Mission Statements are strategic tools to focus employees on the ultimate objective and clearly map out the road to success. They define "what you do" in a single crisp, clear and memorable sentence. Hallmark's working mission statement might be something like this:

> *The working mission of Hallmark is to create unique, high quality products that enrich lives and enhance relationships, and to reflect the warm, friendly spirit of Hallmark products in our stores.*

You might think this statement says as much -- or as little -- as the long, public version. But this statement makes clear that product development is the number one priority, that products must be unique to Hallmark (not available anywhere else), describes a little about what the products do and how they feel, and addresses the store environment. Best of all, every employee could memorize it in 30 seconds -- which is the reason to have a working mission statement in the first place; to give employees an understanding of the strategic goals of the company.

Internal Goal Setting

Marketing Truth

Every department develops a departmental mission to focus their employees on the role that their group plays in meeting the working mission of the overall organization.

The company also creates OPERATING CHARTERS for each department to specify who-is-doing-what-to-whom within their organization, defining interactions and authority across and between groups.

Dr. Edward Deming, the father of quality management system engineering, notes that 94% of problems in most corporations are due to poor systems. The most successful companies spend time and energy continually improving their internal systems -- from internal communications to organizational structure to reporting structures. They clearly define their working mission. They also do two other very important things:

The Departmental Mission & Operating Charter becomes a single document that precisely delineates what everyone within each department in the organization is ultimately trying to achieve, at the same time granting authority, setting parameters and defining limitations. In effect, major corporations create the business equivalent of the Constitution of the United States. They use this document to carefully construct a type of internal business government, complete with checks and balances.

Departmental Mission & Operating Charters reduce the chances of bad decisions and dropped balls. Without a well-defined system, many businesses find themselves recalling the old saying, "I have seen the enemy and it is me." Well-meaning individuals working on their own agendas, and with only a partial understanding of the company's larger goals, can greatly damage both the morale of other employees and the company's overall ability to succeed. They are so intent on checking off priorities on their own private list, they have very little time or interest in the goals of their co-workers. This tendency toward working in isolation or departmental silos is a particularly thorny problem in many privately held or family owned businesses, where employees often have the leeway to carve out their own fiefdoms.

Even the well-organized marketing companies still get tangled in unclear operating systems, usually during internal upheavals such as reorganizations, cutbacks and layoffs, or the development of new departments. At Coca-Cola, we introduced the first departmental mission and operating charter shortly after I arrived to assume the responsibility of Director of Worldwide Olympic Marketing. With Atlanta, the home of the Coca-Cola Company, hosting the 1996 Olympics, the Games became an agenda item for almost every meeting. I quickly discovered that I was a very popular guy. I'd never felt so wanted, being invited to dozens of meetings each day. It seemed that every department within the Company wanted to have its fingers in the Olympic rings.

Instead of powerful synergy, we had absolute business chaos. Marketing initiatives poured in literally by the hundreds. Some ideas sounded good, but they were all over the map -- community projects, promotion ideas, and requests for Olympic athlete appearances, Olympic pins, and merchandise. And that wasn't the half of it. Outside vendors submitted ideas by the thousands. I received a proposal from one consultant for Coke to build an Eiffel Tower in downtown Atlanta to commemorate the Games. Another wanted me to fund the building of the world's tallest totem pole of peace. Still another wanted me to fill the skies over Atlanta with a fleet of Coca-Cola hot air balloons during the Games.

The craziest idea came from a Frenchman who had actually built an airplane that was an exact replica of Charles Lindbergh's "Spirit of St. Louis". He had painted the plane to look like a Sprite bottle and named it "The Spirit of Sprite". His plan was to reenact Lindbergh's famous New York to Paris flight on the eve of the Olympic Games. He wanted me to sponsor him for one million dollars. Needless to say, that historic flight was never made.

It didn't take long to see that unless I defined with senior management exactly where Olympic Marketing fit in the big picture and determined what my group was specifically responsible for delivering, a thousand different projects would be springing up all over the Company with no overall objective and no strategic synergy. Worse still, any spurned department could argue -- with some reason -- that my decisions were unfair, unsound or just plain dumb.

To define our role, my management team sequestered offsite for two days and created a mission statement and operating charter for the Olympic Marketing Department. The mission statement defined our overall goal. The operating charter took a broad stroke view in defining the areas in which the Olympic Marketing Department had authority to operate, listed the tasks we would accomplish, defined our aspirations, specified how we would measure success, and waved warning flags about issues beyond our control that could impede our ability to complete the tasks as planned. While this sounds like we must have been writing a book, we weren't. The whole document was only one page long. The Olympic Marketing Mission and Operating Charter was printed and widely dispersed throughout the Coca-Cola system so that everyone knew what they could and could not expect from our group, and it helped them to shape their proposals to fit our objectives.

Here's an example to demonstrate the effectiveness of the checks and balances created by the Operating Charter. One of my roles was to work with the Brand Groups throughout the company to develop the Olympic consumer strategy for each individual brand. Once the strategy was inked, I was the watchdog to ensure that all marketing elements executed throughout the Company reflected that strategy -- from advertising to promotions to packaging.

Although the Operating Charter gave me the authority and responsibility to ensure that the advertising created for the Olympics was on strategy, the Advertising Department was responsible for developing and producing the actual ads. By the definitions outlined in the Operating Charter, my interaction with their department was strictly limited to judging the advertising for strategic merit. When I saw the advertising, my comments could only be "Yes, that is on strategy", or "No, that is not on strategy." It was not my role to make suggestions about how to change the ads or whether I liked the creative execution -- creative judgment was the exclusive domain of the advertising group. If they asked me my opinion on the creative I could respond -- if they didn't ask, I had to bite my tongue. The Operating Charter defined the parameters within which I could interact with other corporate departments, limiting my power so that I couldn't go wandering off into areas that were exclusively their domain and wreaking havoc where I didn't belong.

The Olympic Marketing Mission and Operating Charter clearly defined our goals as a company and focused our efforts on the job at hand. It worked like a charm. The 1996 Coca-Cola Olympic effort was the biggest and most successful global marketing initiative in the company's history. During the eight months in which the system was executing Olympic initiatives, worldwide volume increased 9%, global profits increased 22%, and Coca-Cola's stock value increased 32%. Why did it work? Because the Olympic Marketing Mission and Operating Charter allowed us to unite the corporate system in one theme, one look, and one objective, and to work cooperatively to achieve spectacular business results.

The point is simple. Many companies don't have a clearly defined working mission. In this evolving business environment, not only do you need a clear, succinct and well-defined working mission statement for the company, but each department needs to develop its own mission that identifies its role in supporting the working mission of the company. An Operating Charter will create a form of "business government" with checks and balances in the system so that everything can move efficiently.

Why Charters Work

The day-to-day operations at many companies can best be described as a state of controlled chaos. Employees are rushing to meet deadlines, crushed under heavy workloads, feeling the constraints of too little time. While a sense of urgency is necessary to keep business moving, employees must also feel a sense of direction. Through the process of defining a working mission statement for both the company and each department and by creating an operating charter, you can:

1. Define management and employee expectations of your business goals and paint a vision of the road to success;

2. Set parameters and define authority that individuals in your department have the right to exert within the organization as a whole;

3. Focus everyone's time, energy and resources on single-mindedly improving the business.

Developing the working mission statement, department mission and operating charter is a very painful and time-consuming process. You need to face reality and become very specific about what you can and cannot do. You must focus, prioritize and determine the goals and responsibilities that meet the overall needs of the company, with an eye to maximizing business results.

Creating A Working Mission Statement

Now that you're a believer in the value of the mission statement, let's take a look at how to write your own.

> *Marketing Truth*
>
> *The working mission statement should answer the question "what do you do?" It is no more than one sentence; must be easily understood; and should be committed to memory by everyone within your organization.*

There are three elements to building a working mission statement:

1) List the core ideas that you think sum up your job activities.

2) List a core principle for which you will stand.

3) Write down whom you are working to help

For example, if you were the operator of a McDonald's restaurant, the three ideas that sum up your job activities could be:

1. Prepare high quality fast food
2. Provide quick & friendly customer service
3. Operate a clean, safe and inviting restaurant

The core principle for which you stand could be: Excellence

And whom you are working to help would be: Our Customers

Now put it all together:

> *The working mission of this McDonald's restaurant is to prepare high-quality fast food, provide quick & friendly customer service and operate a clean, safe and inviting restaurant with excellent service for our customers.*

This concept is relatively simple. Just think of the possibilities and what a difference it would make if every McDonald's employee could recite this working mission by memory and then performed their job in accordance with it!

As another example, assume you are a marketing manager for Avis Car Rental.

The three ideas that sum up your job activities could be:

- Provide clean, quality cars
- Friendly, no-hassle service
- Fast, accurate transactions

The core principle for which you stand could be: being the most efficient company in the car rental business

Who you are working to help: our customers

Again, put it all together:

> *The working mission of Avis Car Rental is to provide to our customers clean, quality cars; friendly no-hassle service; and fast, accurate transactions as the most efficient company in the car rental business.*

This statement should accurately sum up what each employee of Avis is striving to achieve every day when they show up for work.

Creating The Operating Charter

Operating charters are no more difficult to write than mission statements, but may be even more important in saving your sanity -- and your job. Here's how you write a good one.

Marketing Truth

> *The operating charter should be the foundation of your business plan and define how your group will interact with others in the organization. It defines the areas in which you have authority to operate; lists the tasks you will accomplish; defines your aspirations; identifies how you will measure success; and waves warning flags to issues beyond your control which could impede your ability to complete the task as planned.*

Specifically, an operating charter contains the following elements:

OPERATING CHARTER

SCOPE: Defines the parameters in which you work. Is it a particular geography, a particular brand, a particular customer? Be as specific as possible.

PRIMARY OBJECTIVES: List no more than six clearly stated roles your area will provide to the overall organization. These should include primary job responsibilities, areas where your group will provide leadership, and places where your group will provide assistance to others within the organization.

SECONDARY OBJECTIVES: List no more than two other clearly stated roles that are "hoped for" but not mandatory to meet business success.

ASPIRATIONS: List no more than three dreams you hope your work can accomplish within the organization (both short / long term).

QUANTIFIABLE MEASURES OF SUCCESS: List quantifiable means you will use to track whether or not you are accomplishing what you set out to do.

CONSTRAINTS: List external factors you cannot control that could negatively influence your ability to meet all of the objectives as stated above.

The Operating Charter vs. The Business Plan

The operating charter is more than bullet points pulled out of your business plan. The operating charter is different in several distinct ways. First, the charter is the view of your business from 20,000 feet. It gives "The Big Picture" for your work group. Second, it only lists the core tasks you will accomplish in broad strokes, not in the detail demanded by a business plan. Third, it should only be one page long, so that it can be tacked up on the wall over everyone's desk as an easy reference of what your group is striving to achieve.

This may seem like a silly idea, but it works. By having the operating charter in plain sight of all employees every day, it keeps everyone focused on the strategic goals and helps them make decisions on a daily basis, prioritizing tasks. Many times during each day of my Olympic journey I would reference the operating charter to help me decide what tasks to tackle (and more importantly, which to ignore). During the rush of business, it is very easy to get caught up in tasks that feel urgent but don't move the priorities ahead. The operating charter helps you sort the necessary from the minutia and focuses efforts on things that matter.

One of the senior managers at Coca-Cola was so fanatical about having missions and charters defined, he took it all the way down to the individual job level and challenged every employee to develop a one sentence working mission statement for their particular job. He would approach employees in the halls and ask, "What do you do?" If they couldn't give the answer in one succinct statement, he skewered them. While his tactic was questionable, the strategy is right. If everyone in your organization knows and can state in three simple sentences the Company Working Mission; Their Department's Mission; and Their Personal Job Mission, your business will run much more efficiently and effectively.

Think back to the Hallmark example at the beginning of this chapter. If you were the Marketing Brand Manager for Hallmark Cards, you might create the following definitions:

Company Working Mission: The working mission of Hallmark is to create unique, high quality products that enrich lives and enhance relationships, and to reflect the warm, friendly spirit of Hallmark products in our stores.

Marketing Department Mission: The working mission of the Hallmark Marketing Department is to create consumer-relevant and brand-aligned marketing initiatives that drive volume and increase consumer purchase preference & brand equity of Hallmark products.

My Personal Job Mission: My job is to create consumer insistence for Hallmark products.

That, my friends, is strategic clarity and it is what every company must strive to achieve.

Eric D Schulz

Section Two:

Product Strategy

Eric D Schulz

Chapter Four

Developing A Brand

To begin this chapter, I'm going to offer an article written by Mark Gallagher and Laura Savard, Brand Expressionists® at Blackcoffee®, a brand consultancy in Boston, MA. It is one of the best articles I have ever encountered on branding and why we do it. (used with permission).

What is Branding?

A comprehensive look at the origin and function of "branding"

Many people frequently misuse the term "brand" by interchanging it with advertising, marketing, naming or a design. These improper applications have caused much confusion as to what branding is and how it works. As such, "brand" has become a bit of a buzzword. But, what does it really mean and how does it work? Where did all start and how can it create value? To benefit from the effects of branding, a common understanding of "brand" must first be established.

Invented by P&G

Procter & Gamble invented the business strategy of "Brand Management". Brand management focused attention on product specialization and differentiation instead of business function. By distinguishing the qualities of each brand from all other P&G brands, each would avoid competing with one another by targeting different consumer markets with a different set of benefits. This was especially important in product categories that the company manufactured several competing brands, like laundry detergent.

Over the years, P&G and the companies that embraced the brand management concept became extremely successful. In the early 1940s, Ted Bates & Company decided to conduct an extensive research study to find out why and reverse engineer the success of these brands. The company researched "successful advertising campaigns," to see whether they could identify a pattern. What they found was that the most successful brands—

those that lead their category and produced the highest ROI—used what they termed the Unique Selling Proposition or "USP."

The concept of "USP" has three guiding principles:

- The proposition must be clearly stated to the consumer: "Buy this product, and you will get this specific benefit."
- The proposition itself must be unique. It must express a specific benefit that competitors do not, will not, or cannot offer.
- The proposition must be strong enough to pull new customers to the product.

Brand Positioning

In the late 60's and early 70's, the concept of "brand" began to take on new meaning, including the larger concept of image and values. Al Ries and Jack Trout captured this evolution in their Harvard Business Review article and later authored a book by the same title: *POSITIONING: The battle for your mind*. Their concept stated that it was not product superiority that mattered, but rather *consumers' perception of a given brand that paved the road to success*. This concept was dubbed "brand positioning" and to this day it remains the standard for developing successful brands.

In practice: *A brand is an experience living at the intersection of promise and expectation.* Here's how it works. A company expresses its brand as a promise, both overt and implied. That promise lives in consumers' hearts and minds as an expectation. When brand promise and consumers' expectations reflect one another, the brand holds tremendous value for both parties.

Effective businesses view their brands as tools that allow their messaging to cut through the noise of an overcrowded marketplace. Consumers use brands as a method for navigating their way through the marketplace. Each brand distinguishes itself, allowing consumers to identify their preferred products and services from those they see as being less desirable. When brand meaning and relevance are clear, the brand will hold a stronger position in consumer's minds and the more likely they are to choose it.

Consumers use brand as an identification tool

Without brands, the marketplace would be overwhelming. Imagine a world without brands: You're out of ketchup. You run to your local store where you are met by a wall of red bottles with simply the word "ketchup." Without brands there would be no signals to illustrate the differences between the vast array of choices other than size and price. No name, no unique package, nothing! So which one do you choose, why and how?

You can quickly see how making a purchase becomes an ordeal and making a repurchase of a product you liked would be next to impossible. However, we live in a world where consumers have a system for differentiating products and services as well as tracking their experiences. Brands provide a method of classification, differentiation and identification that allow you, as the consumer, to simplify your ketchup buying decisions.

As you scan the many shelves of ketchup bottles, your brain subconsciously translates each brand signal: bottle shape, label, name, logo, color scheme and graphics. You recognize your preferred brand and wham, Heinz. You're on your way!

Brand value

It is important to note that different parties define "value" differently. For example, a politician may measure brand value in terms of votes, a company in terms of profits and a nonprofit as contributions it receives. Consumers place value on many factors ranging from emotional to rational, from exclusivity and rarity to the safety of commonality.

No matter how value is measured, if your brand does not deliver its value, it is merely an empty promise. Without a trusting customer base, a brand is nothing more than a legally protected name, sign, symbol or device.

Branding is managing customer expectations

Branding is not about getting people to choose your offering over the competitions. *It is the act of managing consumers' expectations so as to condition your target audience to see your offering as the only answer to a specific need.*

By defining a realistic and manageable promise of what the brand owner will deliver and what consumers can expect of the brand, branding has become the backbone of modern business strategy. "Brand" drives consumer purchase decisions and affects nearly every functional area of a business. With product offerings converging into sameness, companies are viewing "brand" as the only avenue of differentiation.

Branding defines market position (brand strategy) and, through a series of signals, articulates that position as promise (brand positioning). When strategy and positioning work as one, brands obtain sustainable and favorable market positions. *This has shifted the task of brand building and management to the primary business strategy.*

Mark Gallagher & Laura Savard, Brand Expressionists

Blackcoffee.com

Brands are built on trust

While the concept of brand is ever evolving, its primary purpose is to build a trustworthy relationship with consumers. In other words, what is promised by the brand owner and what is expected by the brand's audience become one and the same—It's that simple and that complex.

- Brands are about *feelings*, not facts.
- How your customers *feel* about your brand isn't a casual question. It is the crucial question.

Tips to achieve a strong brand

In order to develop, cultivate, and nurture your brand, there are definite actions and qualities on which you must focus.

Pay attention to your communications tactics. Every advertisement, brochure, letter, and business card handed out should reinforce your company's core brand message and image.

Focus on that benefit(s) and your means of delivering it. Never lose sight of what it is that your business seeks to achieve for your customers.

You can't fake honesty. You must believe in your brand. If you don't have faith in what you do or sell, you can't expect your customers to believe in you either.

Keep it simple. Find out what you can do well for your target audience and concentrate on doing it.

Be consistent across all your services and products. Never leave your customers wondering if you do a thing well. Do everything well.

Develop a good reputation. A good reputation speaks for itself. A bad reputation is almost impossible to live down.

Actively manage your brand. Be aware of what the competition is doing and monitoring changes in your target audience. Remember, sometimes it is necessary to re-position a brand to keep your client base.

Own your brand. You must pay attention to what customers need and want. You control what you want your brand to mean.

Branding Checklist

As you work on developing your brand, ask yourself the following questions:

What are your company's values?
Who are the target audiences you hope to reach?

What are the unique qualities associated with your products or services?
What are the practical benefits customers can expect from your products or services?
How can you portray those benefits so as to create a positive emotional reaction from potential clients and customers?
What does your brand promise and how can you make good on that promise?
What can you do to generate trust in your relationship with your clients and customers?
What is your brand's personality and how can it be better tailored to reach your target audience?

Don't forget to keep an eye on the competition

It always pays to know what the other guy is doing. Make it a habit to study your competition.

What strategy does the competition use in their branding efforts?
How do consumers perceive the competition?
What are your competitor's strengths and weaknesses?

When you can answer those questions, turn the mirror around and re-examine your own brand. How do consumers perceive you? What are your products and services strengths and weaknesses? <u>Determining and improving your competitive advantage is a major aspect of successful branding.</u>

<u>Above all, be prepared to live up to the brand you create. Good intentions won't get the job done.</u> Keep your promises or better yet, exceed them. Top-ranked brands deliver consistent quality and actively cultivate customer satisfaction. In the long-term, there's no better strategic asset.

<u>In a world of me-too products and abundant choice, the brand must represent a single emotional benefit that is highly valued and difficult to substitute</u>. To create relevance, the brand must be the exception to its category and not the rule. Brands that stay relevant offer a simple, emotional benefit rather than a functional one.

The process of brand development:

1. Identify target audiences – desired action of each
2. Identify core values of your company (drives focus)
3. Identify the brand personality, tone, and manner (drives relationships)
4. Identify the brand promise (drives actions)
5. Create the brand positioning (drives messaging)
6. Create the brand articulation (drives relevance / messaging)

Brand strategy vs. marketing strategy vs. marketing tactics

There is a lot of confusion regarding the difference between a brand strategy, a marketing strategy and a marketing tactic. Here is a simple definition:

<u>***A brand strategy***</u> *defines the unique benefits your brand offers to the target audience. It spells out clearly and concisely what makes your product or service different, better, and special in the competitive marketplace. It clearly defines what it is you want the consumer to think about your product (brand).*

<u>***A marketing strategy***</u> *has a defined business goal, i.e. increase sales; generate more newspaper stories in the local press; attract new distributors. Each marketing strategy uses the brand strategy as the cornerstone in developing "what it will say" to the different target audiences. They will all be "singing from the same hymnal", with a consistent brand message.*

<u>***Marketing tactics***</u> *are the actions you take to execute the marketing strategy. It could include any number of things...advertising, Facebook postings and other social media, new promotional materials, mailers, flyers, etc.*

A great strategy does not depend on brilliant tactics for success. If the idea is strong enough, you can get by with mediocre tactical execution. However, even the best tactics can't compensate for a lousy strategy.

Any number of strategies can be used to achieve a business goal. In fact, it often takes more than one strategy to achieve a lofty goal, and each strategy involves its own unique tactical plan. Unfortunately, a lot of marketing managers simply throw together a list of the tactics they've always used and call it a strategy.

Can you have a marketing strategy without a brand strategy?

Creating marketing strategies and executing marketing tactics in the void of an overarching brand strategy happen all the time. I call these "random acts of marketing". Can they be successful? Sometimes. But without an overarching communication strategy (what it is that makes you different, better, and special), it becomes hit-and-miss often times.

Seth Godin says "*In my experience, people get obsessed about tactical detail before they embrace a brand strategy...* and as a result, when a tactic fails, they begin to question the brand strategy that they never really articulated in the first place.

Articulating your brand promise is the #1 job of marketers.

Chapter Five

Brand Positioning

Suppose you are responsible for developing a marketing campaign for a terrific new car. Where do you begin? You could tell consumers about its luxurious interior and its sporty new look. You could boast about horsepower, safety, handling ability, roominess or German engineering. Or you could create a product image to appeal to a particular type of driver. Is it big and bold like a Cadillac, or irreverent fun like a Kia Soul? Is it as safe and practical as a minivan, or as sophisticated and well made as an Audi?

If you were to produce a TV commercial about this car, you'd have 30 seconds to tell consumers why they should buy it. If your commercial was any good, it would define <u>who you want to buy your car</u> and <u>what the most compelling reasons are that they should want it</u>. You don't have enough time to say that the car is luxurious, roomy, has fine Corinthian leather, is fast, sporty, fun to drive and has a rocking sound system, and you probably can't appeal to everyone watching the commercial. So before you review the first storyboard, you would have to make tough choices about what your product is and whom it's for.

The way marketers define what it is they want to say about their product and whom they are targeting to buy it is accomplished through the development of what's called a <u>brand positioning statement</u>. The crafting of your brand positioning statement is the single most important task you will do as a marketer. This statement is the foundation of all of your marketing, including advertising, pricing, packaging, merchandising, promotions -- anything that the reaches the consumer will be shaped by this statement. But despite its far-reaching effects, it isn't an opus; it is a simple, clearly stated sentence or two -- yes, just <u>one or two</u> sentences -- that defines who to target and what to say.

Think you need more than just this to contain your thoughts? Then you're trying to say too much, and your message is surely becoming diluted. If you can't say it simply, your consumer can't understand it.

The Art and Discipline of Positioning

Successful marketing companies hone the development of brand positioning statements to a fine art. They have files full of case studies to indicate what type of strategies work and what type fail. And let's face it, product managers at these companies are very busy people. So how long do you suppose they spend on that one little positioning statement? Forty-five minutes? An entire afternoon?

Try months. Part of the effort is agonizing over every word to make sure that the brand positioning statement is powerful, compelling and specific. The real work and worry comes in analyzing the roads not taken. If you position your lipstick as old-time glamour, it can't also be youthful and new, so you'd better be sure that glamour has the bigger audience and stronger appeal. If you position sunglasses as the choice of the stars, you can't also be unbreakable sports lenses or most comfortable fit.

These difficult choices make strategy development the most troublesome task in marketing. It involves more than creative thinking in a vacuum; you must collect and analyze all of the information and consumer learning from every available source, then boil it all down to a simple, clear, consumer-focused positioning that will maximize your products consumer appeal. Everything the consumer knows and believes about the product is driven from the brand positioning statement. There is no margin for error.

The ABC's of Brand Positioning

The thinking you invest in your Brand Positioning Statement is hard work, but the statement itself is as easy as ABC:

>   Audience (Target Audience)

>   Benefit

Compelling Reason Why (this is actually sentence #2 of the statement).

It's that easy. Untrained business managers try to hedge their bets by writing the positioning statement as broadly as possible. They hate to make choices about their target audience (wouldn't *all* consumers love this?) or their key benefit (it slices, dices, does the dishes and walks the dog!). The road not taken haunts them, so they position their product squarely at the fork; it's a great product for every consumer and every occasion.

Resist this trap. If your product stands for everything, it stands for nothing. Don't be afraid to define your product in the clearest, most intriguing terms possible. Only then will consumers appreciate your benefit and become loyal to your product.

Think for a moment of Dow Bathroom products and their famous Scrubbing Bubbles. This family of products takes the crappiest job in the house and makes it FUN. How? Because the Scrubbing Bubbles do the cleaning for you!

Note the ABC's of the strategy as follows:

  a. <u>Target Audience</u>: Homemakers seeking a clean, sanitized bathroom

  b. <u>Unique Benefit</u>: Dow Bathroom Products are the easy way to get a clean shine for your tub, tile, and toilet.

  c. <u>Compelling Reason Why</u>: That's because Dow Bathroom Products contain scrubbing bubbles that cut through the dirt and grime, clean to the shine, leaving a clean, sanitized surface.

Developing a Unique Brand Position

The most effective brand positioning statements describe their benefit and reason why in a relevant yet unexpected way. Let's think about Michelin Tires advertising. Recall their campaign featuring a cute baby playing inside a Michelin tire with the copy "Michelin: Because so much is riding on your tires." The brand positioning statement that led to this advertising could be:

a. <u>Target</u> <u>Audience:</u> Parents with young children

b. <u>Unique</u> **Benefit**: Michelin is the safest tire you can buy to protect the lives of your loved ones.

c. **Compelling** <u>Reason Why</u>: That's because duel-wall Michelin tires perform exceptionally well in all weather conditions, gripping the road so you won't have accidents.

Michelin has a specific target, a clear benefit and a compelling, believable reason why. Through the insightful strategic decision to use "babies" as the way to define your loved ones, Michelin created a relevant yet unexpected way to create consumer appeal versus other tire companies.

Now, consider for a moment how different the advertising would look and feel if the strategy were something like this:

a. <u>Target</u> <u>Audience:</u> Adults 18-45

b. <u>Unique</u> **Benefit**: Michelin tires give you the best performance in any driving situation.

c. **Compelling** <u>Reason Why</u>: That's because duel-wall Michelin tires perform exceptionally well in all weather conditions, gripping the road so you won't have accidents.

The second strategy could easily -- and logically -- have been chosen as the brand positioning statement. After all, it has the same "reason why" and all the consumer research probably revealed that performance is a compelling consumer benefit. But alas, this is basically how every competitive tire company is positioned.

So why did the marketing team at Michelin choose statement #1? Because their research, their observations and their gut instincts told them that the strongest emotional tie consumers have to their tires involves safety for the children they chauffeur (think of all those "Baby on Board" signs that used to be so popular and you'll have to agree). Sure, consumers want good performance, but most of them aren't revving fine-tuned sports cars on slippery mountain roads. They're too busy carpooling. Remember, good brand strategy is based on emotion, not function.

Here's a fun exercise: watch a television commercial or take a look at a print ad, then try to restate what you see in the words of a brand positioning statement and analyze how well the strategy works. You'll be amazed at the number of bad marketing campaigns you will discover -- ones that have no clear target, no clearly stated consumer benefit, no believable "reason why." Only rarely will you jump out of your chair and see one that is exceptionally adept at executing a relevant yet unexpected strategy -- and 9 times out of 10 that product will be a category leader!

Here are some tips to follow when doing this exercise:

1) An endorsement (i.e. a celebrity, athlete, chef, etc.), only lends a clue as to who the target audience might be. It doesn't mean the product is targeted to athletes or chefs. Likewise, if an ad has a famous model, or racecar driver, it doesn't mean it's targeted at them either. Try to figure out WHO they are trying to attract with the ad...think lifestyle (active adults, wealthy adults, health-conscience adults), particular needs (cold sufferers, homemakers wanting a clean bathroom, homemakers worried about messy meat germs); age (teens, young adults, older adults, grandparents), life stage (parents, young singles, children, retirees), and gender.

2) FOCUS and be CONCISE. Use as few words as possible in crafting the benefit and reason why.

"3) Make sure "That's because" are the first two words in your "Reason Why". It is sometimes hard to figure out what is the benefit and what is the reason why. If you put "that's because" in front of your reason why, it helps clarify if you got it right.

4) Make sure the name of the product is in your brand positioning. <u>Always</u> start your benefit statement with the name of the product. For example:

Target Audience: For cold sufferers,

Benefit: <u>Comtrex</u> offers customized relief for your cold symptoms.

Compelling Reason Why: That's because <u>Comtrex</u> offers four different relief formulas (Acute Head Cold; Deep Chest Cold; Sinus & Nasal; Cold & Cough) that treat and work against your <u>specific</u> cold ailments.

It's OK to have the product name in both the benefit and reason why.

Here's another example:

Target Audience: For consumers seeking a whiter smile;

Benefit: Crest Whitestrips whiten teeth five times better than the leading paint-on whitening gel.

Compelling Reason Why: That's because Crest Whitestrips gel-coated strips hold the peroxide on teeth longer, to whiten stains below the tooth surface.

Defining a Target Audience

I can't think of any product that can be marketed to the population en masse. Even water has an image and an audience, depending on the brand. If you want to deliver your message, you have to know whom you're talking to. The target is usually described in <u>demographic terms</u> (teens, young adult's 18-35, parents with children living at home, moms with young children ages 2-9). Or you can describe your target in <u>psychographic terms</u> (football fans, outdoor types, animal lovers, homemakers, working women). The target audience is the group of consumers that has the greatest potential for purchasing your product. Of course, you will nearly always find some consumer outside of your target that will also purchase your product. Don't include them in your definition. A target audience doesn't exclude other consumers; it merely describes your core group. You must be specific and knowledgeable about your core target to develop effective consumer communications.

For example, consider Vitaminwater. Both men and women drink the brand. It's targeted to adults 18-35 seeking a flavorful yet healthy beverage alternative to soft drinks. Why? Simply because that segment of the population consumes the most soft drinks and water annually. Furthermore, the smaller slices of other demographic groups who also drink water (men on a diet, older women) drink it for the same reason as the core group; they want a flavorful, healthfully refreshing, no-calorie or low-calorie beverage. By marketing to the core group, the product benefit and personality are maximized -- it's youthful, healthful, and sexy. These are the attributes that the core group -- and a few members of other groups -- value most. So despite the fact that other segments of the population also drink Vitaminwater, the Brand group has focused all marketing efforts on the core target group, and the non-core consumers are merely a bonus.

Functional Consumer Benefits

The most important piece of the brand positioning strategy is stating the consumer benefit -- what the consumer receives in return for buying the product. The benefit can be functional (cleaner, brighter, fresher, more power, lasts longer) or psychological (feel refreshed, feel sexy and beautiful, have fun, gain freedom, no hassles).

Psychological Consumer Benefits

Psychological benefits are much more touchy-feely than functional benefits. In advertising jargon, this type of approach is known as "sell the sizzle, not the steak." In other words, focus on the most appealing benefit of the product (often, how the product makes you feel), not on what the product actually is.

Disney does a brilliant job of tapping into the psychological benefits of its classic videos; instead of simply selling tapes of Snow White or Cinderella, for example, they remind us of how it felt to believe in the magic of those stories as a child. Special K cereal does a great job with its advertising showing a beautiful young woman modeling sexy dresses. The ads clearly imply that if you eat Special K for breakfast each morning, you can look this good -- a powerful promise -- while completely ignoring the usual cereal benefits (doesn't get soggy in milk, tastes great, and so on). Pantene shampoo has a campaign that combines both functional and psychological benefits: "It's your time to shine." This clever positioning overtly celebrates the feeling of confidence and success while subtly reinforcing the product benefit (beautiful, shiny hair).

Developing a Believable "Compelling Reason Why"

Consumers are skeptical of companies, and are on the lookout for over-promises. That's why you need to tell the consumer exactly what they will get for purchasing your product (the benefit), and back it up by telling them HOW you are going to do it! The "compelling reason why" of your brand positioning strategy is of equal importance as the benefit.

The best "reason why" statements use what I call "Kitchen Logic", which means that you need to ensure that you've stated your reason why in a clear, uncomplicated way such that two housewives sitting at the kitchen table could explain it easily to one another. If what you are telling them makes sense, they will believe you. If you say something that doesn't make sense, is complicated, or sounds like you're stretching the truth, they will be skeptical. It's that simple.

Citibank tested the strength of the "reason why" with a "Citi shopper" service offered with Visa and MasterCard accounts. In the first group, telemarketers called consumers and offered the Citi shopper service, telling them "Citi shopper can find you the lowest prices on over 200,000 name brand items." They explained the "consumer benefit" but failed to offer a plausible "reason why." Only a small percentage of consumers signed up.

In the second group they added a "reason why" statement. Here, the telemarketers said "Citi shopper can find you the lowest prices on over 200,000 name brand items. That's because our computers continually monitor prices at over 50,000 retailers nationwide, ensuring that you get the lowest price available anywhere." With only that change in the script, enrollment skyrocketed. Why? Because Citibank told shoppers of the benefit -- finding the lowest prices nationwide -- then backed it up with a plausible reason why -- through their computers continually monitoring pricing at over 50,000 retailers nationwide.

The Power of Passion

The final part of the brand positioning statement puzzle is to develop the relevant yet unexpected positioning to create meaningful differentiation in the mind of the consumer. To do this, you must align the consumer benefit with the most relevant "passion point".

A passion point is the characteristic within the product category that evokes a strong consumer reaction, and one which the consumer has a definite point of view. Often, this is a "pet peeve" problem that you are solving for the customer. You must effectively communicate your understanding of the passion point (and possibly the pain it is causing) and convince them that your product is the ONLY answer to providing for their need.

Think back to the Michelin example used earlier. The consumer "passion point" was "safety for my loved ones." That's a passion point, and Michelin OWNS that benefit versus all other tire manufacturers.

This strategic principle is the cornerstone of success. Nothing you will ever do will be as important as developing your brand positioning statement, and the key to developing a effective relevant yet unexpected positioning is to find and integrate the most relevant passion point.

Why Passion Points Are Essential

The biggest change in consumer purchase behavior in the past ten years is that most no longer base purchase decisions on product performance alone; instead, consumers are using a criteria that combines product performance and passion points. Some of this shift can be credited to evolving technology that has enabled many different products to achieve high quality performance. You don't have to buy a Wham-O Frisbee anymore; plenty of flying discs work just as well. Without a significant difference in product quality, consumers use the passion criterion as the differentiating factor that leads to the purchase decision.

Like most matters of the heart, passion criterion often isn't based in reality. Brand loyalty -- or brand avoidance -- can be triggered by overall brand equity ("this company always makes good products"), by childhood memories of Mom using the product, from a bad experience with another product in the category, or by any number of associations or experiences. Digging to find the most relevant "passion point" can be the most difficult and challenging task you will face in developing a strategy.

A Honey of a Story

Passion points were the key to successfully repositioning of the Winnie the Pooh videos at Disney Home Video. When I inherited the brand, there were 14 Pooh video titles available in stores. Sales were dreadful. Pooh was getting stomped by Barney the Dinosaur. Four of the Pooh videos were in a product line entitled "Walt Disney Mini-Classics." These were the classic Pooh videos you remember from childhood storybooks: Winnie the Pooh and the Honey Tree, Winnie the Pooh and Tigger Too, Winnie the Pooh and A Day For Eeyore, Winnie the Pooh and A Blustery Day. The other 10 videos were in a product line entitled "The New Adventures of Winnie the Pooh." These were compilation tapes each containing two episodes taken from the Saturday morning cartoons that aired for years on ABC network.

At the time, Disney used what I call the "Field of Dreams" marketing approach. They believed that if you put anything with the "Disney" name out on the store shelves it would sell. They applied no marketing discipline within the video division. No strategy, no positioning. The brand groups spent all of their time designing packaging and putting out new videos, paying no attention to titles they had previously released.

A transition period began after my arrival. The Disney creative well was beginning to run dry. Disney Home Video had exhausted nearly all of the offerings in the studio vaults. Our task was to figure out how to stimulate consumer interest in buying tapes that were already available in stores --- like Winnie the Pooh.

When we began the research to try to figure out why Pooh wasn't selling, we unearthed many fascinating tidbits. First, Moms still loved Pooh. We had a solid consumer base and interest in Pooh; that was the good news. The bad news was our titles and packaging -- "Mini Classics" and "The New Adventures of Winnie the Pooh" -- were turning Mom off. Why?

"Mini-Classics" meant "short in length" and "not as good as a Disney classic." The title of "The New Adventures of Winnie the Pooh" was bothering Mom, because she didn't think of Pooh as an "Adventurer." The packaging in both cases was inadvertently sending subliminal negative messages.

Further research revealed what connected Moms with Pooh -- the passion points. They remembered him fondly from the storybooks they loved as children and that they now read to their own kids. They loved the gentleness and innocence of Pooh and his friends Tigger, Piglet, Eeyore and Christopher Robin. Moms believed that Pooh stories taught their children good values -- sharing, trust, caring, friendship, and love. They were pleased that their children liked to play along and pretend with Pooh.

We had found the Holy Grail. We immediately recalled all of the Pooh videos from stores, creating a panic attack that garnered some media attention and helped drive sales to clear off the store shelves. We began a new branding and brand positioning initiative, aligning the product with the passion points.

Three months later we released Pooh under three new brand positioning's: Winnie the Pooh Storybook Classics, Pooh Learning, and Pooh Playtime. In effect, all we had done was repackage existing product, but sales soared. In the first year after the relaunch, Pooh videos sold over 30 times what they had sold the year before. The product didn't change, but the strategic brand positioning aligned to the passion points of consumers paved the road to success.

Where to Find Passion Points

In the words of Star Wars guru Obewon Kinobe, "you have the power within." Inside you is the best place to begin looking for "passion points." What are your reactions to the product? Try to remember the first time you used it. Ask your friends what they think when they use the product, or a competitive product. Ask your Mom what she thinks. Try to learn everything about what normal everyday people think about the product and the product category. Try to find pet peeves. You don't need focus groups to do this. Look at the grocery shelf or the consumer marketplace in which you compete. Is there an unfulfilled need that no product is addressing? Is some competitive product addressing a consumer need better than yours? How can you capture a proprietary positioning within the category that is meaningful to consumers and provides a competitive edge?

To illustrate, let's look at the airline industry. As a consumer, what are the relevant and meaningful product attributes that consumers use to decide in choosing their airline? If you do standard consumer research, the list, in order of importance, will look something like this:

-- Low Fares

-- Recognized Carrier

-- Convenient Flight Schedules

-- Good Frequent Flyer Program

-- Friendly Service

-- Good Safety Record

-- Adequate Leg Room / Seat Width

-- Good Food

-- Good Movies / In-flight Entertainment

-- Careful Baggage Handling

-- Perks for the "Best" Frequent Fliers

Now that you've got your basic research, you can dig for the passion points.

Assume that you are a marketing manager for a major airline. Put on your strategic analyst hat and look at the above list. What attributes are pretty much at "parity" between most of the major airlines? Are there any attributes upon which you perceive that a distinct point of difference could be or has been carved out for one airline in particular? Do any of these attributes fall into the "pet peeves" category for you?

If you are anything like me, my pet peeves with airlines are seat width and leg room. Either my rump is expanding or the seats seem to be getting smaller, and the row of seats in front of me keep inching their way back. On a recent flight, I literally had only 2 inches of breathing room between my nose and the seat back in front of me when that passenger reclined. That's my pet peeve, and a problem I want solved.

If I were to develop a strategic positioning statement for an airline, it would probably be something like this:

    a. <u>Target Audience:</u> Business flyers

    b. <u>Unique Benefit</u>: Eric's Airline offers wide body service on every flight, even if you're skinny.

    c. <u>Compelling Reason Why</u>: That's because on every Eric's Airline plane, we've installed seats wide enough for all bottoms to comfortably fit, with ample leg room and plenty of distance between you and the row in front, ensuring a comfortable, relaxing flight.

Relevant yet unexpected. The play on the word "wide body" gives it an edge without being insulting. Now think about the current brand positioning strategies of the major airlines:

    United: Rising

    American: OneWorld

    Delta: On Top Of The World

    Southwest: Freedom To Fly

    Eric's Airline: Wide body Service On Every Flight

Which of these strategies are a consumer proposition that communicates to the consumer that the airline is different, better and special -- relevant yet unexpected? Only Eric's Airline. The big boys are so caught up in trying to craft a corporate image, they've fallen into the trap of conventionalism and sameness. Nothing about their brand positioning strategies separates them from the competition.

Different, Better, and Special. Everything communicates. That's why you must create a strategic, relevant yet unexpected brand positioning statement to define how you address the consumer. It will separate you from competition and define how your product is better.

Developing a brand positioning statement is hard work, combined with a good sprinkling of insight and creativity. Slow down, take a deep breath, and commit yourself to the process. It takes time to find the right brand positioning for your product. Even Pooh, a bear of very little brain, would sit down at his Thoughtful Spot from time to time and say, "I think this may require some...thinking." Find your Thoughtful Spot, do your thinking, and watch your product develop a unique benefit, a compelling reason why, an identity, and a personality right before your eyes.

Chapter Six

Innovation

Working on innovations and new creating products is the sexiest job in the marketing world. Here you have the opportunity to experience the exhilaration that the great inventors like Benjamin Franklin, Thomas Edison and others must have felt; bringing new ideas to life, creating something from the vast void of nothingness, using only visionary insights to bring thought to creation.

The dream of every new product manager and entrepreneur is to originate a great idea that can catapult business into the sales stratospheres. Unfortunately for most, this dream is about as close as they get to nirvana. It is far more likely that they will end up feeling like Dr. Frankenstein, with a mutated idea that might have seemed pretty at the start, but ultimately must be destroyed in order to save mankind (or more likely, the company's bottom line!)

Academic studies claim that eight out of every ten new products introduced into the marketplace fail within the first 12 months. Despite these daunting odds, innovation is what drives the world economy, and companies continue to invest millions of dollars each year in new product research and development, searching for the big idea that will propel their business into the next decade.

The road to new products success is lined with many perils. Recognizing these problem areas before you stumble upon them is the first step to reducing the risk of failure.

The First Hurdle: Who Will Sell It For You?

Researchers estimate that the average large retailer will be inundated with over 40,000 new product offerings this year, in categories ranging from new foods, beverages, health & beauty to household cleaners, pet supplies and others. That's a rate of nearly 150 new items foisted upon buyers each and every business day!

The failure rate of new products is largely attributable to this fact alone. Most offerings never survive their presentation meeting to the retail chains. The retailer refuses to stock the new product, and lacking distribution it dies a slow and painful death without ever seeing the light of a store aisle.

Many retailers require companies presenting them with new products to pay what is called a "slotting allowance" fee in order to get a new product onto store shelves. This fee is used to offset the retailer costs of resetting their store shelves to make room for the new product, and to pay to get the item into the store computer and inventory systems. Slotting allowances are required to get most new items onto store shelves. But retailers still may refuse to bring in the product despite the cash on the table if they think the product won't sell. The seller must demonstrate to the retailer that his product has consumer appeal and offers unique consumer benefits that other products, currently in the store don't provide.

The Second Hurdle: Will Consumers Buy It?

This leads us to **The Law of Laziness**: Consumers are lazy. Once they have made a conscience decision to purchase a particular product or service, it's almost impossible to get them to change to a competitor's offering, so long as prices and the competitive landscape remain relatively stable.

If you regularly buy Dove soap, it's almost impossible to convince you to switch to Dial soap. If you prefer Heinz Ketchup, it's highly unlikely you will switch to Hunt's. That's the Law of Laziness in action.

For brands, products and services in market leadership positions, that's great news. Consumer lethargy makes it almost impossible to screw up. For everyone else, it sets a clear challenge – *in order to successfully introduce a new product or service and capture significant sales, you must disrupt marketplace equilibrium by offering the customer something significantly different, better and special versus the current product or service offerings.*

This is a high hurdle. Think about maps for example. For a hundred years, when we went off on our summer vacation, we bought a few paper maps (remember how fun they were to try to fold up?), a road atlas, and off we trekked to adventure. Do we use paper maps anymore? No. We now have GPS maps on our Smartphone's or Garmin maps installed in our automobiles that automatically navigate us to our destinations. The GPS disrupted marketplace equilibrium in the paper maps and road atlas categories, offering customers a significantly better product than what already existed.

VCR's are another example. In 2000, 99% of households used a VCR as their primary appliance for watching movies and recorded programs. In 2006, DVD players for the first time were in more homes (84%) than VCR's (79%). High Definition Televisions were in only 10 percent of homes.

Fast forward to 2012 – just six short years later, and 69% of homes have at least one HDTV, 90% own a DVD player, 38% have a Blu-ray DVD player; 41% have a Digital Video Recorder (DVR); and VCR usage has plummeted to under 10%. Did the DVD player kill VCR's? No. In fact, it took DVD players 14 years to push by VCR players in home penetration. It wasn't until HDTV's started getting into homes that VCR's died. Why? Because played on a High-Definition TV, a digital picture from a DVD was significantly better than that from an analog VCR tape. When the two formats were played on old analog TV's, there wasn't much difference in picture quality. But high-definition TV's made the digital pictures come to life, making DVD players suddenly a significantly better product for movie playback than a VCR.

The Third Hurdle: Underestimating Introductory Marketing Costs

Another major reason for new product failure is low marketing budgets for the product launch. Introductions are no time to get queasy about spending. You have to tell consumers about your product to sell it, and you have to spend money to do it.

Procter & Gamble has a principle to follow on new product spending that seems to work pretty well. Their marketing managers are permitted to spend all of the projected profits generated from the first 18 months of sales. P&G knows that it must invest heavily to establish any new product in the marketplace. Only in month nineteen is the product expected to have earned back the marketing investment and begin showing a profit to the corporation.

Of course, most companies and entrepreneurs shudder at the thought of an 18-month payback window, but that's what it takes if you're going to give your product a fighting chance for long-term survival.

The Fourth Hurdle: Flawed New Product Creative Process

Many roads to failure in new products begin with the organizational chart. Companies establish a flawed system for creating new products. Instead of having the process driven by the marketing department out of consumer insight, they put the creation process in the hands of the technical engineers and product formulation scientists -- probably the least creative minds in the company!

Let's face it, how many brilliantly creative and insightful engineers or scientists do you know? People who are trained in these areas of expertise are disciplined. They aren't encouraged to think outside the box; it's their job to *define* the box. They spend their days locked in technical centers hunched over their chemical sets, not mulling over marketing sales data, competitive advertising or consumer trends -- the places where seeds for new product ideas await.

The soap and detergent division at P&G for years was the prime example of product initiation in the wrong hands. Its scientists and engineers continually dreamed up new product innovations, but most of their ideas provided corporate benefits, not consumer benefits.

The classic example was the creation of concentrated Ultra Downy, which was distributed in a small milk carton type package that required the consumer to pour the concentrate into another container and mix with 3 cartons of water. P&G scientists figured "hey, we can ship this in a small biodegradable carton and the consumer can mix in the water at home, saving us in both packaging costs and shipping costs, while making us appear environmentally friendly to the consumer!"

While they were half-right in their environmentally friendly stance, even loyal Downy consumers turned away from the new product in droves.

They didn't like knowing the fact that their fabric softener was 1 part softener and 3 parts their own tap water. They didn't like mixing the product in another bottle, and the small carton in comparison to the large plastic bottles offered by competitors for the same price confused the consumers' price / value relationship. After a year of treading water, P&G returned to their big blue plastic "bottle" packaging, but not before damage was inflicted on the Downy brand franchise and loyal consumers lost to competition.

Ignoring History

Another ticket to new product failure is ignoring what your predecessors have tried. Within every company is a hidden trove of new product ideas that others have been tried and tested in the past. Finding these files can keep you from avoiding the same mistakes, save time, and soften your learning curve.

With the high rate of employee turnover within most large corporations, old information is often buried and forgotten, leaving the current crop of marketers susceptible to re-testing ideas that have already failed. Most likely, whatever you've dreamed up, somebody else already thought of some time ago and the test results are sitting somewhere in a dusty cabinet.

In addition to internal snooping, another great place to learn what has been tried and failed is to buy a plane ticket to Ithaca, New York and visit the New Products Showcase and Learning Center, run by Robert McMath. He has collected an array of new consumer products that have been introduced over the past four decades -- about 100,000 items in all -- covering virtually every product category. It's a fascinating trip and worthwhile for understanding what roads your predecessors and competition may have traveled, and where opportunities may have been missed.

Distribution Debacles

One particularly thorny path to new product purgatory is creating products that require a different distribution system than the one you currently use.

Kellogg's suffered one of the classic new product meltdowns. In the summer of 1998 they introduced Kellogg's Breakfast Mates, which has a bowl of cereal and MILK packaged together in the same box along with a plastic spoon. Just tear off the cereal bowl top, open the small milk carton and pour the milk over the cereal, grab your spoon and eat away.

At first glance the product seems like a great idea, since cereal requires milk, a bowl, and a spoon, right? Now you can buy this one package and have everything you need!

When you look at it from a practical consumer point-of-view however, Breakfast Mate's didn't really offer a meaningful consumer benefit. Most consumers always have fresh milk in their refrigerators, so it's no big deal to grab the milk out of the fridge when you get your box of cereal out of the cupboard. Opening the refrigerator certainly doesn't require any more effort than opening the pre-packaged box. Kellogg's intended the product to address the growing "breakfast on the go" trend, but a bowl of cereal and milk still isn't a very portable meal; you can't eat it in the car like an Egg McMuffin, you need one hand on the bowl and the other on a spoon, and it doesn't have any appreciable benefit over those handy cereal and fruit breakfast bars.

Kellogg's management ignored the product flaws because it lusted to expand their brand offerings beyond the limitations of the cereal aisle and crusade into the grocer's refrigerated section -- a place where Kellogg's didn't have any products. But in addition to the lack of a meaningful consumer benefit, Breakfast Mates created a slew of logistical distribution problems.

First, Kellogg's distribution system was set up to ship boxes full of dry cereal in trucks to stores for stocking in the grocery aisle, a relatively simple process. Their trucks aren't set up for delivering products that require refrigeration, and since Breakfast Mates include milk, they must be refrigerated at all times. This meant Kellogg's had to partner with local dairies in every market to get the product delivered to the stores, or find a refrigerated distributor who was willing to deliver and stock the product for a price. A daunting task, and one that reduces the profit margin by putting another hand in the distribution chain.

Another key issue is that unlike dry cereal, which is can sit on a store shelf for months without spoiling, milk can only stay on the grocery store shelf for 10 days. Stock must be continually monitored and rotated, and out-of-date product discarded. Kellogg's didn't have a sales force equipped to visit stores to monitor and stock the shelf this diligently.

Refrigerated trucks, dairy partners, and product spoilage – all key issues Kellogg's didn't have to deal with in their basic cereal business. So, they decided that instead of dealing with all the issues that came with "fresh" milk, they instead put "canned" milk inside the Breakfast Mate boxes. Problem solved, right? Canned milk didn't need refrigeration so it could ship in Kellogg's regular trucks, didn't need a dairy partner to distribute, and had a long-shelf-life that didn't need to have stock rotated with expiration dates.

But this also meant the product didn't need to go into the grocery's coolers, so retailers started displaying it in the regular cereal aisle. Customer Red Flag #1 – how could something with fresh milk be stocked on the cereal aisle? Mom's immediately figured out it was canned milk, and that was the end of Breakfast Mates.

Brand Extensions

Many new products get their inspiration from what are termed "brand extensions", which take a well-established brand name and creates new products leveraging its popularity. Examples would include Gillette, which started as a popular men's razor and blade brand but through smartly using brand extensions has transformed Gillette into a men's personal care brand, including razors, blades, shave gel and foam, skin care, body wash, and anti-perspirant / deodorant. Dove bar soap has likewise leveraged its brand strength to expand into the personal care market, with brand extensions that include bar soap / body wash, deodorant, hair care and shampoos / conditioners, skin lotions and Men+Care products.

Other examples of brand extensions would include Marie Callender's, which started as a restaurant chain featuring comfort foods and fresh pies, into a line of frozen meals, entrees, pot pies and dessert pies sold in grocer's freezers. Starbucks coffee liqueur, Milk Bone brand dog toys,

Tide-to-Go stain removal pens, and Iams pet insurance; all are good examples of brand extensions. Frito-Lay introduced Doritos brand Taco Shells in Taco Bell. Brilliant idea.

Brand extensions should leverage your core brand strengths to extend and strengthen the overall brand. Choosing the right brand extension depends on brand fit and brand depth. The new offering should fit with the existing brand identity. Does it deliver similar meaning and value? Is the relevance of the new offering clear? Do the personality and character of the brand still apply? Without brand fit, the extension will be confusing and you may weaken existing brand equity.

The Wrong Way To Extend Your Brand

While it seems like a pretty simple idea – leverage your brand strength and create new products that will build even more brand equity -- the new products graveyard is littered with brand extensions that leveraged their brand name into areas where their brand equity had no meaning. A few of the notable include:

- Lifesavers (the candy) Soda
- Bic (the pens) Disposable Women's Underwear
- Cheetos (snacks) flavored lip balm
- Hooter's (restaurants) Airline
- Everlast (boxing equipment) fragrance and grooming products
- Starburst (candy) bath and body collection
- Diesel (jeans) wine
- Chicken Soup for the Soul (book) pet food
- Colgate (toothpaste) Kitchen entrée's
- Play-Doh Perfume

Many marketers try creating brand extensions in product channels where they don't have expertise. The problem with this is that if you do land on a truly great idea, someone who does have the competencies and economies of scale in distributing through that channel will steal the idea from you and execute it cheaper and more efficiently.

When I was working on the Folgers Coffee brand I invented a Fudge Crème coffee creamer that young consumers loved. It turned coffee into hot chocolate with a hint of coffee flavor. In our test market at a college university, we couldn't keep it on the store shelves. However, even though Folgers coffee creamer seemed to make strategic sense as a brand extension, P&G did not compete in the coffee creamer category. We would have had to pay someone else to manufacture the product for us (more expensive), and General Foods (our main competitor) owned coffee creamer plants and could make a Fudge Crème knockoff cheaper and more efficiently than we could. Rather than jumping into a product category where we would have had a competitive disadvantage from the get-go, we discontinued work on the Fudge Crème product.

General Foods learned this lesson the hard way when it invaded the frozen dessert business. In 1979 it created Jell-O Pudding Pops and built a $100 million dollar brand within a year of launch. By 1984 it had grown to a $300 million dollar business. Soon thereafter, Pudding Pops were discontinued. How could this happen? Why would General Foods throw away a $300 million dollar business? The answer was simple. Competitors had the expertise in delivering to the frozen food case that General Foods lacked, and General Foods had to pay dairies to manufacture the Pudding Pop product and frozen food distributors to get the product from the manufacturing facilities to the store freezers. Despite $300 million in sales, the Pudding Pops business was not profitable -- the more Pudding Pops they made, the more money General Foods lost. The extra hands in the manufacturing and distribution chain taking their cut of the profits killed the goose that laid the golden egg.

Me-Too Products

The sure road to new product failure is in creating products that do not have a perceptible and meaningful point-of-difference versus current product offerings.

Me-Too products are the disease that afflicts a majority of new products. The fundamental problem is that they aren't really "new" products -- they are copies of an existing product sold by somebody else! Store shelves are littered with Me-Too products.

Go to the household cleaners and see how many knock offs of the popular brand "Pine-Sol" there are. The knock-offs come and go, but Pine-Sol lives on. Just like in politics, Me-Too's have a tough time unseating the incumbent. To succeed with a Me-Too product, you must be prepared to spend like a drunken sailor on advertising to convince consumers that your product is different and better than the entrenched competition (even though it probably isn't), and you have to be prepared to fight protracted price wars in which profitability might dwindle to nearly nothing. Net, Me-Too's are much more trouble than their worth.

Line Extensions

Nearly three-quarters of all new product introductions are "line extensions" -- new products that borrow the name and brand equity from an existing product and create new products WITHIN the same product category.

For years the cereal "Cheerios" has been a breakfast staple. In the early 1990's General Mills launched its first Cheerios line extension -- Honey-Nut Cheerios. The success of that product spawned even more line extensions; Multi-Grain Cheerios, Apple-Cinnamon Cheerios, Chocolate Cheerios, Dolce de Leche Cheerios, Peanut Butter Cheerios, Cinnamon Burst Cheerios, Frosted Cheerios, Fruity Cheerios, Oat Cluster Crunch Cheerios, and Banana Nut Cheerios, giving consumers a dozen different variations of the popular cereal to choose from. These line extensions helped grow Cheerios to the #1 brand in the US cold cereal category.

The benefits of line extensions are many: they are much cheaper to introduce than an entirely "new" product; you can use your primary brand as a sampling vehicle; and it can expand your brand franchise significantly if done right. However, keep in mind that the Cheerios model is the exception to the rule. Most line extensions fail. They either cannibalize the sales of the "mother" product, or merely slice up the sales pie into smaller pieces.

Often desperate marketers try to cover up fundamental bleeding on the core brand by using a line extension as a Band-Aid. One example is Hawaiian Punch. The brand (just one flavor, Fruit Juicy Red) was getting slaughtered by Hi-C fruit drinks, which had a complete flavor line of twelve different fruit drinks. To try to stop the bleeding, Hawaiian Punch introduced a series of line extensions called "Hawaiian Punch Colors". The flavor of each was identical to Fruit Juicy Red Hawaiian Punch -- only the colors were different. Consumers bought the new offerings once and never came back. Despite success in the first couple of months of sales, Hawaiian Punch Colors soon disappeared off of grocer's shelves, and were virtually extinct within 9 months.

The Best Way To Invent New Products -- Buy Your Ideas

Having tried and failed far too often, many of the top marketing companies have taken a long, hard look at their processes for inventing new products and have turned to a new resource – entrepreneurs, outside new-product think tanks, universities innovation labs, and the US Innovation Marketplace to find their ideas. The growth of the Internet has made it possible to look for new products anywhere in the world with a few keystrokes in Google.

When you stop to think about it, finding your new products out in the world rather than inventing them yourself makes a lot of sense. Just as corporations turn to advertising agencies to tap into great creative minds, it seems natural to use outside creative resources that specialize in new products if you want to increase your odds of success. There is a far greater likelihood that looking to an entrepreneur or new products specialist who has invented and worked on their idea has a higher chance of success over a small cadre of your own employees who may have only five or six new product success stories (if that) to their credit.

Developing New Product Concepts

There are a few simple yet elegant principles that have been found over time to be critical to new product success:

Focus On Consumer Benefits, Not Product Function

The biggest learning when creating new product ideas is to push the consumer benefits and don't focus on the product functions. Consumers buy benefits. They don't care about the nuts and bolts.

To illustrate the principle, a local mother who was starting up a small children's performance group recently came to me to ask for marketing help. She was having a tough time attracting kids to sign up for her program. The name of the group was "Sunshine Generation". In the group, children learned to sing, dance, and offer community service by performing in public at various functions.

Her introductory advertising called out "Join A Kid's Performance Group" and detailed the functions children would learn: singing, dancing, music theory, and performing in front of audiences. She was featuring all of the "functions" of the group, but not mentioning the "benefits" kids and parents would receive from participation.

We developed a new product strategy targeted to moms, encouraging them to sign their kids up for Sunshine Generation to "Give Your Child The Chance To Shine" -- the benefit Mom and the child would receive. What Mom doesn't want to give her child a chance to shine? The new promotional materials highlighted all the benefits the child would receive from participating: develop talents (singing, dancing, performing), build self-confidence, learn to work together with others, and offer community service. Enrollment skyrocketed after the change. She sold the benefits, not the functions.

Far too often product marketers get hung up on telling you how the product does what it does instead of telling you what benefits you'll get from using it. Think about tire commercials that spend 25 seconds detailing how their innovative five layered sidewalls and unique tread designs channel away water to grip the road. OK, sounds good to me, but I'm no tire engineer, so they could draw up just about anything and show it to me and I'd have to agree with it. These companies have their priorities backward. They would be better off spending their time up front telling me about how their tire is the safest in the world, and that by using them on my car I'm showing my loved ones that I really care about their safety. That's the benefit I want to buy. The five layered sidewalls and tread designs are the "reasons why" the tire can deliver the benefit. The "reason why" is important, but the benefits must come first.

The Importance of A Plausible "Reason Why"

New products must have not only a compelling consumer benefit, but also a clear explanation of how the product will deliver that benefit. Consumers are skeptical about new product claims, so you have to use logic in your reasoning. Keep it simple and understandable. Don't try to pull the wool over the consumers' eyes with fluff and hyperbole. Tell them in plain language in a way they can understand.

Good Ideas Must Be Able To Stand Alone

The third key learning is that the death of most line extensions comes as a result of the brand's assumption that a pretty good idea married to a great brand name can pull the new product through to success. Not true. If the new idea can't stand alone on its own without needing the "umbrella" of the brand name as protection, don't try it.

Recently I received a call from a friend whose father wanted to launch a new line of NASCAR-licensed soft drinks. He wanted my opinion on whether or not it was a good idea. The concept was to create the NASCAR brand with 6 different fruit flavored soft drinks. Each flavor would feature a different NASCAR driver and his or her car on the packaging.

Citing this principle, my reply was simple. Take off the NASCAR name and then ask me if you should launch it. Does the world really need another bunch of fruit flavored soft drinks? How would they be different, better, and special versus FANTA fruit-flavored soft drinks? After some thought, they decided not to move ahead with the project.

You've Got To Have A GREAT Name

In this world of new product bombardment, a great name can make a good idea great. New products specialists spend a great deal of thought on creating product names that will peak consumer interest. Research has proven that most successful new products have a product name that communicates the benefit of the product. Gone are the days when you can introduce a new brand of toilet paper and simply call it *MD toilet tissue*. You've got to use the branding as a communication vehicle!

One quick example illustrates the point beautifully. If you are in the market for a new brand of Louisiana-style Cajun hot sauce, which of these would be more appealing: Old El Paso Cajun-Flavored Hot Sauce, or Ass-Kickin' Ragin' Cajun Hot Sauce. You don't have to read the label any further, do you?

The New Product Development Process

The process for new product creation is summarized in four steps:

1. Brainstorm lots of ideas
2. Develop an idea you think has potential
3. Write a "product concept"
4. Test the concept on real live consumers

Let's work through these steps in more detail.

Successful Brainstorming

I often get invited by different groups to participate in on-site brainstorming sessions to help dream up new products, marketing and promotion ideas. I love the art of strategic creativity, so I jump at the chance whenever offered. To crank up the creative juices, I have a personal routine I go through before I get to the group called "gittinjiggywidit". It includes loud music, looking at wild colors or beautiful landscapes, and turning loose the adrenaline. By the time I arrive, I'm wild-eyed and fired up, ready to rock n' roll.

Many times, an expert moderator supplied by the clients advertising agency hosts the creative session. The brainstorming is held in a staid office conference room somewhere on the corporate campus. Typically some "toys" like PlayDoh or blocks are tossed out on the tables in a feeble attempt to create a playful environment. Then the corporate participants march in -- often in the middle of a work day for an hour or two session -- dressed in their business suits, men's neckties smartly tight around their collars (brain tourniquets, as I like to refer to neckties), with corporate decorum and rank in full effect.

Unfortunately, most of the time these sessions provide very little out-of-the-box thinking by the corporate participants. They produce run-of-the-mill ideas. The one or two outsiders like me usually out-produce the entire corporate team by a 10-to-1 margin. The question I am asked by my corporate clients in the follow-up meeting from these sessions is always the same -- if we have a bunch of very smart people in the room, why does the brainstorming exercise always fail to produce great creative results?

The answer lies in the brainstorming methodology and the environment. To get breakthrough creative results, you have to break out of traditional paradigms. Great ideas aren't usually found sitting around a corporate conference table at 2 o'clock in the afternoon.

Braindraining

My friend Doug Hall has a great way of describing the problem. He calls this typical corporate method of brainstorming "braindraining" or alternately the "suck" method of creativity. This method presupposes that all great ideas already exist within the gray matter of one's brain, and all you have to do is somehow siphon the ideas out. People sit down in a room, think, sweat, use their brains as reference libraries and try to squeeze out a few hard-thought ideas. For most, this is a very short and laborious experience.

Stimulus Response

The alternative method of creativity is one that uses the brain as it was intended -- to absorb and process stimuli, then make new connections. This method is called "Stimulus Response". In his book "Jump Start Your Brain", Doug writes:

> "With Stimulus Response, your brain is used more like a processing computer and less like a reference library. Instead of withdrawing ideas from a finite collection of thoughts, your brain reacts off stimuli to create new associations, new Eureka's.
>
> Stimuli act as a fertilizer for your brain; they set up the chain reaction of ideas, many with the potential

for brilliance. Stimuli can be anything you see, hear, smell, taste, or touch. Stimuli can be anything that spurs your brain to make new connections, new associations, and new-to-the-world ideas."

Validation studies by Dr. Arthur VanGundy of the University of Oklahoma, one of the nation's leading authorities on the creative process, have found that the Stimulus Response method cranks out over 1,000 percent <u>more</u> new ideas than the aforementioned braindraining technique used by the average corporation. Going further, the studies concluded that Stimulus Response generated 558 percent more "super-smart" ideas with above average marketplace potential. Said another way, it can make your brain five times more effective at coming up with THE BIG IDEA.

Preparing For Brainstorming Success

There are three keys to creating an atmosphere where great brainstorming can occur. First, **provide an environment that's fun**. Get out of the corporate office. When I was at Coca-Cola, I held my creative sessions at a place called Dave & Busters. It is an adult's playground, with thousands of video games and virtual reality simulators. We'd rent out the back room, do some creative exercises, and then go out into the game room to play for a while before coming back in to create again.

Fun is critical to the creative process. A University of Maryland study indicates that when people are laughing, they're three to five times better at generating successful ideas.

Music is also crucial to the process. Loud, upbeat and eclectic are the best. Food is important as well. M&M's, soft drinks, coffee, and anything laced with sugar to keep the blood racing works great as creative snacks and munchies.

Second, **bring lots and lots of stimuli to provoke ideas**. Stimulus can be anything you can see, smell, taste or touch. Magazines, toys, products, pictures and lists of interesting words can all work wonders. It is important to keep feeding the brain with stimulus for the duration of the session. If you are planning on doing a full-day creative session, you'll need about 1,000 different items of stimulus to maximize your effectiveness.

Third, **invite creative people who don't work for you to participate**. You need to seed both business sense and non-sense into the invitees. Why have people that don't work on your business there? Simple. Remember when you first started your job and you came in all fired up with exciting new ideas? Then you started learning the business: corporate culture, personal agendas and biases, and were told by others what you could and could not do. Over time, those new ideas dried up. One day you woke up and discovered that you'd been beaten into the mold of corporate conventionalism.

This is not an unusual transformation. In fact, it's often part of the company system. Corporate culture makes its employees fit like pegs into holes. Employees learn what their job is and stop thinking. They perform the task to which they are assigned. Only "rebels" continue to press for new ideas. But over time, most rebels abandon the company out of frustration. It's a strange dichotomy. Corporations need these free spirits to spur them on, but the system can't handle them because they don't fit with the culture.

You need outside thinkers who are unbridled by the confines of corporate conventionalism. It's the only way to get out-of-the-box thinking.

Marketing Truth

The recipe for brainstorming success is simple: blend together people who know everything about your business with a healthy serving of creative folks that know absolutely nothing about what you do. Pour fun all over and serve in a wild, loud environment with lots of stimulus, great music, and munchies.

Creating The Perfect Brainstorming Session

There are a few very important steps to take at the beginning of the brainstorming session to foster the creative environment. First, **tell everyone to show up in CASUAL clothes**. Absolutely no ties are allowed. Heck, T-shirts, shorts and bare feet are the preferred attire for brainstorming. Comfortable clothes are important in allowing each individual to feel free of restraints and "be themselves".

Second (and this one is absolutely critical), **the playing field must be level among all participants**. Vice-Presidents and other corporate muckity-mucks must store their egos in their pockets and participate sans titles. Everyone in the session must feel equal to everyone else -- from CEO to administrative assistant. There are no titles in brainstorming sessions, just people all having fun working together to create. High-ranking executives must be made aware of this philosophy before arriving at the session so that they can help facilitate the leveling process with their underlings.

Third, **you must have a curriculum developed for the day with a full itinerary of different creativity exercises**.

Fourth, **you must have a moderator that can motivate the group and keep the energy at a frenetic level**. One executive coming out of a Stimulus Response brainstorming session remarked that "it seemed at times like a train wreck in there. But the amazing thing is that the chaos really was quite structured and we got a lot of great ideas".

Fifth, **as the brainstorming session commences, the participants should be assigned to small groups of no more than 5 or 6 people to work on each exercise**. Studies have shown that small groups are much more effective at creating new ideas than individuals working alone or larger groups. Groups should be reorganized after each exercise to create different connections and exposure to different thinking styles.

And finally, **you should break after each exercise and have a spokesperson for each group report back the highlights of their brainstorming**. This breather gives everyone in the session the opportunity to use the seeds of ideas generated to "build" on for even better ideas. After ninety minutes of brainstorming, take a 15-minute break for everyone to unwind and relax, then fire it back up.

The Truths of Brainstorming

Over the years, I have found that for me to be most effective at brainstorming, I have to remember what it was like to be five years old. All of the sudden, this mundane world is a fantastic new adventure. I start feeling things I haven't felt since childhood. Once I get rid of preconceived notions and business sense, my ideas run wild and true creativity can bubble to the surface.

Great Brainstorming Exercises

When conducting a brainstorming session, you have only one rule: ALL ideas are sacred and great -- protect the newborns.

The analogy is simple. Sometimes when a child is born, he looks a little funny; squishy, or blotchy, or hairy or pointy-headed. The wonderful thing is that often these ugly babies grow up to be attractive adults like Jennifer Aniston or George Clooney. For the same reason, we don't kill ugly ideas during the brainstorming session. While they may appear to be hideous and deformed when first uttered, sometimes this is where BIG IDEAS are born. When the brainstorming is in session, every idea is a great idea, no matter how outlandish or ridiculous. I've never met an organization that isn't skillfully adept at killing ideas. The key is to try to keep the ideas alive long enough so that they can mature and be refined.

There are hundreds of different exercises that have been developed for brainstorming. Here are six of my favorites. They all originate from Doug Hall and are used extensively at Eureka! Ranch. For more great exercises and brainstorming ideas, get his book "Jump Start Your Brain" published by Warner Books. It contains a plethora of great exercises, plush a wealth of creative knowledge from the master marketing inventor himself.

Exercise #1: Mind Dump (Individual Exercise)

This exercise is critical to starting a brainstorming session. At most sessions, participants have already thought up some ideas before they get there. Until everyone can get these preconceived ideas dumped out, their brains are constipated and nothing else can be thought of.

Pass out a handful of 3 x 5 cards to each individual. Give the group 5 minutes for everyone to "dump" the ideas they came into the session with on the cards, one idea per card. This helps "flush" everyone's mind so that creativity can begin.

Exercise #2: Stimuli One-Step

Provide each group with a box of miscellaneous stimuli. The objective of the exercise is to make direct connections between the stimuli and the task. Rifle through the stimuli quickly, making quick connections.

This exercise may appear to ridiculously simple to yield worthwhile results, but you'll change your mind once your try it. Often the simplest, most straightforward paths are the most effective.

Exercise #3: 666

The objective of this exercise is to force-associate related elements.

Give each group three dice -- each a different color. On a piece of paper, create three separate columns containing six words, thoughts, ideas, or product attributes -- anything that might be used to describe the task and a few that don't relate at all. Label the three columns the colors of each of the dice. Pass this list out to each group.

Now roll the dice. Look at the number that comes up each and look to the word or idea that corresponds in each colors column. Force yourself to make associations between those the three unrelated thoughts. When the ideas lull, re-roll the dice and force-associate another three ideas. Use the combinations that emerge with each toss as starting-gate stimuli. They don't have to be taken literally. The point isn't to make literal sense of the three ideas. It's to stimulate thoughts outside of normal thought patterns.

Exercise #4: Catalog City

Get a stack of different catalogs and pass them out to each group for stimuli. Use the photography and products as stimulus to get outside the box.

Exercise #5: Tabloid Tales

This exercise pushes you to the extremes. It takes the spirit of P.T. Barnum and the rank exploitiveness of The Enquirer and applies it to the task at hand.

The objective is to make your task larger than life. To emphasize, magnify, and overstate various aspects of your task to create new applications for individual elements, new approaches to improving the total package, or new solutions for your task.

First, hand out copies of the supermarket rags -- Enquirer, Weekly World News, or others to each group. Then list four thoughts about your task or problem in the middle of a piece of paper. Find ways to make them more provocative -- sensationalize them. Distort one aspect, then another. Look for facts that spark exaggeration. Use the tabloid rags as stimuli. Where has Elvis been spotted? Force-associate the wild, the bizarre, and the eye-popping.

Exercise #6: Pin Pricks

This is a devilishly fun exercise where you take on the persona of a madman. The objective is to spot vulnerabilities in your competition and turn them into advantages for you -- to engage in one-upsmanship, to make the other guy gnash his teeth, pull out his hair, and curse the day he was born.

To start the exercise, identify competitive candidates, anyone with whom you compete for time, sales, dollars or attention. Map out a plan to gig your rival in any one of the following ways:

-- What is your competition's greatest source of pride?

-- Who could endorse your effort and in so doing most annoy your competition?

-- How could you change your product to annoy the competition?

-- What customers could you steal to bother them?

-- How could you irritate competitors by changing pricing or sizing?

-- What elements of your competitor's product, packaging, marketing, or advertising could you learn from?

-- What humorous or outrageous claim could you make to drive the competition crazy?

--How could you shame them into taking steps they'd rather not?

Brainstorming Imaginatively

Your only limitation is your own imagination. There are literally thousands of different ways you can brainstorm effectively. The key is to provide your mind with stimulation. Get out of your comfortable everyday environment. Go someplace where creativity abounds. For me, when I need an injection of creativity I go to Walt Disney World Resort. At EPCOT they have a ride I just love. It's a silly ride called "Journey into Imagination". It features a jovial inventor and his little purple friend "Figment". The theme song chorus that plays throughout the ride says something like this:

Imagination

Imagination

A dream can be a dream come true

With just one spark, from me or you.

As you journey through the inventor's imagination, you encounter whims and whimsy from horror books to outer space. It's a delight, and it's inspirational. Don't miss it on your next trip to Florida. You'll be whistling the song for the rest of your life.

Developing A Concept

Finding an idea that has real potential is a numbers game. The more ideas you generate in your brainstorming session, the higher the likelihood that one of them is a big idea. Think of it this way. If you have ten ideas to choose from, what are the chances that you've developed the next multi-million dollar idea? Slim and none. But if you have two hundred ideas from which to choose, you improve your chances immensely.

Once the brainstorming is over, it's time to start weeding through the idea seeds and looking for the big ideas. When you find one you like, you turn it into what is called a "Concept". A concept has three parts:

1. Determine the key benefits and reason why for this idea. Why should the customer care? How is it different, better, and special versus what already exists in the marketplace?
2. Create a great name for the product. You improve the chances of success if your name aligns with the customer benefits.
3. Write a one paragraph "ad" for the product – we call this the concept statement.

Here is an example. Suppose you had been the one that came up with the idea to put your picture on your credit card, to reduce the possibility of theft. You start with the benefit and reason why:

> Benefit: Protects you against credit-card fraud if you card is ever lost or stolen.

> Reason Why: That's because you picture and signature are embedded on the front of your card, making it virtually impossible for someone other than you to use it.

Then, you come up with a great name, one that aligns with the benefit:

Photo-Protect Credit Cards

The perfect way to protect your account if your card is ever lost or stolen

Then you write a one paragraph "ad":

Introducing Photo-Protect credit cards from Citibank, the safest credit card ever made against fraudulent use. That's because YOUR photo and signature are actually embedded on the front of the card, STOPPING thieves from even thinking about using it! In fact, Photo-Protect cards have been proven in testing to significantly reduce credit-card fraud versus a normal card. Sign up for your Photo-Protect card today and protect your credit!

Now, put it all together:

Photo-Protect Credit Cards

The perfect way to protect your account if your card is ever lost or stolen

Introducing Photo-Protect credit cards from Citibank, the safest credit card ever made against fraudulent use. That's because YOUR photo and signature are actually embedded on the front of the card, STOPPING thieves from even thinking about using it! In fact, Photo-Protect cards have been proven in testing to significantly reduce credit-card fraud versus a normal card. Sign up for your Photo-Protect card today and protect your credit!

This is now a completed concept that is ready for testing!

Here is another example. During a recent brainstorming session, I started thinking about my kitchen, and in my mind's eye I was looking around…the fridge, microwave, range, oven, sink, dishwasher, cabinets. Then, the breadbox in the corner caught my eye. It started me thinking "How could I change a bread box to make it keep the bread fresher?"

Then I dove deeper. The question isn't "how could I change the bread box to make it keep my bread fresher", the real question is "how can I make the store-bought bread inside the bread box taste and smell like it just came out of the oven?" That's what I really wanted – to make store-bought bread taste and smell fresh baked.

Then I started brainstorming a product solution…a new kitchen appliance. What would we call it? We need a name that describes the benefit and seems provocative and new. *Bread Fresh.*

What would be the benefit? It turns every slice of store-bought bread into a warm, delicious indulgence that tastes and smells home-baked!

What would be the reason why? That's because the Bread Fresh machine warms each slice of store-bought bread in a patented moisture controlled chamber to both heat and naturally refresh it to its just-baked goodness. Just put a slice of bread into the Bread Fresh machine, and in 20 seconds it will smell and taste like it just came fresh out of the oven!

Finally, I put it all together into an "ad":

Bread Fresh

Turns every slice of store-bought bread into a warm, delicious indulgence that tastes and smells home-baked!

Introducing Bread Fresh, the new kitchen appliance that turns store-bought bread into home-baked goodness! The Bread Fresh machine warms each slice of store-bought bread in a patented moisture controlled chamber to both heat and naturally refresh it to its just-baked goodness. Just put a slice of bread into the Bread Fresh machine, and in 20 seconds it will smell and taste like it just came fresh out of the oven! Ohh, the smell. Ohh, the taste. Your family will love it!

Once again, we now have a fully developed concept ready for testing.

Concept Testing

Concept testing is the final piece of the new product innovation process. Once you have a fully developed concept, it's time to get it in front of customers for feedback.

Today's socially connected society makes getting quick feedback easy. You first have to put together a small online survey at a site like www.surveymonkey.com. Surveymonkey allows you to design a survey with up to 10 questions that you can get up to 100 responses for free.

When creating your survey, there are two key parameters that have been proven over time to be the keys in predicting new product success. They are:

> **Purchase Intent**: If this product were available in stores, how likely would you be to buy it?

> **New & Different**: In thinking about this product idea against products already sold in stores, how new and different is this product idea?

The ideal new product has high purchase intent and is very new and different versus what already exists. When you can find ideas that are high on both these scales, you are in the promised land of new product success!

Once you have designed your survey, get a link from the Surveymonkey "Collect Responses" tab and post it on your Facebook feed, asking friends and associates to take the survey for you. This will get you fast, first-cut feedback that costs $0 to see if you are possibly onto a good idea.

Rapid-Cycle Testing

Often, the first set of test results are mixed. In these cases, you may consider revising the concept and testing again. Research has shown that in many cases, it takes four-cycles of test-and-improve to optimize a new product concept. The key is to do it fast. If your idea is going to fail, you want it to "Fail Fast, Fail Cheap", before you have to invest time and money. Set a 30-day deadline for making the "Go-No Go" decision. This testing platform allows you to do just that with zero out-of-pocket costs.

Product Prototyping & Testing

Ideas that have tested well – with high purchase intent and which seem new and different versus what already exists – move on to the next phase of product development, which is product prototyping and small tests. In this phase, your goal is to "Make A Little, Sell A Little, Learn A Lot." Again, the goal is to find out if it really is a good idea, once it has been translated from just a written idea into a real product. But you again need to follow the "Fail Fast, Fail Cheap" model. Think like an entrepreneur. How can I get a few samples of the product put together as cheaply as possible and then try selling them? Ideas that require lots of time and investment to make a prototype are risky. Can you make something close to what you are thinking to test it?

Many entrepreneurs have new product ideas that are perfect for testing at Saturday Farmers Markets during the summer. Make a little, sell a little, and see if people will buy it. Only then will you know if you have a great idea! The ultimate test of new product success is when people pay you for your creation!

Risk and Reward

When you work on new ideas, you're a bit like a trapeze artist working without a net. When you fly through the air and catch the bar, it's a beautiful thing. But if you miss, you go splat. Scary, yes, but still the best act in the whole show. If you prepare carefully, troubleshoot diligently, and avoid making mistakes, you can take the risk. Where you'll end up is strictly unknown. But as Ray Bradbury once said, "Jump, and find your wings on the way down."

Eric D Schulz

Section Three:
Pricing Strategy

Eric D Schulz

Chapter Seven

Pricing Strategies

I often attend major sporting events on the spur of the moment, showing up at the stadium with the intent of purchasing tickets from some fan or scalper wandering around the parking lot. These exercises in free market pricing and negotiation are some of the most interesting business experiences I've ever had. If you've never tried it, you really should. Haggling over ticket prices exposes the naked underbelly of free market economics and quickly illustrates how pricing for the same product can vary wildly depending upon who's doing the selling.

The sellers have a ticket in their hands with a price printed on it -- face value -- but they have no idea what I am willing to pay for that ticket. I shop around with different sellers. To my amazement, I can usually find people with virtually identical seat locations offering them anywhere from below face value to nearly double the price.

When I'm dealing with professional ticket scalpers, it's tough to negotiate them down, but I can usually get them to a price about $10 to $15 above the amount printed on the tickets. When I'm dealing with non-scalpers -- regular fans or season ticket holders who have extra seats -- I almost never pay above face value, and the first price offer they make to me is usually either face value or below. I love dealing with these people. I gleefully pay for the tickets and head to the concession stand for a hot dog, a bag of peanuts and a Coke.

How can the ticket sellers know how to price to their tickets? If they don't do some asking around, they can't. Good ticket scalpers know precisely what every person in the parking lot is charging for their tickets and the location of their seats. They shop around and ask others what they are selling, and when they locate naive fans significantly undervaluing their tickets, they snap them up and quickly resell them at a profit. The scalpers understand the competitive environment and the market price of the tickets.

The scalpers also know when to hold 'em and when to fold 'em. When they see an oversupply of tickets, they sell what they are holding for the best price they can get and go home. They know you can't make a profit if the market is flooded with cheap tickets.

The same concept of knowing the pricing within the competitive landscape is what you must use if you are selling anything from yo-yos to yachts. You must understand what all competitive products are selling for and determine what price is best for your product to maximize your profitability.

Pricing Strategies

There are a multitude of different pricing strategies that have been developed and tried. Here is a list along with brief descriptions of each:

Cost-plus pricing

Cost-plus pricing is the simplest pricing method. The firm calculates the cost of producing the product and adds on a percentage (profit) to that price to render the selling price. This method, although simple, has two flaws; it takes no account of demand and there is no way of determining if potential customers will purchase the product at the calculated price.

This appears in two forms, Full cost pricing which takes into consideration both variable and fixed costs and adds a % markup. The other is direct cost pricing which is variable costs plus a % markup; the latter is only used in periods of high competition as this method usually leads to a loss in the long run.

Creaming or skimming

In market skimming, goods are sold at higher prices so that fewer sales are needed to break even. Selling a product at a high price, sacrificing high sales to gain a high profit is therefore "skimming" the market. Skimming is usually employed to reimburse the cost of investment of the original research into the product. It is commonly used in electronic markets when a product such as the latest iPad, are introduced into the market at a high price. This strategy is often used to target "early adopters" of a product or service. Early adopters generally have a relatively lower price-sensitivity -

this can be attributed to their need for the product outweighing their need to economize; a greater understanding of the product's value; or simply having a higher disposable income.

This strategy is employed only for a limited duration to recover most of the investment made to build the product. To gain further market share, a seller must use other pricing tactics such as economy or penetration. This method can have some setbacks as it could leave the product at a high price against the competition.

Limit pricing

A limit price is the price set by a monopolist to discourage economic entry into a market, and is illegal in many countries. The limit price is the price that the entrant would face upon entering as long as the incumbent firm did not decrease output. The limit price is often lower than the average cost of production or just low enough to make entering not profitable. The quantity produced by the incumbent firm to act as a deterrent to entry is usually larger than would be optimal for a monopolist, but might still produce higher economic profits than would be earned under perfect competition.

The problem with limit pricing as a strategy is that once the entrant has entered the market, the quantity used as a threat to deter entry is no longer the incumbent firm's best response. This means that for limit pricing to be an effective deterrent to entry, the threat must in some way be made credible.

Loss leader

A loss leader is a product sold at a low price (i.e. at cost or below cost) to stimulate other profitable sales. This would help the companies to expand its market share as a whole. Retailers often use this tactic on popular products to lure customers into their stores, making up the loss by selling other items to the shopper.

Market-oriented pricing

Setting a price based upon analysis and research compiled from the target market. This means that marketers will set prices depending on the results from the research. For instance if the competitors are pricing their products at a lower price, then it's up to them to either price their goods at an above price or below, depending on what the company wants to achieve.

Penetration pricing

The price charged for products and services is set artificially low in order to gain market share. Once this is achieved, the price is increased.

Price discrimination

Setting a different price for the same product in different segments to the market. For example, this can be for different ages, such as classes, or for different opening times of a theatrical production (i.e. Matinee discounts).

Premium pricing

Premium pricing is the practice of keeping the price of a product or service artificially high in order to encourage favorable perceptions among buyers, based solely on the price. The practice is intended to exploit the tendency for buyers to assume that expensive items enjoy an exceptional reputation, are more reliable or desirable, or represent exceptional quality and distinction. This approach is used where a substantial competitive advantage exists and the marketer is safe in the knowledge that they can charge a relatively higher price.

Predatory pricing

Aggressive pricing (also known as "undercutting") intended to drive out competitors from a market. It is illegal in some countries.

Contribution margin-based pricing

Contribution margin-based pricing maximizes the profit derived from an individual product, based on the difference between the product's price and variable costs (the product's contribution margin per unit), and on one's assumptions regarding the relationship between the product's price and the number of units that can be sold at that price. The product's contribution to total firm profit (i.e. to operating income) is maximized when a price is chosen that maximizes the following: (contribution margin per unit) X (number of units sold).

Psychological pricing

Pricing designed to have a positive psychological impact. For example, selling a product at $3.95 or $3.99, rather than $4.00.

Dynamic pricing

A flexible pricing mechanism made possible by advances in information technology, and employed mostly by Internet based companies. By responding to market fluctuations or large amounts of data gathered from customers - ranging from where they live to what they buy to how much they have spent on past purchases - dynamic pricing allows online companies to adjust the prices of identical goods to correspond to a customer's willingness to pay. The airline industry is often cited as a dynamic pricing success story. In fact, it employs the technique so artfully that most of the passengers on any given airplane have paid different ticket prices for the same flight.

Price leadership

An observation made of business behavior in which one company, usually the dominant competitor among several, leads the way in determining prices, the others soon following. The context is a state of limited competition, in which a market is shared by a small number of producers or sellers.

Target pricing

Pricing method whereby the selling price of a product is calculated to produce a particular rate of return on investment for a specific volume of production. The target pricing method is used most often by public utilities, like electric and gas companies, and companies whose capital investment is high, like automobile manufacturers.

Target pricing is not useful for companies whose capital investment is low because, according to this formula, the selling price will be understated. Also the target pricing method is not keyed to the demand for the product, and if the entire volume is not sold, a company might sustain an overall budgetary loss on the product.

Absorption pricing

This method of pricing is one in which all costs are recovered. The price of the product includes the variable cost of each item plus a proportionate amount of the fixed costs and is a form of cost-plus pricing

High-low pricing

Method of pricing where the goods or services offered by the retailer are regularly priced higher than competitors, but through promotions, advertisements, and or coupons, lower prices are offered on key items. The lower promotional prices are designed to bring customers to the retailer where the customer is offered the promotional product as well as the regular higher priced products. This is the pricing strategy of most department stores (Dillard's, Macy's, Kohl's, etc.).

Premium decoy pricing

Method of pricing where a retailer artificially sets one product price high, in order to boost sales of a lower priced product.

Marginal-cost pricing

This is the practice of setting the price of a product to equal the extra cost of producing an extra unit of output. By this policy, a producer charges, for each product unit sold, only the addition to total cost resulting from materials and direct labor. Businesses often set prices close to marginal cost during periods of poor sales. If, for example, an item has a marginal cost of $1.00 and a normal selling price is $2.00, the firm selling the item might wish to lower the price to $1.10 if demand has waned. The business would choose this approach because the incremental profit of 10 cents from the transaction is better than no sale at all.

Value-based pricing

Pricing a product based on the perceived value and not on any other factor. Pricing based on the demand for a specific product would have a likely change in the market place.

Pay what you want

Pay what you want is a pricing system where buyers pay any desired amount for a given commodity, sometimes including zero. In some cases, a minimum (floor) price may be set, and/or a suggested price may be indicated as guidance for the buyer. The buyer can also select an amount higher than the standard price for the commodity.

Giving buyers the freedom to pay what they want may seem to not make much sense for a seller, but in some situations it can be very successful. While most uses of pay what you want have been at the margins of the economy, or for special promotions, there are emerging efforts to expand its utility to broader and more regular use.

Freemium

Freemium is a business model that works by offering a product or service free of charge (typically digital offerings such as software, content, games, web services or other) while charging a premium for advanced features, functionality, or related products and services. It has become a highly popular model, with notable success in phone apps.

Odd pricing

In this type of pricing, the seller tends to fix a price whose last digits are odd numbers. This is done so as to give the buyers/consumers no gap for bargaining as the prices seem to be less and yet in an actual sense are too high.

Product line pricing

This is useful when there is a range of products or services where the pricing reflects the benefits of parts of the range. For example car washes - a basic wash could be $2, a wash and wax $4 and the whole package for $6. Product line pricing seldom reflects the cost of making the product since it delivers a range of prices that a consumer perceives as being fair incrementally – over the range.

Optional product pricing

Companies will attempt to increase the amount customers spend once they start to buy by offering "add-ons". Optional 'extras' increase the overall price of the product or service. For example, car dealers will often offer service programs, and airlines will charge for optional extras such as guaranteeing a window seat or reserving a row of seats next to each other. Airlines are prime users of this approach when they charge you extra for additional luggage or extra legroom.

Captive product pricing

Where products have complements (such as blood sugar testing strips that are required with diabetes blood sugar monitors), companies will charge a premium price since the consumer has no choice. For example a razor manufacturer will charge a low price for the razor handle and recoup its margin (and more) from the sale of the blades that fit the razor. Another example is where printer manufacturers will sell you an inkjet printer at a low price. In this instance the inkjet company knows that once you run out of the consumable ink you need to buy more, and this tends to be relatively expensive. Again the cartridges are not interchangeable and you have no choice.

Product bundle pricing

Here, sellers combine several products in the same package. This also serves to move old stock. Blu-ray and videogames are often sold using the bundle approach once they reach the end of their product life cycle. You might also see product bundle pricing with the sale of items at auction, where an attractive item may be included in a lot with a box of less interesting things so that you must bid for the entire lot. It's a good way of moving slow selling products, and in a way is another form of promotional pricing.

Promotional pricing

Pricing to promote a product is a very common approach. There are many examples of promotional pricing including approaches such as Buy One Get One Free, money off vouchers and discounts. Promotional pricing is often the subject of controversy. Many countries have laws that govern the amount of time that a product should be sold at its original higher price before it can be discounted. Sales are extravaganzas of promotional pricing!

Geographical pricing

Geographical pricing sees variations in price in different regions of the same country, or in parts of the world. Some countries tax goods such as alcohol or gasoline in order to increase revenue, and it is noticeable when you do travel overseas that sometimes goods are much cheaper, or more expensive.

Value pricing

This approach is used where external factors such as recession or increased competition force companies to provide value products and services to retain sales e.g. value meals at McDonalds and other fast-food restaurants. Value price means that you get great value for money i.e. the price that you pay makes you feel that you are getting a lot of product. In many ways it is similar to economy pricing. One must not make the mistake to think that there is added value in terms of the product or service. Reducing price does not generally increase value.

Every-Day Low Price

This approach is made famous by Walmart and was recently adopted by JC Penney. In this method, the retailer sets price at the lowest price that they are willing to sell the product at. They calculate the price from their cost price + profit margin. The retailer rarely if ever offers discounts off that price.

Charge Your Customers A Fair Price

Most of us are in business for the long haul and would like to have repeat customers. In order to achieve success, we must price our products to maximize profitability and still satisfy the consumer that he paid fair market value for our goods.

Every monetary transaction is an exercise in balancing <u>value</u> (both intrinsic value and actual value provided through product benefits) versus price. If the value that I as a buyer attach to the product is about equal to or more than the price being asked, I'll buy it. If the price being asked is significantly higher or lower than the value I attach to the product, I won't buy. This is not an equation of absolute dollars; the same consumer who willingly shells out $35 for an attractive silk tie may balk at spending an extra 20 cents for his usual brand of disposable razor. He'll switch razor brands before he'll forego the tie, not because he can't afford the razor, but because his brand isn't worth an extra 20 cents to him. Figuring out just where the right price lies is often a tricky proposition.

Price Elasticity

In economics classes, the fundamental technique for determining product pricing is called price elasticity. This principle follows the basic idea that the lower the price you offer, the more product you will sell; the higher the price, the fewer items you will sell. This pricing strategy makes sense for many consumer products. The goal of price elasticity is to find the right combination of price and sales volume to make the most profit. Here's an example of how it works.

Assume for a moment that we are selling baseballs to major league teams. The balls cost us $1.75 each to manufacture. As a test for the last two months, we've let our sales force sell the baseballs for whatever price they could negotiate with each team buyer. The prices have been all over the map. Some of the salesmen have sold them for as much as $8.00 per ball. Others have let them go for as little as our cost price of $1.75 each.

TEAM	# Balls Sold	Price
Phillies	200	$3.50
Dodgers	500	$2.75
Braves	200	$5.00
Reds	100	$4.75
Giants	50	$6.00
Red Sox	100	$6.50
Yankees	300	$5.50
Padres	700	$1.75
White Sox	400	$5.50
Cubs	50	$8.00
Angels	75	$7.25
Brewers	50	$6.75
Diamondbacks	200	$6.50
Marlins	75	$7.00

Our sales team figured out that the average price paid per ball was $3.96. The management team thinks that a price of $4.00 per ball must be the right price to go with, but you and I are still not sure if that price point will maximize our profits.

We decided to graph the sales figures to see if a picture makes any sense. The graph looks like this:

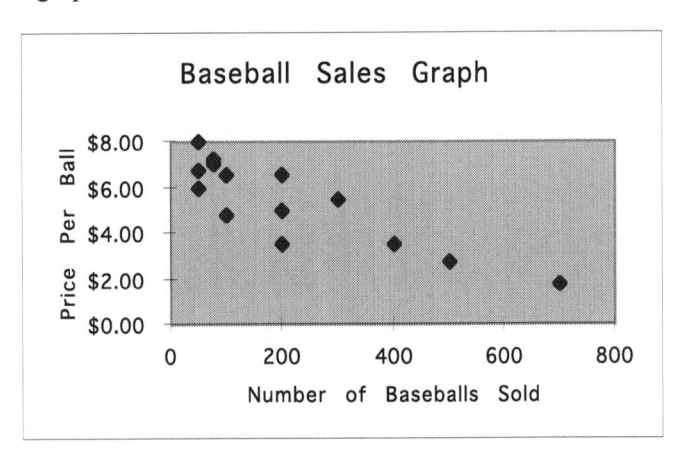

Baseball Sales Graph

[Scatter plot: x-axis "Number of Baseballs Sold" from 0 to 800; y-axis "Price Per Ball" from $0.00 to $8.00]

Looking at this chart, we can draw the conclusion that the right price appears to be somewhere between $4.00 and $6.00. Next, we draw a straight line between the different data points to quantify the price/sales relationship (this is called a regression analysis. The line represents what is called a price elasticity curve).

It looks like this:

Baseball Sales Graph

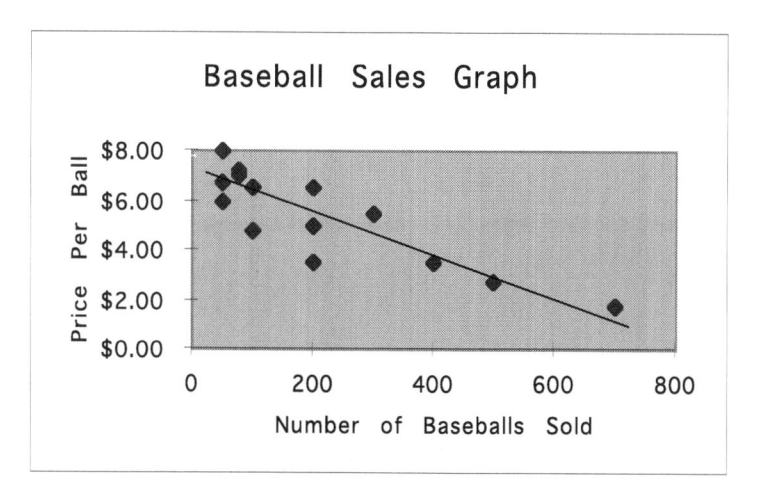

The elasticity curve represents our best-guess of how many balls we'll sell to each customer as we raise or lower prices, based on the actual sales experience of our sales team over the past several months. Remember, each ball costs us $1.75 to manufacture, so now let's add profit to our scenario. The price elasticity graph converts to this financial picture:

Price	# Balls Sold	Revenue	Profit
$6.00	175	$1,050	$743.75
$5.00	300	$1,500	$975.00
$4.00	400	$1,600	$900.00
$3.00	550	$1,650	$687.50

The elasticity analysis shows that somewhere around the price of $5.00 per ball is where our company will make the most profit! To find the exact price, we refine the analysis:

Price	# Balls Sold	Revenue	Profit
$5.50	250	$1,375	$937.50
$5.25	275	$1,443.75	$962.50
$5.00	300	$1,500	**$975.00**

$4.75	325	$1,543.75	**$975.00**
$4.50	350	$1,575	$962.50

Notice how at both the price of $5.00 per ball and $4.75 per ball we end up making the exact same profit! We'd naturally select the price of $5.00, because we don't want to invest the manpower in making and selling another 25 balls for no additional profit.

By performing the price elasticity analysis we found the _right_ price instead of using the average of $4.00 each that the sales team wanted. If we had accepted the lower price, we would have been leaving $1.00 on the table for every ball we sold, worked harder to sell more balls, and gone home with less money in our pockets.

The Sales Commission Quandary

Look again at the financial comparison between selling the balls at $4.00 versus $5.00:

Price	**# Balls Sold**	**Revenue**	**Profit**	**Margin**
$4.00	400	$1,600	$900.00	56.25%
$5.00	300	$1,500	$975.00	65.00%

Lurking behind those innocent numbers is a brewing conflict between sales and marketing. These two departments work off of different incentive programs, and therein lay the problem.

Typically, marketing personnel are awarded their salary bonuses based upon how their products perform against certain overall profitability targets. Sales personnel are usually rewarded sales commissions for attaining specific sales revenue figures (remember, revenue doesn't take into consideration the cost of producing the product; it only factors in price x number of units). Often, these reward systems are in direct conflict. Looking at this example, you can see that the sales team will earn much more revenue, thus bigger personal paychecks, if they can sell the product for $4.00 per ball because at that price they sell 100 additional balls. The marketing team receives bigger paychecks if they set the price at $5.00 per ball to maximize overall profits. No wonder these departments have a hard time getting along!

So which is the right price? If your company has shareholders, the right price is $5.00, because you have a responsibility to the stockholders to maximize shareholder wealth -- which means maximize profitability. If you work at a privately held company, then the discussion can become a bit livelier, since mere profitability might not be the owner's primary motivation.

Price Sensitivity

In order to understand how much leeway you have in pricing with consumers, you must determine how sensitive they are to changes in prices within your product category. The price elasticity analysis can answer this question nicely. If you are selling a commodity with virtually no product differentiation between you and competition -- like bags of sugar -- you won't have much flexibility in price before the consumer switches to your competitor's product. At the other extreme, if you are selling airline tickets, you have a great deal of latitude, since nearly every person on the plane paid a different price for his seat and nobody knows what anybody else paid.

Airlines are the masters at understanding price sensitivity. They have elaborate pricing models built into their computer ticketing system that continually adjusts pricing based on each plane's seats sold and seat occupancy. Most major airline computers automatically change over 100,000 fares daily!

Price Insensitivity

The best business to own and operate is within a category in which buyers are price insensitive, meaning they will pay just about any amount for your goods and the sales volume doesn't change much no matter what you charge. Microsoft has lived in this world for a long time with its popular Windows platform and biannual upgrades. No competitive product can serve as an alternative to Windows, thus no market leverage exists to hold down the price Microsoft chooses to place on the product. Gates & Company continue to roll in the dough as all PC users are virtually forced to purchase the Windows upgrades in order to keep their computers current and utilize new software, all of which is designed to run with the newest version of Windows. Product monopolies like Microsoft are a wonderfully profitable machine.

One Man's Trash Is Another Man's Treasure

In Park City, Utah there is an old shop on Main Street filled with collectibles and artifacts from years gone by. I love going into this store and looking at product prices. You can find worthless stock certificates from defunct Park City silver mines selling for $25.00; old 6 oz. glass bottles of Coca-Cola for $15.00 each; neon signs that don't work priced at $300.00, along with hundreds of other trinkets of the old west -- horse shoes, rusty buckets, miners lamps and so on.

The first time you walk into this store, you look around and say "Geez, what a pile of junk". But this junk has made the owners wealthy. They have succeeded by transforming the consumer's price / value relationship -- setting high prices on their funky goods to make consumers believe that they are buying prized collectibles, not trash. Since there is no competition or value comparison for the items, the strategy works. The old circa 1920's cash register in the store is constantly cranking up new sales as the gullible tourists snatch up pieces of what they consider to be Park City and old west history.

Now what would happen if the owners priced their goods at flea market prices and sold the junk for what it was really worth? Let's say the stock certificate was priced at $1.00, the Coca-Cola bottle at $2.00, and the broken neon sign for $5.00. Nobody would buy any of it. Consumers would walk into the store and instead of seeing prized collectibles, they'd see a pile of junk. The high pricing creates a perception that their products are highly valuable!

Why do people pay $100 for a haircut at a fancy salon versus $12 at Supercuts? Because consumers believe that the stylist at La Boutique De Bouffant is more skilled than her counterpart at Supercuts, and the huge price differential supports that conclusion. In reality is there that much difference? Probably not.

Marketing Truth

Everything communicates something to consumers about your product; this is especially true of pricing. The price you ask makes a statement about the value you are offering to the consumer. If you offer a low price, consumers assume lower value. If you offer a high price, they infer that the product has a higher value and that it truly delivers the benefits.

I have a friend who does marketing consulting for a living. When he first went into business, he charged $50,000 for his unique services, sometimes discounting to $35,000 to get the business. He was doing fine, but not great. Finding clients was a constant struggle. Instead of lowering the price of his services even lower to attract new clients, he decided to raise his price to $75,000 and eliminate the discounts. Without any other significant changes to his program, he suddenly saw more business come his way. Now he charges $150,000 and his calendar is booked out 8 months in advance. He didn't change what he was selling. He changed the perception of the value of his services by jacking up the price. The more he charges, the more successful and sought after he's become. Now he is considered to be the world's top "guru" within his specialty! Price perception IS reality!

Super Low Prices

It doesn't take a brain surgeon to try to compete on the platform of lower prices. Many retailers have tried to establish themselves with this strategy. Most have disappeared, including Woolworth's, People's Express, and many more. And let's face it; if low price were everything, we'd all be driving a Yugo. Why doesn't lowest price equal success? Because consumers don't shop for the lowest cost – they shop for the highest value! Products and services that deliver the most value (both intrinsic and through product benefits) are what consumers purchase.

This truth is why generic products didn't wipe out all name brands years ago. Consumers find intrinsic value and better product performance in the brand names of many of their favorite products -- Tide, Windex, Folgers,

Bounty and others. The lower price of the generic items doesn't compensate for the performance value of the name brands.

Products and businesses that rely on a positioning of lowest prices are usually destined for failure. Low price is important to consumers, but it can't be the sum total of the brand's positioning. Sooner or later (and usually sooner) somebody will come along with a way to either deliver the product benefit in a better or cheaper way, and at that point it's turn out the lights, the party's over.

The Psychology of "Cheap"

Even though many consumers are poor, no one wants to think of himself that way. Poor people want to enjoy the fruits of life just as much as the country club set. Purchasing name-brand products can offer a degree of comfort and pride to consumers; they may not be able to afford a new car, but they can provide small luxuries like a favorite cereal or premium ice cream. Studies have shown families living below the poverty line purchase significantly more name-brand items for everyday use than the average consumer -- soaps, beauty products, prepared foods -- as well as mid-range luxury items such as watches, TV's and stereos.

So if the poor don't want cheap generic products, what does that tell you about the middle and upper classes? Consumers want quality and are willing to pay for it. The price you set for your product translates to a value statement with consumers. Is a Rolex Presidential watch really worth $5,999? Not in my world, but for some select buyers the brand provides intrinsic value that justifies paying the exorbitant price. Every consumer makes a value judgment based upon the benefits the product delivers and the cost associated with purchasing those benefits.

Best Value Pricing

On any given trip to the grocery store I can find a dozen or so brands with a highlighted burst on their packaging stating "Best Value", which is another way of saying "lowest price". This promotional packaging suggests to the consumer that your brand performance is inferior to the competitive shelf set. Consumers aren't strictly looking to spend the least amount of money; they're shopping for the best performance for their dollars. They buy the product with the most compelling benefits, and that's what you should highlight!

Pricing Through A Product Life Cycle

The concept of product life cycle is helpful when considering pricing options. To illustrate the idea, think about the introduction of DirecTV Digital Satellite receivers in the mid 1990's. In the beginning, DSS was priced everywhere at $499 for a basic system. Those media-loving consumers who were fed up with their cable companies and techies who wanted the newest TV toy happily ran to stores to gobble up this new window to the world. DirecTV used these high profits to fund more production and lower their costs. After two years, the average price tag of a basic system was $299; three years later it fell to around $199. Now, the system is free, just for subscribing.

Where did DirecTV make its big profits? At the beginning. Now that competition has forced the system price down to nothing, they are making virtually no profits on the receivers, but instead are raking it in from selling the programming, with over 50 million units now in homes! By pricing the product differently at various stages of the product life cycle, DirecTV was able to maximize profitability.

When determining the price for your products, you must have a bit of selfishness in you, but at the same time temper the quest for profits with the understanding that you must make your consumers believe they are receiving fair value for your product. Your products must deliver the benefit to the consumer. You should always assume that each customer you sell product to will be back for more at some time in the future, and you need that consumer to want to deal with you again.

Fool me once, shame on you. You'll never get the chance to fool me twice because once you've stiffed me; I'll be dealing with your competitor next time around. Deception and greed are short-term business strategies. If you want to find long-term success, you must act with morals and conviction. It's not a sin to charge a high price for your product if the product benefits are commensurate with the consumer's personal definition of value. If your price is right, you'll buy business success.

Eric D Schulz

Chapter Eight

Life Currencies

YOU ARE AT THE STORE considering buying a new pair of running shoes. As you look at the store display, it tells of many new features in the shoe – spring-loaded heels, gel-cushioned insoles, sweat removing dry-fit casing. It all looks great, but you really want to talk to a salesperson about it to get more **information**. You look around, but there's no one in sight. You try on the shoes, but still want to get some insight. Finally you put the shoes down and walk away in **frustration**. You just used life currencies.

The only currency we ever talk about is money, but the reality is that every individual has a combination of currencies continually being evaluated in their subconscious that they measure and use when contemplating a purchase decision. These subconscious currencies are called "life currencies", and are often more important to the purchase decision than the currency in your pocket.

What are life currencies? They are the things besides money that affect purchase decisions. In almost every transaction, there is a combination of life currencies in play that affect the decision on whether or not to purchase something. The twelve life currencies we as marketers can manipulate in purchase decisions are:

- Information
- Time
- Space
- Human Energy
- Expertise
- Fun
- Fear
- Frustration
- Convenience
- Love
- Quality
- Money

Using Life Currencies

Here are some examples of how life currencies work. Have you every purchased a good or service because having that would save you a lot of time? *Time* therefore is one currency that you value and use as a consideration when making the purchase decision, along with **money**.

Have you ever walked away from buying something because you were frustrated standing in line or waiting on the phone, or the website was just too slow? *Frustration* or lack of *convenience* is the primary currency that makes that purchase (or non-purchase) decision.

Have you ever wanted a giant LCD HDTV, but haven't bought it because you don't have a place in your home to put it? **Space** (or lack of space), is the primary currency that sways the (non) purchase decision.

Step back for a moment and think about the purchases (and non-purchases) you've made in the past several days, I'll bet that one of the other life currencies was the determining factor in the many of your purchases, though you were likely unaware of its influence.

When business schools teach marketing, they focus on the 4-P's: Product, Placement, Promotion, and Price. When they talk about price, they only talk about money. That's wrong. Smart marketers know that for most products, money is only one factor in the purchase decision, and it's often a minor one at that.

> <u>*Marketing Truth*</u>
>
> *The monetary cost of items is often not a factor in the purchase decision. More often than not, one or more life currencies drive the purchase (or non-purchase) decision.*

Think about the decision on whether or not to purchase the services of a professional tax preparer. You may think it is wise to purchase the service because you lack the **information** to know the minutia of the tax code.

You don't have the **expertise** of a tax preparer. You **fear** and have **angst** that if you do your own tax return, you'll mess it up and get audited by the IRS. You hate having to take the **time** and expend the **mental energy** to do the return yourself. It's more **convenient** to have someone else do it. The professional tax preparer will likely do a more **quality** job.

All of these currencies are likely more valued in the overall decision than the price of the tax preparer. So if you were a marketer for a major tax preparer, wouldn't it make sense to focus on the benefits of these life currencies in your consumer communications, more so than it would be to have a person costumed as the Statue of Liberty out dancing on street corners holding a "Tax Preparation" sign?

When buying a ticket to a sporting event, what life currencies play a factor? **Fun** is probably high on the list. You may do it because you are a big fan of the team, (a more masculine way to say "I **love** my team"). You may go because it is a release from life, a way to recharge your **human energy**. You may pick to attend a particular game because you have **information** that this will be a good game. All of these in combination add up to justify the value of purchasing your tickets!

Virtually any purchase decision can be linked back to life currencies. The key to smart marketing is to peel back the layers of the onion, recognize the existence of life currencies, and figure out how to maximize their value in your consumer offering! Let's look at each life currency individually:

Information

Information is a collection of related data or knowledge about a business, product or service. Marketers often use a combination of advertising, packaging graphics, websites, flyers, and salespeople as vehicles to communicate information about their product or service.

Not providing customers with adequate information to make an informed decision is the #1 reason customers walk away from purchasing items that they otherwise are interested in. For many businesses, products or services, just fixing this one thing will boost sales significantly.

Time

Time is the only life currency besides money that we often refer to as "spending", i.e. "spending time with my family". We often use the time currency in deciding how to spend it. "How long is this movie? Do I have three hours free tonight?"; "Wow, it takes 9 hours to drive to Vegas. Guess I won't go gambling tonight". "It will take an hour to load this program on my computer. Do I want to spend my time doing that?"

In all these cases, money isn't the issue at all. It's TIME driving the purchase decision. All of us only have 24 hours in a day. Time, for many of us, is one of our most valued currencies. Any time you can offer your customer the opportunity to save time they otherwise wouldn't have, you are on the path to success.

Space

No one has unlimited space. Our homes aren't going to grow (without considerable expense). We only have so much wall space, cabinet space, and floor space to put our stuff. Our desktops are limited in the room they have to accommodate our phone, books, computer, modem, and printer. Our electronic gadgets, from iPads to laptops, only have so much memory space.

Lack of space is why we see so many yard sales signs up in our neighborhoods during the summer. Every once in a while we all need to purge and get rid of things we don't need – freeing up extra space! Offering customers something that doesn't require a lot of space, or de-clutters space, or creates free space, is a big motivator.

Human Energy

Everything we do requires some sort of human energy, from sitting at a keyboard typing to shoveling snow or mowing lawns. Some are mindless; some require great concentration and focus.

Often we use human energy as an excuse not to do something – "I'm too tired to cook dinner tonight", "I don't feel like going out tonight". Our society is zapped of its human energy – why else the explosion of artificial human energy drinks in recent years (Monster, Red Bull, 5-Hour Energy, Rockstar and dozens more) and coffee consumption. If you can save people from having to expend energy, you have found a great life currency to leverage.

Expertise

Our society has become so complicated, with so much information available, it can make your head swim. This has helped create the phenomenon of "experts" cropping up in virtually every nook and cranny of business and life. There are expert cooks, expert bathroom remodelers, social media experts, marketing experts, and even experts at lounging (go ahead and Google it!).

With the explosion of experts, it has created a society where many well-educated people sometimes feel inadequate or lacking knowledge when it comes to some of these emerging areas or those with massive details (like the IRS Tax Code). Even flat screen televisions are changing so quickly (Plasma, LCD, LED, 3-D, Smart TV, OLED) that the average customer has no idea what the differences are in order to make an informed purchase choice. Any time you can offer your customers access to unique expertise, you are living in the promised land of life currencies.

Fun

Face it. Life is fundamentally boring. You get up, go through the same morning routine every day, go off to school or work, come home, have dinner, watch some TV, and go to bed. Then do it all over again the next day, and the next day, and the next day. We crave a little fun in our lives. We don't like doing things that aren't fun.

You can give customers fun in lots of different ways. A local newspaper recently offered its readers fun by assembling a group of local businesses to give away gifts to "lucky number" readers for shopping in their stores over the holidays. Newspaper subscribers each received a lucky number in their newspaper. They then took the paper with their number into each of the 20 retailers to see if their number matched winning numbers posted in the retail stores. A business school offers its students a little Harry Potter fun by converting itself to "Hogwarts School of Business" for Halloween week, complete with their professor / wizards wearing their robes to teach class on Halloween. Figuring out how to give your customers a little fun is a great way to create happy customers – and happy customers buy more.

Fear

Everyone has fear. Fear is a distressing emotion aroused by impending danger, evil, or pain, whether the threat is real or imagined. It can manifest as foreboding feeling, apprehension, consternation, dismay, dread, terror, fright, panic, horror, or trepidation.

For example, you may fear going to the dentist. I fear that if I buy this chain saw, I'll cut off my arm accidentally. I fear that if I buy that computer program, I won't be able to make it work right. I fear that my level of expertise is below what it takes to accomplish this chore successfully.

Marketers need to address and alleviate fear in order to maximize their products sales potential. Reassure customers. Offer guarantees, have 24-hour customer service and tech help lines. Figure out what fears customers have, and make sure you can assure them that your product or service has it covered. Fear is one of the biggest reasons customers don't buy products or services that they are interested in. They just can't overcome their fear. Marketers that figure this out have a huge leg up on the competition.

Frustration

Frustration is a feeling of dissatisfaction, often accompanied by anxiety or depression, resulting from unfulfilled needs or unresolved problems. Certainly you have walked out of a crowded restaurant lobby because you were frustrated that the wait time would be unacceptably long. We've all been frustrated in a store when we couldn't find a sales associate to help, and end up buying nothing instead.

Frustrated customers are the worst kind of customer. Every frustrated customer on average tells 4 other people about their frustrating experience. As a marketer, you don't want that! Case-in-point: Netflix. In early July of 2011, it was being hailed as one of the fastest-rising companies out there. Its stock price was trading as high as $340 a share. Then, they shot themselves in the foot, announcing a restructuring and subscriber fee increase, taking away "free-streaming" video for all its customers to make it a separate subscription fee from its home-delivered DVD business. The immediately lost over 20% of its subscribers – four million customers -- which sent its stock into a free-fall, dropping as low as $62.37 before recovering to just below $100 / share. Wise marketers look at their competitive landscape and determine just what frustrates customers in their product category, and figure out ways to alleviate and eliminate all points of potential frustration with their customers to set themselves on a path to success.

Convenience

A convenience is anything that saves or simplifies work, adds to one's ease or comfort, or makes something easy to obtain, use or reach. We've all been in a convenience store and grabbed a candy bar our waistline probably didn't need, because it was convenient and easy to obtain. Most impulse purchases happen because the retailer has made it convenient for you. We pay for a drive-thru car wash because it's much more convenient than slopping out a bucket full of soapy water and washing it ourselves. We buy our music on iTunes because it's easy and convenient. We buy a Smartphone because it makes it easy to access our emails and everything else, anywhere we go. We buy microwave TV dinners primarily for convenience sake.

Giving your customers complete and total convenience is a great way to differentiate your product and service. Make it easy for them to buy!

Love

Love is a feeling of warm personal attachment or deep affection, to have a strong liking for; to take great pleasure in. You love NFL Football, you love the Broncos; you buy Bronco jerseys, t-shirts and the like to show the world your love. Jeweler's make a living out of convincing you to spend lavishly on gold, diamonds, and watches for the ones you love. Why do you spend $80 for a dozen roses on Valentine's Day? Because you need to show your spouse or partner that you love them.

Love is a powerful driver in retail sales. After Kobe Bryant's problems in Colorado back in 2003, he bought his wife a $4 million dollar, eight-caret purple diamond "Apology" ring! Playing the "love" card is a great way to move the focus off of money and onto something much more difficult to value – love! Trying to buy love is a game fools play – and play every day.

Quality

Quality is defined as producing or providing products or services that are considered high grade, superior, or excellent. This is the fundamental essence of brand marketing. We often pay premiums for brands that have a reputation of quality. At Best Buy, you can buy a Visio 55" HDTV for $899.00; right next to it is a SONY, same size, for $1199.00. The SONY TV sells five times better than the Visio, because SONY has a reputation for making good electronic products. After the release of the iPad ($499.00 for the base model), dozens of competitors, from HP to Sony, released their own versions of a Tablet. All failed, despite significantly lower prices. The only competitor to make a dent in the market was the Kindle Fire at $199.00.

Movie studios often try to leverage the quality card when promoting their movies. They'll say in their advertising "From Stephen Spielberg, the director of ET, comes …" in a way of leveraging the quality of the previous product as an indirect endorsement of the second. Anything that Apple creates instantly has a halo of quality generated from all the previous Apple products.

When competitive products are pretty much at parity from a performance perspective, a way to swing the sales pendulum in your favor is to play up the quality and heritage of excellence that your company has provided over time.

Money

The most basic form of economic exchange is that we trade money for products and services. We earn money by providing services or selling products; we spend money in order to acquire goods and services that we desire. In this most basic form, price would always be the determining factor. But I hope you can see by now that price in terms of money is just the final means of completing the exchange. The actual "price" is determined by the value each individual places upon each of the life currencies. A vintage bottle of wine has a much higher intrinsic value to a wine connoisseur than it does to someone who only drinks Vitaminwater. If money were all that mattered, we'd all be driving the cheapest cars out there, all our food products would be "Great Value" brands from Walmart; and nobody would pay extra to see a movie in an IMAX Theatre. But we do.

Life currencies are a key way to differentiate your products and services, and can be the difference between success and failure. It is the first stop when trying to gain customer and marketplace understanding.

Eric D Schulz

Section Four:

Placement Strategy

Eric D Schulz

Chapter Nine

<u>Powerful Packaging</u>

If you have observed any of the number of celebrity court cases grabbing headlines in the past several years, you have an idea of how much work, research and energy -- not to mention theatrics -- goes into preparing the closing arguments. The jury has often been presented with a complicated collection of arguments and theories, and only during the closing does that the mass of information begins to take shape. Lawyers painstakingly reiterate the key evidence, but this time they insert it into an emotional context that they hope will lead to a vote for their client. They create feelings of sympathy, rage or confidence in the jurors that provides a filter for sifting through the dry information.

When a consumer steps into the retail environment, she becomes a juror who decides whether your product is worthy of purchase. Her primary piece of evidence is your packaging. Like a good closing argument, strong packaging not only trumpets the functional benefits of your product, it also conveys an emotional message about whether your product is reliable, effective, friendly, prestigious or easy to use. But unlike a lawyer who enjoys unlimited time and space to make his argument, you must do all of your communicating in 3 seconds and three inches of shelf space. That is why packaging is the cornerstone of product performance.

<u>*Marketing Truth*</u>

> *Packaging is the best way to communicate to consumers the most compelling reasons to buy your product. Packaging delivers messages to consumer's right up to the moment they pluck the product off the shelf. Your information must be both succinct and tantalizing to win their attention and their purchase.*

Advertising Only Reaches So Far

One of the harsh realities of marketing is that advertising won't reach all your potential consumers. Even the best, most expensive campaigns only reach up to 70% of target consumers. Moreover, many products aren't good candidates for advertising. The only place where you are absolutely guaranteed the opportunity to speak to consumers about your product is at the point of purchase. If a shopper is standing at the store shelf ready to select an item to buy, and your product is displayed as part of the competitive set, only then do you have a 100% chance to communicate why they should buy your brand instead of somebody else's.

Extra - Extra - Read All About It!!!

Consumers make purchases because they are seeking the benefit the product provides. Obvious, isn't it? So it follows that the best place to trumpet the benefits of your product is on the front of your packaging. That's where you tell the consumer that your brand delivers the desired benefit better than all those other Joe-schmo competitive products on the shelf.

More often than not, marketers overlook this apparent no-brainer. They mistakenly assume that consumers know what their product is and what it does, so they just slap the brand name on the label with the required legalese and very little fanfare. Big mistake. Sure, shoppers who have used your brand in the past know what your product does and how to use it, but unless you control 100% market share and have no competition, you are losing potential consumers who for one reason or another are buying your competitor's product. These are precisely the folks to whom your packaging should be talking! If a shopper is using your product and likes it, you won't have to work hard to get him to buy again. Savvy marketers know that the real money lies in attracting new users and stealing competitive share!

Package copy is no time to be shy -- you need to think like a carnival barker. Go take a look at the products in a typical store that are category leaders. Most of them shout to the consumer what benefit the product delivers. A sampling of the front package copy from some powerhouse brands:

Windex Glass Cleaner: More Cleaning Power! Streak-Free Shine with Ammonia

Dow Disinfectant Bathroom Cleaner with Scrubbing Bubbles. Removes Soap Scum Easily!

Drano Clog Remover: Opens Drains Fast! Safe for Pipes.

ChapStick Lip Balm: Helps heal and prevent dry, chapped lips.

Dove: 1/4 Moisturizing Lotion Beauty Bar.

Lubriderm: Seriously Sensitive Lotion For Extra Sensitive Dry Skin.

Purell Instant Hand Sanitizer: Kills 99.99% of Germs Without Water or Towels.

Downy Ultra Care: Helps Keep Clothes Soft and Looking Like New.

Bounty Paper Towels: The Quilted Quicker Picker-Upper.

Kleenex Cold Care Tissues: Softest Tissue Made! Ultra Comfort.

Developing Unique & Proprietary Package Shapes

When you go to the grocery store for a gallon of milk, do you browse the aisle to consider which brand to purchase, or do you simply grab the jug that has the best freshness date and lowest price? If you're like over 90% of consumers, you only look at the freshness date and have no idea what brand of milk you just bought. Why? Because they all look exactly alike. Big plastic jugs, same shape, different color caps for whole, 2%, 1% and skim milk. There is no apparent difference between dairy brands, so nobody cares to notice.

When you move over to the juice aisle, same problem. All of the glass bottles offered by each of the different apple juice brands such as Mott's, Treetop, White House, Juicy Juice, Red Cheek and others look virtually alike --- except one. Martinelli's bottle is in the shape of an apple! The apple-bottle not only makes the Martinelli's brand stand out from the crowd, but it subconsciously makes you believe that it contains a better quality apple juice than the others, allowing the brand to command a premium price in a commodity market.

Marketing Truth

Everything communicates! You must use every available weapon in your marketing arsenal to differentiate your brand from competition. This includes development of proprietary packaging that reinforces your special uniqueness to consumers.

Coca-Cola understands the power of proprietary packaging. The company has moved all plastic packages of Coca-Cola classic (including 2-liter bottles) into contour bottles, rekindling the nostalgia consumer's hold for the original package shape. In the quest for differentiation and specialness, the marketing team at Coke has even attempted to develop a contour aluminum can for Coca-Cola classic! Expensive? Yes. . .until you look at the profits.

Creating Preference Through Improved Package Performance

The world's best marketers are always searching for new ways to create competitive advantage through packaging innovation. Developing packaging that performs better than the competition is a great way to differentiate your product to consumers. Patents can usually protect packaging innovations, which provide your consumers with a demonstrable and meaningful reason to purchase your product.

When liquid laundry detergent was first introduced, consumers loved the product and how easily it dissolved in their wash, but they didn't like the messy bottle caps. The caps were designed for measuring and pouring the detergent into the wash, but when consumers replaced the cap on the bottle, the liquid detergent leaked around the cap edges causing a gooey mess. To solve this problem, the Tide brand team developed an innovative package design for no-spill tops on their liquid Tide bottles. The bottle top was designed to channel the liquid detergent from the cap back into the bottle, leaving the cap edges clean. The Liquid Tide bottle is protected by no fewer than 13 patents, making it difficult for competition to mimic and offers Tide a distinctive long-term competitive advantage.

Citrus Hill Orange Juice was another P&G brand that gained competitive advantage through packaging innovation. Citrus Hill was the first major juice brand to introduce the carton "pouring spout". The development of the spout was driven by the consumer desire to shake orange juice before pouring in order to mix up the pulp that settles to the bottom of the carton. In a typical cardboard carton, the juice would often spurt out of the top when shaken. The pouring spout eliminated this problem, and gave Citrus Hill a distinctive point-of-difference versus competition. The package design became so popular with consumers that today, every half-gallon carton of refrigerated orange juice has a pouring spout.

Many brands outside the grocery channel have also developed proprietary packaging. Ortho Lawn Care has done a terrific job creating brand preference in this way through the innovation of a quick-attach sprayer that allows the user to stand upright and pump the stream of lawn & weed chemicals accurately and powerfully. Ortho also captured an advantage in the granular lawn food arena through the introduction of Ortho brand spreaders, with correlate settings listed on the granular Ortho lawn food packaging to help consumers understand how much food to put on their lawns. If consumers buy a lawn food brand other than Ortho, they don't know how to use the spreader settings correctly!

Why did it take until the mid-2000's for shampoo brands to start installing the large flat caps so that you can stand your bottle upside-down to get the last 20% of shampoo to come out of the bottle? Seems like a no-brainer. Same with the ketchup bottle.

When you consider these examples, it's easy to see why they work. The tricky part is developing the packaging strategies in the first place. It is common to become so caught up in the process of choosing colors and fonts, developing labels and solving manufacturing problems that you stop asking the question, how could it be different or better? How does the consumer use my product? How could I make her life easier or more pleasant?

Step back from the creative process, and get functional once in a while. Worry about pull-tabs versus screw tops, and whether your product reseals easily. These are the unglamorous steps to successful packaging, yet can lead to huge gains. Think about the re-sealable Oreo Cookie package and how that innovation has made that package much more desirable and functional than any other cookie brand? Do you think it's helped grow sales? You bet it has.

Creating New Product Categories Through Packaging Innovation

If you are disciplined -- and creative -- about considering how packaging affects the ways consumers interact with your product, you may be successful not only in creating compelling packaging, but perhaps even in creating new usage occasions and new product categories through packaging innovation.

Kraft Cheese is a terrific model for this notion. The brand team saw a gap in which school-aged kids weren't eating a lot of cheese for lunch. Why? Because a hunk of cheese isn't a great lunch or snack food by itself - it's better when combined with crackers or lunchmeat. The brand team's response to this opportunity was simply brilliant. It created Kraft Lunchables -- putting crackers, lunch meat, cheese, and a candy snack together into a single box to create a convenient way for consumers to enjoy Kraft Cheese as part of a complete lunch, and an easy way for moms to pack the lunch box. By focusing on the consumer need (convenient, complete lunch) and expanding the definition to include product categories other than just cheese (luncheon meat, crackers, and candy) the Brand group developed an entirely new product category. Kraft now had a sensational, proprietary means of fulfilling a consumer need and selling cheese free from competition.

Taco Bell, the leading Mexican fast-food restaurant chain in the USA, instigated a commando raid on the Mexican food aisle in grocery stores using the same proprietary packaging technique. Taco Bell leveraged its high consumer awareness and brand appeal by introducing an entire product line of Taco Bell branded Mexican foods. The most insightful of the new products was Taco Bell Taco Kits, containing corn tortilla shells with Taco Bell seasoning and Taco Bell hot sauce. Instead of competing with the established brands like Old El Paso and Rosarita on their own terms by offering only standard products, Taco Bell leveraged its key difference -- the restaurant experience -- into a competitive benefit, by enabling consumers to make real Taco Bell Tacos at home. No one else could do that.

At Procter & Gamble, I worked on a project aimed at changing the way consumers bought cake mixes. This change was to be accomplished -- you guessed it -- through creative packaging. We studied the cake habits of consumers and noted that they had two basic options; buy a cake mix for 79 cents and a can of frosting for $1.59 and bake it yourself, or go to the in-store bakery and buy a cake that was ready to go with icing & decorations for between $15.00 - $25.00. We were sure there was an opportunity to fill a gap in the middle.

So, we developed a new product line called "Pantastic Party Cake Kits", which included everything you needed to create a great cake in your own home in one box. The box included the cake mix, frosting, a coloring packet for the frosting, and a proprietary "paper baking pan" that allowed the consumer to bake great looking shapes at home. The kits came in Kermit the Frog, Miss Piggy, Garfield, Major League Baseball, Sweetheart, and Party Bear varieties. In test market the product sold wildly, and we knew creative packaging had succeeded once again. Unfortunately, you haven't seen this product because technological problems with the paper baking pans emerged and P&G killed the project.

Creating Brand Personality Through Packaging

Just as Harley Davidson clothes communicate intangible messages about the person wearing them, the graphic treatment and design of your package can communicate attitude and personality. It may seem silly, but yes, a package can sport an attitude. Dark packaging connotes upscale and fashionable; pearl white is high-class; multi-colors can be wild and irreverent.

Many brands have created a very specific brand personality as part of their overall packaging strategy. Dow Bathroom Cleaner with Scrubbing Bubbles is an example. The personality of the scrubbing bubbles gets carried through all advertising as well as packaging -- whimsical and fun, not at all what you would think the personality of a cleaning product would be! But it works, because the brand has focused on reinforcing the brand personality in everything it does, including packaging.

Breakfast cereal brands are kings at developing and reinforcing a personality and attitude through packaging. In fact, they go so far as to develop characters that embody the product's personality; Rice Krispies - Snap, Crackle & Pop; Cap'n Crunch; Frosted Flakes w/ Tony The Tiger, to name but a few. Coors Beer reinforces the brand's use of pure Rocky Mountain Spring Water through the graphic of a mountain waterfall on its cans. In all, brand personality and attitude can be quite powerful if considered as part of the communication objectives for packaging.

Line Extensions and Family Packaging of Products

I was in a grocery store recently and saw a woman on her hands and knees in the juice aisle, peering at different boxes of Capri-Sun juice. She was perplexed, searching for a specific Fruit Punch flavor. As I looked at the boxes lining the shelf, I understood her dilemma. The brand had seven rows of product, and all of the boxes looked absolutely identical from a standing position in the store aisle. Only by dropping to hands and knees could I find and read the flavor listing, which was buried within the graphic elements of the design.

As I moved to the men's personal care section I encountered a similar problem. The brand "afta", manufactured by Mennen, makes a terrific Pre-Electric shave lotion that I have used for years. But every time I shop the section I have to be extremely careful to pick up the right bottle, because several different "afta" products are packaged in virtually the same gray bottle with identical graphics and colors. I have to squint at the extremely small print at the top of the label to differentiate one product from another. It's so confusing that about one in every 5 trips to the store I end up picking up the wrong bottle, and this after being a loyal user for over a decade!

Often brands have several different product varieties to sell to consumers, requiring that the packaging differentiate between options yet still reflect a "brand family" look. Sometimes this can be accomplished with as little as different color stripes on the packaging, and at other times it requires more radical alterations. Creating a "line look" can often be a challenging task, but consumers must be able to identify your brand and differentiate between products to obtain the benefits they value most.

Creating An In-store Billboard

In the mid 1990's, Disney Home Video undertook an entire repackaging effort to make shopping for their videos easier for consumers. At the time of the initiative, the video aisle was a mish-mash of packaging, with no thought to how one product line looked in relation to others. Each line had been designed independently. As the Disney segment of the category had grown to include over a dozen different product lines, the Brand teams wanted to ensure that consumers could quickly and easily find the Disney videos of their choice.

Packaging experts were hired to develop the line look. The goal was simple: blindfolded consumers were brought in and placed in front of a video aisle containing all of the different Disney videos in their new packaging -- about 120 different video titles in all. The consumers would be told to find a specific video when their blindfold was removed -- for example, "Ariel's Undersea Adventures". The consumer had to be able to find that video line in three seconds or less or the packaging was deemed unacceptable.

It took several iterations, but we finally achieved our goal. How? By creating a "billboard" effect on the shelves with the packages. Each of the different Disney Video product lines had very distinct graphic designs that when stacked next to each other on the shelf created a miniature billboard, making it very easy to find the right section to look in: Masterpiece Collection; Sing-Along Songs; Favorite Stories; The Little Mermaid; Walt

Disney Film Classics; Winnie the Pooh and others each were designed to "pop" off the shelf, while at the same time maintaining a distinctive "Disney" feel. When introduced into the marketplace, Disney Video sales increased significantly and consumer satisfaction was high.

Minute Maid Orange Juice does a fantastic job of creating a billboard effect with packaging that reflects the familial look yet communicates effectively the different options of juices available. The brand communicate the different products through a simple colored bar across the lower third of the packages front panel. It is very easy to read, yet the family grouping of packages makes a very bold statement on the shelf that is appealing and grabs your attention.

Packaging Can Make or Break Sales

Procter & Gamble learned the hard way what a small mistake in packaging could do to brand sales. When introducing Folgers Coffee Singles (an instant coffee product in single-serving sizes) into test markets, the product failed because of packaging issues.

The first problem was a disadvantageous price comparison to instant coffee because the Brand Group had designed the boxes to hold too many Coffee Singles packets:

Average Retail Pricing

Folgers Coffee Singles	**Instant Coffee**
20 ct. Box = $2.99	8 oz. jar = **$2.79**
40 ct. box = $5.99	16 oz. jar = **$5.59**

A second issue concerned the way the product was stacked into cases when shipped to the grocery stores. The cases did not fit correctly onto a normal shipping palette, overhanging on each side by about 1.5 inches. This overlap resulted in crushed cases as forklifts moved things around in the stock room, causing abnormally high returns for damaged goods.

To fix the problems, P&G managers reduced the number of Coffee Singles in each box, lowering the package counts to 18 and 36 from 20 ct. and 40 ct. Now Folgers Coffee Singles had a pricing <u>advantage</u> versus instant coffee while maintaining an identical profit margin to the original packages:

Average Retail Pricing

<u>Folgers Coffee Singles</u>	<u>Instant Coffee</u>
18 ct. Box = **$2.69**	8 oz. jar = $2.79
36 ct. box = **$5.49**	16 oz. jar = $5.59

The resulting smaller shipping boxes fit perfectly onto the palettes, virtually eliminating damages. The difference? By making this seemingly insignificant change, Folgers Coffee Singles went from a disappointing one-half of one percent share of the instant coffee market to over a 5 percent share. Fixing the packaging problems increase sales by a factor of 10x, turning Coffee Singles into a profitable success story for P&G.

Developing Packaging In A Competitive Vacuum

A common mistake that leads to problems is developing packaging concepts in a competitive vacuum. Many times I've seen new concepts being evaluated in someone's office or by placing the packaging mock-ups alone on a desk or on giant conference table for everyone to admire and make comments. The issue is that the ideas are not viewed in the context of the environment in which they will be displayed and sold to the public. I've seen hundreds of sample packages that have looked great when they are sitting alone on a conference room table, but get lost or look horribly out of place when put into the store selling environment!

> *<u>Marketing Truth</u>*
>
> *Top marketers re-create a typical store shelf setting inside their offices so that they have at hand a ready reference of the*

competitive environment. As new packaging options are considered, they place them onto the shelves and see what each option looks like within the context of the competitive setting to ensure that their packaging "pops" off the shelf.

Rule of Thumb: If a consumer cannot spot your package from 15 feet away, and within 3 seconds of looking, your packaging needs improvement.

Points To Ponder BEFORE Developing Packaging

There are several steps required and questions that you must answer before embarking on any packaging initiatives. First, look at the competitive set of products that your product will be situated next to on the store shelf. Analyze all brands carefully. What primary colors are they using? Study their unique packaging designs -- both graphic designs and engineering designs of the packages. Read the words on the labels very carefully. Notice the size of each product, the shape of each product, and the number of packages that fit on the store shelf. What consumer benefits are the competitive products communicating well with their packaging? Can you think of consumer benefits that the competitive packages fail to communicate, offering you an opportunity? Does your product have performance superiority versus competitors?

Consider how the package will be displayed and stacked in the store. How tall can it be to fit on the shelf at a typical store? How deep is a store shelf, and how should your product set on the shelf? Are there an ideal number of packages that will stack on the shelf?

Most large retailers measure the success of products by how much profit a particular item will return to the store commensurate to the amount of shelf space the item requires. Retailers want to maximize their profits, and so those brands and items that return the highest profit (both in terms of gross margin and penny profit) per square inch are the ones that receive the most shelf space. It is important to design packages that utilize space efficiently. Along these lines, you should carefully consider the number of items packed into shipping cases so that when store personnel restock the shelves, they always put out a full case and do not have to return partial cases to the back room. This logistical allowance enables the retailer to efficiently use his money to keep products on the shelf and not incur carrying costs for product in the back room. Stores HATE having partial cases of products in the back room!

Even if your product is an established category leader, you should always be asking questions like: how does the consumer open the package? Is there a way of making it easier to use? Can it fit into a consumer's hand more comfortably, or function more effectively? Is the package thrown away immediately, or is product dispensed from the package over time and stored? Is there a way to make it more storable? Are there other products that are typically used with this one? Could I package them together?

Trendy vs. Classic Graphic Treatments

The choice of graphic treatment is critical to the success of the product. Trendy graphics commit products to long-term problems. Trends are short lived. Packages that reflect short-term thinking often have to be revised time and time again, and each change confuses consumers.

Classic packaging that will stand the test of time is what every product should strive for. The most successful brands in the world all have logos and packaging graphics that have endured decades with very little change -- Coca-Cola, Tide, McDonald's, Shell Oil, Gillette, Hershey's, Heinz, Campbell's Soup, Jell-O, and Domino's Pizza to name but a few.

Preparing A Packaging Strategy

The final step in undertaking a packaging project is the development of a document call the *packaging brief*.

A packaging brief contains all of the information that is relevant to development of the packaging assignment. It outlines:

1. The competitive environment;

2. Addresses important issues and insights;

3. Specifies opportunities to create competitive advantage;

4. Delineates important consumer benefits;

5. States the positioning strategy for the product, brand personality & attitude.

The reasoning behind developing a packaging brief is to think through all of the functions the package must perform and specify the information the package must communicate BEFORE you begin looking at different artistic options. Why? Because as soon as the pretty artwork and packaging ideas start streaming in, strategic thought goes out the window. It's easy to become infatuated with packaging proposals. Seeing new artwork is a little like seeing your own newborn child for the first time. Your baby is the most beautiful baby in the world. Other people might have ugly babies, but not you. The package is the personification of your brand. It becomes very easy to lose perspective. You need to develop the packaging brief to have strategic focus to ensure everything the package needs to accomplish is ultimately achieved.

Marketing Truth

The marketing team, not manufacturing, must drive packaging strategy. Let the people at the plant tell you how the machines work and try to understand the limitations as well as capabilities, but do not let a machine limitation kill a great idea. Most innovations require changes to the way things are currently done. If a new machine or part is required to create a killer packaging idea, then buy it!

Packaging development is perhaps the most rewarding task marketing managers perform, as the fruit of their labor appears in stores all over the world. Great packaging can sustain a brand. Poor packaging can kill one very quickly. It is critically important that all initiatives are developed in line with strategic objectives and that those objectives are adhered to.

When the great baseball legend Yogi Berra once said, "You can observe a lot by watching," he could have been talking about packaging development. You can learn a lot by studying and paying attention to what other brands and competitors are doing. Don't try to design your packaging in isolation. Here, more than anywhere else in the marketing game, you must force yourself to step back from the excitement and glamour of logo treatments and colors, and take a long, analytical look at the job you aim to do. Look at other product categories to steal ideas. Figure out pet peeves consumers have with your package and fix them! Delight your customers, and they will be loyal customers!

Eric D Schulz

Chapter Ten

Distribution & Merchandising

Let's pretend you're in the market to buy a Rolex Presidential watch. You've shopped around and found the watch you want at Cartier Jewelers for $5,995. You go home to think about it, and on the way stop for a bag of chips at the neighborhood 7-Eleven. There at the checkout counter, to your amazement, you see the very same watch at the discounted price of only $1,999!

How would you decide where to make the purchase? Would you have a nagging suspicion that the quality of the watch at the 7-Eleven might be inferior to the one at Cartier -- that maybe the 7-Eleven models had some sort of flaw? Would you worry about the credibility of the 7-Eleven salesperson and could you trust what he said about the watch between ringing up Slurpee sales at the cash register? Would you have a concern about getting the watch serviced under warranty at 7-Eleven should something go wrong later? Would you think that the convenience store Rolex models were illegal knock-offs imported from who-knows-where?

Of course you would! A Rolex display inside a 7-Eleven store is completely out of context. You'd have a hard time believing that the watch at 7-Eleven was truly the premium Rolex quality watch that you wanted. The sales environment inside the 7-Eleven is not a match with the kind of place you would expect Rolex watches to be sold based on the brand's premium image.

> ### *Marketing Truth*
>
> *Where your product is sold, and how it is displayed, creates a powerful communication message about your brand in the mind of consumers – more powerful in fact than your advertising message. Everything communicates. Proper distribution and display will maximize sales and reinforce your brand positioning strategy.*

Distribution Strategies

You can choose from any number of distribution strategies ranging from *"ubiquity"* -- wanting to have your product everywhere -- to *"exclusivity"* only selling it in a few handpicked locations. Each has its own merits and pitfalls, and as a marketing manager you must consider the options.

Ubiquity

The distribution strategy developed by former Coca-Cola CEO Roberto Goizueta for his flagship brand was "to have Coca-Cola products available within an arm's reach of desire". By that statement he meant that he wanted Coca-Cola products available everywhere and anywhere a human being could possibly be: ubiquity.

The company's stunning success through the 1990's was largely tied to this simple mandate: find more and more points of distribution for Coca-Cola products. Ten years ago who would have predicted vending machines in remote National Parks locations or inside most office buildings? Or all-you-can-drink fountain dispensers at McDonald's and other fast-food restaurants? Or Coca-Cola coolers at the checkout at Target and Walmart?

In pursuit of ubiquity, Coke employee's work cooperatively with established retailers to find new and better ways to offer Coke products to consumers. Inside many grocery stores, for example, you can find a cooler full of single-serve Coca-Cola products, a Coca-Cola vending machine and a Coca-Cola fountain dispenser in addition to the product available in the soft-drink aisle. By focusing on finding ever more points of distribution, Coca-Cola management continues to believe double-digit annual growth is possible, even with a brand nearly 150 years old.

Exclusivity

At the opposite end of the distribution spectrum is the exclusivity strategy, which limits the product to specific selling environments or even one particular retailer. Why would a marketer choose this strategy? Simple math would lead you to believe that the more places you sold your product, the more product you'd sell. But remember the Rolex example; selling your product everywhere isn't always the smartest way to go.

Marketing Truth

When choosing a distribution strategy, match brand image with the consumer perception of the potential distribution point to find those channels that enhance and synergize with your product identity.

Consider for a moment the men's fashion brand Brooks Brothers. The brand image is upscale and elite, targeted at households with annual incomes above $100,000 and fashion wannabe's that like the well-heeled image. The brand has historically adopted an exclusivity strategy of selling primarily through dedicated Brooks Brothers shops. This strategy matches the nature and tone of the brand and has worked well for years to differentiate Brooks Brothers from other brands of apparel.

If you were the brand manager for Brooks Brothers considering new distribution opportunities, think about which of these potential retailers would enhance and synergize with consumer perception of their brand: Walmart (no), Kmart (no), Bloomingdales (yes), Saks Fifth Avenue (yes), Costco Warehouse Club (no), The Men's Warehouse (no).

But wait a minute; aren't discount outlets the hot new trend in outdoors malls? How do you explain the success of Outlet Malls, or Nordstrom's Rack, or the Anne Taylor Loft -- which all sell exclusive product at discount prices? There's a big difference between offering your product at a club store or mass merchant, and selling it at one of those brand name outlet stores that are cropping up all over. Outlet stores are a terrific way to sell overstocks and out-of-season items to price-conscious consumers. Instead of devaluing the product, outlet stores actually reinforce the upscale image by making consumers believe that only in this specialized outlet can they obtain authentic product at bargain prices. The displays, merchandising and general look of the stores is all carefully crafted to support the premium image -- no dump bins or bargain basement piles here!

Disney is that rare company that manages both ubiquity and exclusivity strategies with real intelligence and flair. Disney DVD's, for example, are available everywhere: supermarkets, drug stores, and airports. People snatch them up wherever they see them. But Disney also knows when to create consumer demand -- and command higher prices -- by holding back on product distribution. Some brands, like Winnie the Pooh, have actually been segmented into separate looks (and separate price points) for the different channels. The colorful, cartoonish "Disney Pooh" line is designed with bold palettes and playful graphics, and it's available everywhere, from mass merchants to groceries. However, the gentler, more abstract "Classic Pooh" products modeled on the original watercolor artwork from the Pooh storybooks are only available at upscale boutiques and Disney stores. Both brands are tremendously popular.

The classic case study of a powerful exclusivity strategy is the shrewd placement of Disney's "The Art of Disney" hand-painted animation cels. Through proper distribution, and little else, the marketing whizzes at Disney were able to transform a windfall into a highly lucrative long-term business. Faced with huge warehouses bursting at the seams with original art cels from over 60 years of Disney animation, they looked at the pile and figured "why not try to sell them off?" For perspective, one hour of Disney animation yields 64,800 original cels. You can only imagine the millions upon millions of cels available inside the Disney vaults after all those years of work!

Disney considered different distribution options, and the most obvious choice was to offer the cels to Kmart, Target and Walmart and price them between $30 - $50 each. This was an appealing and financially tempting idea and seemed a safe bet with consumers. Running the numbers, if Disney sold a million cels per year, they could net around $30 million dollars annually, since the only real cost associated with selling each cel was its frame.

But the brand team walked away from the easy money. Instead, it opted for an exclusivity distribution strategy -- limiting the availability and selling only through The Disney Store, Disney Catalog, and Fine Art Galleries at a price of $250 -$500 per cel.

Why did the brand team pick exclusivity over mass availability? On the surface, the decision seemed foolhardy; after all, this is Disney, the most commercialized brand on the planet! But the Disney marketers knew better. They chose to create a premium image and stoke consumer passion for original Disney art, thereby establishing a long-term business. They knew that if these one-of-a-kind artworks were available at mass, consumers would no longer believe in the "magic" of the movies themselves. By selling the cels at a high price in limited upscale outlets, they accepted the fact that they would sell fewer cels each year than if they'd blown them out at the mass retailers. But with the new lofty price point, they'd only have to sell a fraction of the volume -- only about 100,000 units each year -- to net the same profit. By choosing the exclusivity strategy, they elevated owning original Disney art cels far above the mere purchase of an upscale poster. And the Disney art business is on solid ground for decades to come.

An exclusivity distribution strategy usually works best for brands that are either high-ticket -- Rolex, Mercedes-Benz, Porsche -- or that have a real or perceived limited supply -- for example, UGG boots, footwear and accessories imported from Australia, fine art, hand-made goods, etc. This type of product must provide more than function and value; it must impart status as well.

Channel Strategies

One way of looking at the distribution issue is to define what kinds of retailers should carry your product, or defining a "channel strategy". If your company sold canned green beans, would you want to sell them at your local O'Reilly's Automotive store? Of course not. But you would want to have your beans available at Costco and Sam's Club Warehouse stores, in addition to traditional supermarkets and independent grocers. And what about institutional food services for schools and hospitals? Restaurant suppliers? Convenience stores? Bodegas in the many Hispanic communities? You'd definitely want them to sell your green beans.

There is no magic list of distribution channels to review and select the ones you'd like a la carte. The channels of distribution are numerous and ever changing, and opportunities within these channels must be searched out separately and painstakingly for each individual product. If you manufacture scoreboards, for example, your distribution channels would likely be pro sports venues, high schools, colleges and universities and city recreation departments. For audio speakers your channels might be electronics stores, audiophile shops, automotive retailers and high-end electronics catalogs. Each brand must specifically define its distribution channel strategy to place product where the target audience shops and in the retail environments that support the overall brand positioning.

Thinking in terms of channels is usually the best way to develop a distribution strategy. Most top companies plan distribution this way, developing separate placement objectives within each channel. For example, the green beans brand manager may expect his channel strategy to achieve distribution in 90% of grocery stores, 60% of convenience stores, 85% of institutional food services, etc. By quantifying these objectives, the manager can develop annual volume projections and set the benchmarks for placement and sales within the organization.

Marketing Truth

> *Until you achieve distribution in excess of 70% of the outlets in your consumer-targeted selling channel, do not advertise broadly to consumers. Consumer advertising prior to a 70% penetration is a waste of money. Think of it this way...even at 70% distribution, three of every ten customers who go looking for the product can't find it!*

The Wrong Distribution Strategy Can Devastate A Brand

Levi's jeans learned the hard way that even a popular established brand could sabotage its business through a poor distribution strategy. Throughout the 1970's, the brand had a virtual lock on the jeans market. The corporate distribution strategy was to offer Genuine Levi's products exclusively at upscale department stores. This strategy had paved their road to success for several decades, and they believed it would keep them on that profitable path for decades to come.

As the '70's ended, shopping malls became the rage, obsolescing traditional stand-alone department stores. Department stores chains were forced to move into the malls to stay where the shoppers were, but here they became vulnerable to increased competition, especially in the apparel category. At most malls, boutique shops such as GAP and Banana Republic as well as a variety of young, contemporary 'teen shops" quickly became the favorite clothes shopping stop for teenagers.

As sudden as an unexpected lightning strike, Levi's weren't cool anymore -- because they weren't sold in the teen clothing boutiques. Arizona, Calvin Klein, and private label jeans all became much more fashionable -- primarily through the image transference from the stores where they were being sold. Levi's was in the department stores where "my parents buy their clothes" -- Yuck! Ever since this distribution strategy blunder, the Levi's brand has struggled to re-establish a fashionable image with teenagers and has watched its market share plummet from the 70% range in the 1970's to around 20% today.

Product Strategies by Distribution Channel

Many manufacturers adapt their product in some way to fine-tune it for placement in different distribution channels. For example, many consumer products brands that gain distribution within Club Stores such as Costco and Sam's Club will offer a special super-large size, or create double or triple packs of product that are not generally available in traditional retail environments such as grocery stores or pharmacies.

They do this for two reasons. First, they attempt to raise the "dollar ring" price of the sale (the amount paid for the group of product). They know consumers in these channels buy in bulk (since consumers perceive they're receiving a much lower price per unit), and they have a good chance at selling more products at one time than they could in any other channel. Second, by selling more units, they ensure that the consumer will be using their product longer and won't be back in the store anytime soon. Some categories, like facial tissue and snack foods, know that consumers actually use more products if they have more around the house. For all of these reasons, creating customized "bulk" packages at Club stores makes good marketing sense.

As unlikely as it might seem, television manufacturers also follow this customization strategy. When you shop for a 47-inch Sony HDTV television, you can find several different variations available, depending upon which stores you shop. At Kmart and Walmart you'll find a somewhat "stripped down" model (just a standard TV) at an attractively low price. Inside a Best Buy you'll often find two or three different models of the 47 inch Sony, with a variety of "add-on's" such as multiple HDMI connectors, Smart TV, Surround Sound, Wi-Fi connectivity for video streaming and various plug-ins for audio and video jacks, selling for as much as $200 to $600 more than the 47 inch Sony TV's at Kmart.

Why the variation? Same reasons as there are Mercedes and Hyundai's. Some consumers have caviar tastes while living in trailer parks. They want the personal gratification associated with owning a big 47 inch TV, but don't need the extras. A big screen is all that matters to them, and Kmart and Walmart are stores where this type of consumer is more likely to shop. Technophiles want to hook up their Blue-Ray DVD players and surround sound, or stream shows wirelessly from the internet, so they'll shop at the higher-end electronics stores and pay much more to get the add-ons. Sony tailors the product to fit the consumer needs of the shoppers in the different distribution channels.

Merchandising: Creating An In-Store Presence

Once you have decided where you want your product placed, the next piece of the puzzle is how you influence the way it is displayed and sold in the retail environment. It's not enough to put the product on the shelf. Where it sits, and what it sits next to, are critically important questions.

Marketing Truth

The Consumer Strike Zone – the focal range in which consumers are most likely to shop for products on a store shelf, is almost identical to the traditional baseball strike zone – the top of the shoulders to the knees. Products that are placed on shelves "in the zone" have an 85% greater chance of being purchased than those shelved higher or lower.

On your next trip to the supermarket, watch a few shoppers as you make your way up and down the aisles. See how their eyes scan the shelf. Notice how many of the products they purchase are "in the zone". Studies have shown that while the shelves in the Consumer Strike Zone only hold about 50% of the products in a typical retail environment, they produce about 85% to 90% of total sales!

Capturing Incremental Shelf Space

Often, the marketing game is very simply played. The deciding factor is *the products with the most shelf space wins!* When this is the case, the battleground for top marketers is to develop a rationale to convince store managers why your product merits more space than the competitive product.

Through the 90's and early 2000's, most consumer product manufacturing companies used a specialized computer program to help them illustrate their placement argument with retailers. The program analyzed each individual item for sales velocity and profitability, considering how many units of the product fit onto the store's shelf, then spit out a list of the number of facings each product in the category deserved in order to maximize the retailer's profitability.

This program was a successful sales tool for years. The sales people for the top consumer products companies would perform the analysis free of charge and share the results with the stores, who were thrilled to have the data. Procter & Gamble brands used this service as a primary sales tactic for nearly a decade. Of course, the analysis was often skewed in favor of the company's products, but that bias was to be expected. Retailers took the information with a grain of salt and acted from there.

The retail chains have consolidated and grown larger and more sophisticated over the years, and they now perform regular profitability analyses on their own and don't need manufacturers to do it for them. But any good marketer still runs the numbers to understand the competitive sales environment and profitability landscape. This knowledge gives him ammunition to approach the retailer for more shelf space.

Savvy marketers now create their own personalized versions of a profitability model with any spreadsheet program by plugging in sales information and running the numbers. The calculations are fairly straightforward. Obtain the store sales numbers in your product category for a month or two, and then load in pricing and cost information (most large companies always have competitive sheets so that they know what prices are being offered to the Trade). Multiply sales volume time's profit per item. This calculation will render a "profit by sku" and can be sorted to produce a rank order from top to bottom for each of the items the store carries in your product category, showing which are producing profit and which are not, as well as documenting the differences.

Remember, stores are most interested in maximizing profits for every square inch of shelf space. Products that aren't producing profits are vulnerable to being replaced by something that sells better. The "profit by sku" ranking identifies the products in peril. Looking at the bottom of the list (let's hope none of your products are there), you can create a rational argument with the retailer for dropping that item, adding more of yours, and increasing your shelf space.

The advent of profitability analyses caused the death of many small brands that simply could not generate the sales velocity to compete effectively with major brands. It's a shame too, because many of these small local brands were actually better products than the national competitors.

Blocking Strategies

If you're managing a brand with multiple products in a typical store -- like Folgers Coffee with Regular, Automatic Drip, Decaffeinated, and Gourmet Supreme flavors, each offered in 13 oz., 26 oz., and 39 oz. sizes -- you can create an in-store advantage by developing a "blocking scheme" that maximizes your brand recognition and aids the consumer in finding your product.

A blocking scheme is really nothing more than designing the way you want the products to be displayed on the shelf. A good blocking scheme will increase sales and call attention to your products.

Wander by the coffee section in your store and notice how the Folgers (red) and Maxwell House (electric blue) "pop" off the shelf. These brands are so easy to find because they have convinced the retailers to display their products in a block section on the shelf. In the soft drink aisle, you can always find the Coca-Cola section by quickly scanning the aisle for the bright red cans and bottles. Most top brands devise a blocking strategy for their products. If you don't, you leave your product shelf placement in the hands of store clerks and even worse, your competition!

Special Displays

For some brands, proprietary special displays are the best place to spend merchandising dollars. These displays can be permanent, like the McCormick's Spice Displays or the new Campbell's Soup displays popping up in many stores, or temporary displays that are discarded when the product sells out.

Permanent displays are the most desirable merchandising a marketer can ask for. They "mark your territory" against competitors and allow you to directly control the way your product is presented to the consumer. You'll often spot permanent branded displays for products such as sunglasses and watches in mass merchandisers, but sometimes a very important part of the display is something you can't see.

Have you ever been in a jewelry store with a display for DeBeers Diamonds? Not only will you see the diamonds displayed with highly effective branding, but also what you don't see is that the lights in that store are part of the display provided by DeBeers. Lighting can have a significant effect upon the way a diamond appears to glitter, so stores carrying DeBeers diamonds are offered this special halogen lighting by DeBeers as part of their display program in order to optimally showcase their products. Very smart and very effective.

Temporary displays usually work only if your product is seasonal in nature or a quick hit-and-run, like a DVD release for a hot movie or a new CD. Most retailers are predisposed against taking in temporary displays because they think they look junky. To get yours in, you have to make it gorgeous!

When I was at Disney Home Video, the Halloween seasonal movies were part of my domain. Sales of these videos had been sluggish for several years, and so my brand team decided to take an aggressive position by dreaming up a totally new temporary display concept that would drive retailers to want to take in these titles just to get the great looking displays in their stores. The team in Creative Services used the inspiration of Disney's Haunted Mansion (one of the classic rides in the Magic Kingdom) to create The Haunted Mansion Video Shoppe, a display containing 48 videos in a wickedly cool and spooky display. They sold like a cold glass of ice water in hell, and retailers loved them! These displays became the centerpieces of the seasonal section, which not only ensured our distribution, but nabbed us a premium location for shoppers as well.

Music stores are effective in using temporary displays to capture the cutting-edge attitude of the music industry and feature hot, contemporary artists. Have you ever noticed that when you walk into a Virgin store or other dedicated music shop, the mood is suddenly really cool and the lights are just a little dimmer than in the rest of the mall? It's all part of the merchandising scheme. The environment is designed to make you feel the music, to feel like you're cutting-edge, even if you go in shopping for Tony Bennett and not Lady Gaga.

Marketing Truth

Top marketers try to influence everything associated with the display and sale of their product. Lighting, ambiance, and product displays in the retail environment are all powerful marketing tools that can directly increase the appeal of your product to consumers and ultimately increase sales.

So here's a question for you. If you are a retailer looking to increase sales, should you expand your product lines to offer virtually every possible product offering in each product category to consumers, or cut your product offerings by as much as 50%, offering just the top sellers in each category?

The answer probably will surprise you -- cut your product line. In multiple studies of retailers, it was found that oftentimes less is more. More products just confuse the consumer, making the sales selection more difficult. Give consumers fewer choices, and it makes it easier for them to make a purchase. In one test with a small jam maker, by cutting her product lines from 24 different varieties down to 6 choices, her sales increased 6x.

Did you know that at a typical grocery store there are over 30,000 items stocked, but only about 250 items make up over 80% of sales? It's true. It is a concept in retailing known as the Big Head and the long tail. You need to have a good selection of the 250 "Big Head" products, and the rest are shelf-fillers.

Kevin Nealon, an old *Saturday Night Live* comedian used to portray a character who peppered his conversations with subliminal messages to convince others to do his bidding. Distribution and merchandising strategies work in almost the same fashion. They can subtly influence consumers to effectively and proprietarily enhance products sales, increase consumer appeal, and stay off the radar screen of competition, creating a scenario to develop competitive advantage.

Everyone defines success differently. A very successful college basketball coach once told me his definition of success was to have $20 in his pocket so that he could go to McDonald's any time he wanted and grab a Big Mac. Only you can define your terms of success both in life and in business. Sound distribution and merchandising strategies are one way to find increased business prosperity.

Eric D Schulz

Chapter Eleven

Product Mix

When it comes to functional, no-frills products, men's underwear is about as basic as they come. But even guys whose primary interest in underwear is sitting around in it on a Sunday morning, who don't mind sagging elastic or holes or fading, even guys whose wives have to threaten legal action to shop for new ones -- even *these* guys have definite opinions about their underwear. Some of them have worn the same brand since boyhood. Others got in the habit of wearing their particular brand or style in college and never switched. A few even have "lucky underwear" for watching the big game.

The point is this: even with a humble product like men's underwear, consumers have their preferences. And no matter how terrific your product may be, it's probably can't satisfy the demands of millions of different people. As your research will verify, consumers have very specific -- and often quite different -- ideas of what they want. Sometimes the differences will arise from personal preference (like tighty-whity or boxer's), or from the various ways consumers use products (I need something sporty vs. I want the basic blue). Just as often, the variety of consumer demands simply reflects the quirks of different personalities (it's the kind my father wore).

Not even the craftiest marketing whiz can make his product appeal to everyone. But you can come close. The trick is in knowing your category, and your consumers, well enough to offer a selection of products that meets consumer needs better than anyone else. Finding the right product mix is a bit more complicated than simply quantifying consumer research and churning out a product for every taste and occasion. If you want to own your category, you must understand how benefits motivate purchase, and whether alternative options in your line will be a strength or a weakness for your brand. In this chapter we will look at a variety of strategies that can help you win the product mix game and dominate your product category.

Segmentation Analysis

Categorizing consumer needs is a rigorous task we call "segmentation analysis". Segmentation analysis is just a fancy way of stating the consumer question "When you go to the store to buy this type of product, what product benefits are most important to you?" After compiling a list of answers, marketers group the results into categories that suggest a rationale for a series of products -- a product mix.

Take a look at the analgesic pain reliever category. It contains such popular brands as Bayer Aspirin, Bufferin, Excedrin, Tylenol, Advil, and Aleve. When these companies perform a segmentation analysis, they ask consumers the question "When you need a pain relief product, what product benefits are most important to you?"

Tylenol is the category leader, a pain reliever containing acetaminophen that is manufactured and marketed by McNeil Consumer Products Co. Tylenol is offered to consumers in a variety of package sizes and product forms. It is available in tablets, gel caps, and liquid forms. It has segmented the market into a variety of usage occasions (with products targeted to each):

HEAD & BODY: Tylenol Extra Strength, Regular Strength Tylenol, Tylenol 8-Hour Muscle Aches and Pain.

ARTHRITIS: Tylenol Arthritis

SINUS & ALLERGY: Tylenol Sinus Congestion & Pain Severe; Tylenol Sinus Congestion & Pain Daytime; Tylenol Sinus Congestion & Pain Nighttime; Tylenol Sinus Congestion & Pain Day/ Night Pack.

COLD & FLU: Tylenol Cold Multi-Symptom Severe; Tylenol Cold Multi-Symptom Daytime; Tylenol Cold Multi-Symptom Nighttime; Tylenol Cold Multi-Symptom Day/Night Pack; Tylenol Cold & Cough Daytime.

PAIN & SLEEPLESSNESS: Tylenol PM; Simply Sleep.

CHILDREN: Infant's Tylenol Oral Suspension; Children's Tylenol Oral Suspension; Children's Tylenol Meltaways Chewable Tablets; Tylenol

Meltaways Chewable Tablets; Children's Tylenol Plus Multi-Symptom Cold.

Why all the choices? Because the brand team at McNeil learned through its segmentation analysis that each of these variations are necessary to meet the numerous -- and distinct -- needs of consumers who are interested in purchasing pain relievers. Importantly, none of these many variations is redundant; each offers consumers a specific benefit to meet a specific need. Some treat specific ailments (Muscle aches / arthritis, etc.); others are for specific times (day / night); others are for specific ages (adults, infants, children); while other segmentation is on product form (caplets, gel-caps, chewable, liquid).

You may wonder, what if Tylenol were available in just one version -- one that effectively controlled pain for everyone -- wouldn't consumers buy it? Don't they all want the same thing -- to feel better? Surprisingly, the answer is no. Consumers experience different types of discomfort, and the relief they seek is to treat their specific need. The folks at Tylenol understand this dynamic and want to make sure that you can get precisely what you want to deliver the exact pain relief you need. So while the brand Tylenol has one consistent message -- fast, reliable pain relief -- the product mix reassures consumers that the scientists at Tylenol have developed a specialized remedy for their particular ailment, in the size, dosage or form that most favorably delivers relief. As a powerful fringe benefit of this strategy, segmentation not only encourages the consumer to purchase Tylenol instead of a competitive brand; it may also spur the purchase of several different Tylenol products (one for night, one for headaches, one for kids, another for muscle pain, or a small dosage container for my office desk…the list goes on).

Marketing Truth

The adage "One size fits all" is not true when it comes to consumer products. "One size fits no one" is more like it. The most successful brands craft their product mix in a variety of sizes, shapes, colors, forms, and occasions in order to specifically meet consumer's needs and their expectations, resulting in maximized brand appeal.

Product Proliferation

Look inside any grocery store and you'll find many examples of top companies that have successfully implemented a segmented product strategy to own their category. The Coca-Cola Company is the classic example. For the flagship flavor Coca-Cola classic, it also offers Coke Zero, Diet Coke and Caffeine-Free varieties. Coke is available in 2-liter bottles, 20 ounce plastic bottles, 1-liter plastic bottles, 10 ounce glass bottles, 12 ounce and 8 ounce aluminum cans. Whatever the consumer prefers is usually available on the store shelf. The company extends this strategy across the entire soft drink category by offering many brands that cover virtually every flavor of soft drink. It is nearly impossible to find a successful soft drink brand for which The Coca-Cola Company doesn't produce an alternative purchase choice:

The Coca-Cola Company makes sure that every time you reach for a soft drink, one of its products is uniquely suited to quench your thirst.

Developing New Usage Occasions

The trick to forecasting when a segmentation strategy will work lies in careful interpretation of your research. There are many angles to consider, but at the top of the list next to your product benefits category should be "usage occasions." In other words, in addition to considering *what* the consumer wants, you must address *how* and *when* the consumer intends to use the product.

Usage occasion segmentation is valuable for two primary reasons. First, because it taps into key reasons the consumer makes a purchase decision (the product is easy / pleasant / convenient to use). But another powerful benefit of analyzing how consumers use your product is that the research will suggest ways to actually increase the frequency of consumer use. Naturally, if consumers use more of your product, they buy more as well.

Band-Aid provides an excellent case study of how usage occasion segmentation works. For decades the adhesive bandage category was one of the most combative product categories in supermarkets and pharmacies. The category had two major competitors: Band-Aid, manufactured by Johnson & Johnson, and Curad, produced by Colgate-Palmolive. There are also a few smaller competitors like 3M and KidCare. Throughout the 60's, 70's and 80's, there was very little "new news" in the category. The only significant product innovation was the development of the "Ouch less" Band-Aid (which did not fulfill the consumer promise and still hurt like heck when you pulled it off), and the licensing of cartoon characters to add a bit of fun and color for kids.

As you would expect in these static conditions, the market saw very little shift in share between Band-Aid and Curad over time. Each competitor held a strong position in the marketplace, and each seemed content to stand toe-to-toe with the other, not backing down, but not taking any real swings, either. Then in the early 2000's Band-Aid broke with convention and jumped out of the pack through innovation, introducing an entire array of products specifically targeted to the consumer needs it identified through a segmentation analysis. Suddenly, consumers could choose from Band-Aid treated with Aloe-Vera and Vitamin E; Band-Aid treated with Antiseptics; Special Band-Aid strips shaped for Finger and Knuckle Cuts; Sport Band-Aid; Waterproof Band-Aid; Clear Band-Aid; Bright-Color Band-Aid and Disney Cartoon Character Band-Aid featuring The Little Mermaid, Winnie The Pooh, and Mickey Mouse.

What had been a tight market share race became no contest virtually overnight. A recent trip to the supermarket revealed Band-Aid controlling over 75% of the category shelf space with Curad, 3M and KidCare splitting the remaining slots.

And here's the beautiful part of the strategy; not only did Band-Aid address specific consumer needs, they actually created a reason to own more than one box at a time. After all, you'll need one for the kids (with cartoon characters to take the sting out of the boo-boo), one for finger and knuckle cuts (the most common kind of injury), Sport Band-Aid for the hubby or teenager's basketball games, and maybe even a vitamin E or "general" box thrown in the first aid kit for miscellaneous cuts and scrapes. Over time, people may not need more adhesive bandages then they used to, but they now have a reason to purchase more than one box of Band-Aids for different usage occasions.

When Product Proliferation Doesn't Work

By now you may be thinking you've found the hidden treasure simply by offering more, more, more to your consumers. But many a seaworthy vessel has been sunk on those treacherous rocks. Even the biggest, savviest marketing captains have been capsized because they couldn't tell the difference between good and bad segmentation choices.

For example, look at a segmentation analysis of the toothpaste category. When consumers were asked: "When you go to the store to buy toothpaste, what product attributes are most important to you?" Consumers responded that the benefits most important to them were:

Cleans & Prevents Cavities	Freshens Breath
Whitens Teeth	Tartar Control
Prevents Gum Disease	Contains Baking Soda
For Sensitive Teeth	For Kids
Won't Damage My Teeth	Mouth Feel Fresh & Clean

Historically, "Crest" toothpaste held a virtual monopoly in the category through the 1960's and 70's thanks to its protective fluoride ingredient. Competitive brands tried to "own" other product benefits: "Gleem" and "Ultra Brite" toothpaste's were for white teeth and a great smile; "Aquafresh" was toothpaste that cleaned, whitened teeth and freshened breath; "Sensodyne" was for sensitive teeth; "Rembrandt" for whitening teeth; "Arm & Hammer" toothpaste cleaned with baking soda. "Colgate" toothpaste simply positioned itself as an alternative to Crest.

In the mid '80's, the category started heating up with a vast array of new product line extensions and packaging options. Top brands such as Crest and Colgate extended into consumer-friendly gels and flavors for the first time. "Pump" and flip-top tubes were introduced to eliminate the old squeezed-out tube complaint. The category that once had only 2 or three product offerings from each brand exploded to 10 or more from each of its major competitors.

As the '90's progressed, the proliferation of products continued. Virtually every major brand offered a complete array of products targeted at each of the specific consumer needs in the segmentation analysis. Most brands developed formulas specific to fighting tartar, stopping gum disease, whitening and brightening, featuring Baking Soda, gentle formulas for sensitive teeth, gel and paste options and kids brands. Selecting a tube of toothpaste had become a major decision, with nearly 80 brand options in a typical store.

In 1998, Colgate got smart. They sensed the consumer confusion that had overtaken the category and switched direction. Instead of trying to figure out what the next "hot" product benefit would be, Colgate introduced Colgate Total, one product that addressed practically all of the consumer needs revealed in the segmentation analysis. It was an instant success, building a 35% market share within 2 months of introduction. Crest followed suit shortly thereafter with the introduction of a cloned product, *Crest Complete*, but the damage was done. Colgate had won the war, because consumers no longer saw a reason to switch. They now had everything they wanted in toothpaste.

KEEP IT SIMPLE, STUPID (The KISS Strategy)

Most of the toothpaste brands became casualties of the segmentation war simply because they carved up their consumer segments into tiny benefit slices. When they performed their segmentation analysis, they categorized the qualities that consumers described as important (whitens, freshens breath, etc.). But they didn't listen very carefully. Consumers didn't say they wanted whiter teeth *or* clean breath; they said they wanted both. Different consumers may have prioritized their needs differently, but chances are none of them said, "I don't really care about fresh breath," or "white teeth aren't at all important to me." Similarly, consumers didn't have distinct usage needs for their toothpaste; in other words, their priorities for what the toothpaste should do for them did not change according to when or how -- or even how often -- they brushed.

Now, think back to Tylenol and Band-Aid. Their product segmentation strategies worked because they identified distinct consumer needs. All Tylenol products promise pain relief. But beyond that basic function, some consumers absolutely could not swallow tablets and wanted only gel caps. Others wanted maximum strength but cared nothing about helping them sleep. Some wanted a sleep aid; others muscle pain relief. For Band-Aid, while consumers all wanted clean, comfortable healing, they described very different uses for the product. Sometimes they wanted a colorful bandage for the kids. Other times they wanted a super-strong, flexible bandage that wouldn't come off during sports. Other times they wanted Band-Aid's treated with antiseptics.

But toothpaste consumers wanted it all. They didn't need toothpaste that cleaned and whitened teeth but failed to control tartar or fight cavities. They wanted toothpaste that cleaned and whitened, prevented cavities, controlled tartar, freshened breath, AND prevented gum disease to boot -- precisely what Colgate Total promised them. In the short term, some brands were able to attract consumers who identified one particular attribute as the most important benefit on their list, but in the end, the complete package won out.

The moral of the story is that the product mix strategy for any particular product category must be determined by whether the consumer needs are independent or linked. If the consumer needs are linked, don't try to break them apart. If consumers need a soft drink that is low in calories and tastes great, don't try to sell them something that's just low in calories. Give consumers a product that specifically addresses their needs.

The Silent Partner -- Developing Fighter Brands

If you truly want to create an unfair advantage over your competitors, you must learn that the public battles for shelf space and consumer attention are only a piece of the puzzle. Some of the most interesting competitive maneuvers actually occur below the consumer radar. It is fairly common for a major company to have in its stable of product a low-profile secret weapon they call a "fighter brand". A fighter brand exists only to wreak havoc against the competition. They are not intended to develop consumer loyalty; they are not designed to increase volume every year. Their mission, like any good soldier, is purely to attack the top competitors in the category.

To the glee of marketing strategists, fighter brands are effective, if covert, members of the product mix. Procter & Gamble used a fighter brand in the Frozen Concentrated Orange Juice category several years ago to help defend Citrus Hill Orange Juice. When P&G purchased a small juice company named Sundor in 1989, it acquired several small brands, among them one called "Texsun".

In the frozen orange juice market, unlike refrigerated juice, generic brands were dominant. Since the product was frozen, consumers no longer valued "freshness" as the key attribute, and most found very little difference between the flavor of the generic frozen oranges juices and the more expensive brand names of Tropicana, Minute Maid and Citrus Hill. When P&G introduced Texsun Frozen Orange Juice into stores nationwide, it was priced competitively with generic brands, not as competition with Citrus Hill or the other premium names.

But Texsun's real purpose was not to corner the frozen juice market; it was to foil Minute Maid and Tropicana from making any profit on their major promotions. Whenever these juices were featured in a store chain's advertising circular (an expensive promotion for the brand), the P&G sales force would offer tremendous discounts on Texsun juice as an "unadvertised special." Consumers at the point-of-purchase would often pick up the heavily discounted Texsun product instead of Minute Maid or Tropicana frozen juices. The strategy was very effective in neutralizing Minute Maid and Tropicana from reaping huge volume bumps during their features.

The strategy had a number of fringe benefits as well. It allowed Citrus Hill to remain safely above the price wars, ever the premium brand, which protected both its image and its price point. At the same time, retailers became increasingly disinclined to feature the Minute Maid and Tropicana frozen juices, since these promotions never seemed to generate the expected sales volumes.

Discovering fighter brands as a consumer onlooker is sometimes quite difficult. Major consumer product companies go to great lengths to distance themselves from these products and keep their secret weapons a secret. They often use the manufacturing names of defunct companies that they purchased in the past to shield their true identities. If you see a "brand" name that you don't recognize being sold at the low-generic price point, chances are it is a fighter brand, acting as a warrior for one of the major brands in the category!

Why You Need A Product Mix

What happens when you don't have a product mix -- when you are a one-trick pony with only one product or service?

Looking back at the long distance telephone wars of the 1990's provides a terrific case study of the dangers of being a brand without a product mix strategy. The market consisted primarily of AT&T, MCI, Sprint, -- all huge companies -- and a host of small resellers (the category equivalent of "generic brands") selling long-distance time over telephone networks. Time is a commodity. Ten minutes of time on AT&T is no different than ten minutes of time on Joe's Long Distance service. Time is time, no matter who is selling it. So why didn't consumers flock to the small resellers who offered the lowest long distance prices? The power of premium branding is what kept them from running away from AT&T, MCI and Sprint.

All through the 1960's, 70's and 80's, AT&T did a very smart thing. They had a monopoly on the phone business, and created a three tiered pricing structure for long distance phone services that made you believe that there was a functional reason why calls placed during the day (business hours of 7 a.m. to 5 p.m.) cost more than calls made in the evening (5 p.m. to 11 p.m.). The cheapest call of all was supposedly during the late night / early morning hours (11 p.m. to 7 a.m.). Consumers were led to believe that AT&T actually incurred greater costs during business hours (because of additional staff? additional technology?), but could offer reduced rates late in the evening, when call volume was lower. As a benefit to consumers, they would pass on those savings to us.

This strategy supported AT&T for years, building it into one of the most profitable corporations in world history. But their pricing strategy was all a scam. The truth? No matter what time a call was placed, there was no cost difference to AT&T. AT&T paid exactly the same for a phone call made at 10 a.m. as for one placed at midnight. Its premium pricing during the day was based on nothing more than the fact that they could get away with it. For years AT&T duped the public into believing their three-tiered pricing lie, and made huge profits as a result of its inflated daytime rates.

Along came MCI and Sprint, each created by former AT&T executives who understood the true cost scenario and knew that there were huge profits to be made by discounting the AT&T rates. MCI and Sprint developed brand strategies based on "AT&T quality at a lower price". The battle began at 25 cents per minute flat rates, 24 hours per day, and escalated from there. The cost savings was sufficient to spur many consumers to switch to MCI and Sprint, and despite AT&T's positioning as the most reliable carrier (you get what you pay for), consumers found no difference in the quality of their phone calls placed on these alternative carriers.

Now AT&T could no longer profit from the strength of its image; it had entered the commodity war. Voice quality was equal, calls got through -- now the only differentiating factor was price. Consumers happily jumped from one carrier to another, one low-cost promotion to the next. Many households switched long distance carriers as often as 6 to 8 times per year.

So how does a premium brand survive in a commodity world? The first attempts were targeted consumer promotions designed to stop the frantic switching. MCI introduced "Friends and Families", offering a discounted rate to your designated circle of friends and family if you convinced each of them to be MCI residential long distance customers. It didn't work. Sprint introduced "Free Friday's" for its business customers -- a more compelling offer. MCI countered with "Free Sunday's" for residential customers to call relatives. Sprint offered "Dime-A-Minute" calls late night. AT&T finally entered the fray with its One Rate plan, offering 15 cents per minute calls 24 hours a day, seven days a week.

Battle over? Not yet. Out of the blue a new competitor emerged and upped the ante. Internet provider America Online (with over 15 million subscribers) in partnership with a small, unbranded long distance reseller offered its customers 9 cents per minute long distance, 24 hours a day, seven days per week. The siege began. All of the premium, branded carriers, AT&T, MCI and Sprint began to lose their most technologically proficient customer base (who coincidentally was more educated, had higher than average income and spent more on long distance each month than the typical consumer). The propensity to switch long distance carriers frequently with relative ease -- a tactic that the big three had nourished and perfected for so long -- suddenly became their worst nightmare.

The final round of battle began. AT&T, after considerable internal resistance, began offering "One Rate Plus", 10 cents per minute, 24 hours per day, seven days per week with 5 cents per minute on Sunday. To lure back the Internet crowd, AT&T made an offer exclusively on their AT&T WorldNet website of 9 cents per minute to customers who subscribed to use AT&T WorldNet as their Internet Service Provider, AT&T as their long distance provider, and provided a discount to the monthly fees of America Online. MCI and Sprint also bundled Internet Service Provider packages with their long distance service.

The contest ended with MCI and AT&T declaring bankruptcy, while Sprint developed a product mix strategy and transitioned itself to a mobile phone service provider. AT&T eventually shut its doors before being purchased and rebranded / relaunched as AT&T Mobile.

So how could one of the USA's iconic brands such as AT&T fail? It all goes back to brand positioning and market segmentation. Perform a segmentation analysis, and start by asking the question "When you communicate with others, what product benefits are most important?" Notice how the question is phrased. It doesn't ask what is important about choosing a long distance carrier -- it asks what is important in communicating with others. This can include pagers, faxes, Internet, long distance, cell phones, mail, television, satellite transmissions, radio, newspapers, sign language and smoke signals. Figure out what besides price is important to consumers. They'll tell you – and craft your offering to meet their need better than anyone else. Craft a product mix that allows you to compete on several fronts aligned to consumer needs.

Marketing Truth

You cannot win a price war, so don't join the battle. Instead, research and understand your customer needs, then build added-value into your brand that will clearly separate your product from competition and justify the price / value relationship to consumers.

It is possible for even the most established and sedate product categories to be overrun by a competitor with some innovative flair. The key to owning your category, today and in the competitive fray of the future, is in dedicated and careful segmentation analysis. If you do it right, and listen carefully to what consumers say, you can own your category and ward off competitive threats, because YOU already have a product specifically targeted to every significant and meaningful customer need within the product category.

Eric D Schulz

THE SMART MARKETER'S TOOLBOX

Section Five:

Promotion Strategy

Eric D Schulz

Chapter Twelve

Advertising

Early in my marketing career I stepped into the office of a category manager at Procter & Gamble and asked him a simple question: "Since P&G does so much advertising and creates so many different campaigns over the course of a year, why don't we make the advertising ourselves? Wouldn't it be more cost effective to develop an in-house advertising agency and hire our own creative teams, saving the millions upon millions of dollars we pay to the dozen or so ad agencies in New York, Chicago and Los Angeles that work on our different brands? And wouldn't we have more control over the finished product that way?"

His answer was simple. "We need different creative perspectives for our many products. Most creative people have a certain perspective and a personal style to the way they develop their creative campaigns. If we hired our own creative people to work on all of our brands, the content would begin to look very similar over time. It's the nature of the beast. Without new blood, new visions and challenges to our ways of thinking about our brands, we would quickly land in an advertising rut. But by hiring different agencies, each brand receives its own unique creative approach and we can tap the brains of many talents, not just a few of our own, to achieve consistently great and unexpected results."

That is probably the best explanation I've ever heard of why advertising agencies exist. As my career has unfolded, I have experienced both incredibly wonderful and horrifically painful interactions with ad agencies. I have discovered along the way that developing a good working relationship with an agency -- one that fosters a creative environment and consistently produces great work -- is a learned skill. It begins with a thorough understanding of the agency business, and ends with the development of good client skills that mesh with the agency's needs.

To develop a positive working relationship with an agency that results in consistently strong campaigns, you must first understand some realities of the advertising agency business.

Reality #1: Advertising Agencies Are Businesses With Profit Motive

Advertising is the area in which most marketing people have the least amount of hands-on practical experience. Understanding "fair market value" for agency services is difficult to do, and costs can vary widely from agency to agency. If you don't know what you're doing, an advertising agency can fleece you faster than a three-card monty player in Central Park, and the stakes are astronomical.

So here are the basics behind the razzmatazz. Agencies make their money from three primary channels: 1) a monthly retainer fee, usually locked in for a 6 to 12 month duration; 2) a mark-up on all of the advertising materials they produce for you, usually in the 30% to 50% range; 3) a commission on all advertising they "buy" and place for you, usually in the 10%-15% range.

To understand the magnitude of the dollars, let's examine an average brand's financial interaction with an agency over a one-year period:

	Annual Agency Income
Monthly Retainer of $15,000:	$180,000
Materials Development Markup @ 40%:	
$250,000 of Print Materials	$100,000
Two TV Spots @ $400m each	$320,000
Ten Radio Spots @ $10m each	$40,000
Ad Buying Agency Commission @ 12%:	
$5 million campaign	$600,000

That's $1.24 million dollars. If you assume advertising was the biggest marketing effort of the year, the agency hauled in 19% of the budget!

Just think what a bonanza it is for an agency to land an account like McDonald's or Coca-Cola, who spend hundreds of millions of dollars each year on advertising! It's no wonder so many agencies can afford huge digs on Madison Avenue.

Reality #2: Advertising Agencies Are Not Your Partners

Advertising agencies are not your friends, and they certainly are not your partners. They are suppliers, the same as any other supplier. Unfortunately, they can have a much more dramatic impact upon your business than most suppliers depending upon how well they do their jobs.

Agency folks will vehemently disagree with this assessment, but if they were your partners, they would share the risk of failure with you. I have yet to come across an agency with a money-back guarantee if the campaign they develop for you flops. If you ever do find one with that promise, hire them!

I remember a budget meeting for Folgers coffee several years ago where the brand team was presenting its annual marketing spending recommendation to senior management. The Brand team had determined through a usage and attitude study that Hispanics presented an opportunity for incremental volume. It recommended that a new Hispanic campaign be developed, and that an agency that specialized in Hispanic marketing be hired to develop the campaign.

Senior managers for N.W. Ayer, the ad agency that worked on the Folgers account, were in the room. You should have seen the blood rush to their faces when the Brand team recommended that $5 million of the annual advertising budget be diverted to this new Hispanic agency. You've never seen such vigorous objections in your life. They were watching $600,000 of commissions walk out the door! If they were truly partners, they would have acknowledged the benefits of the recommended Hispanic campaign. But they were watching their piggy bank!

Reality #3: Advertising Agencies Are Not Research Groups

Some of the large agencies claim they are the best because they have developed proprietary intellectual models and research tools to understand consumers that give them unparalleled insights into buying behaviors.

They brag that their experience is so vast and extensive they alone truly understand the consumer.

The truth? It's all poppycock. While some of the consumer research that agencies generate is genuinely useful, data is only data until it can be transformed into action. And most creative people within the agency abhor research and statistical information, so the net result is that the insight is never exercised in the development of creative materials. The account executive will lay it on you as a part of the razzle-dazzle during the pitch for your pocketbook, but 9 times out of 10 the consumer learning's are not reflected in the campaign concepts.

Reality #4: Good Creative Teams Are Not A Guarantee Of Success

Many agencies will try to convince you that their creative teams are so gifted and insightful that they are virtually privy to divine revelation. Some lay it on so thick, you'd think the Dali-Lama himself sits in their conference room!

It is true that agencies are only as good as their creative teams. Now allow me a horrible generalization: most agency creative's are usually slightly off-centered people, functioning on the fringes of reality. That off-kilter quality in itself is not necessarily a bad thing, but you have to understand that these folks come from a different world than you and I. They see their work through rose-colored glasses. While the last campaign they created for a client might have been absolutely brilliant and insightful, it's no sure bet that the concepts they develop for you won't stink. Think of it this way. Steven Spielberg brought you such wonderful films as *"Jurassic Park"* and *"Saving Private Ryan"*. But he's also the guy who made *"Howard The Duck"* and *"1947"*. Even with talented and proven creative people, sometimes you win, and sometimes you lose big.

> *Marketing Truth*
>
> *The most critical piece in working with an advertising agency is knowing the creative team that is working on your campaign. Insist on seeing the full portfolio of the creative teams work, not just their highlight reel. Agencies, just like every other business, have new-hires and inexperienced rookies in their ranks. Insist*

that only experienced creative's are working for you! Let the rookies earn their stripes on somebody else's nickel.

Reality #5: Bigger Isn't Necessarily Better

Most advertising agencies like to make a big deal out of how many millions of dollars of billings they do each year. As a client, why should you care? When you're buying a car, do you consider as part of the decision set that Ford has sold $10 billion dollars worth of cars this year? In my experience with the agency world, bigger isn't necessarily better -- in fact, bigger can be worse.

What Drives Agencies To Succeed

That said, advertising agencies can do amazing work if you manage them well and give them good direction. The work an agency produces for you is only going to be as good as the foundation you provide. If you give them a solid brand positioning strategy to work from, an understanding of the target consumer, and allow them the freedom to explore, often they will develop campaigns that both captivate and inspire, bringing your strategy to life in ways you'd never dreamed possible.

But you won't taste that sweet success unless you see the agency for what it is and understand the motivations that drive it. Agencies live and breathe because they want to win awards. Creativity is their primary motivation, fueling a desire to be as innovative as possible with your brand; their industry rewards are Clio's and accolades for beautiful ads. Nobody gives out medals to agencies for campaigns that generate the most sales. Your business results are down on their priority list, and are there only because good business results allow them to keep your account and stay in business.

Personality Counts

Managing your relationship with an agency is like walking a tight rope in many respects. Advertising agencies are loaded with people with inflated, and fragile, egos. Many of the creative folks are incredibly insecure. You need to understand how to manage your relationship with both ends of the personality spectrum and everything in–between. Happy people are a critically important element to success!

That said, you must still establish right off the bat that you are the client and the agency is a hired gun. You drive the business; they don't. While this may sound aggressive, I've encountered several agency executives over the years that thought they knew more about my business than I did, and tried to ignore the strategic direction they were given. I've seen smaller consumer product companies who have let their agencies work as de facto brand teams, and when it happens, invariably strategic focus is lost in creative maelstroms. The brand gets advertising that is incredibly creative but consumer's walk away thinking, "huh?" The campaigns do nothing to communicate product benefits or convince consumers to purchase the product -- but boy, are they creative!

Keeping A Focus On The Brand Positioning Strategy

Often, agencies will take the brand positioning strategy you've given them and rework it to fit their own frame of reference or business style. For example, they may have a specific type of language or format that they use for all of the strategies across their different clients. You should usually give them the leeway to organize themselves internally if their creative teams work better off of their own structure. Be aware, however, that reworking your strategy is a big yellow caution flag. When the agency rewrites your brand positioning strategy, make sure that your strategic underpinnings are still in place – the target audience, the benefit, and the reason why. Often in the translation, agencies will try to dilute the strategic direction, providing them with more creative latitude and offering less restrictive strategic guidelines. So even if you think you've ordered a steak, the agency may try to feed you a lamb shank.

One very famous and well-respected agency tried to pull this trick on me. When I was working with them in developing the Coca-Cola Olympic advertising campaign, I had to keep a reminding them to adhere to the strategy. They didn't like the strategy we had provided to them, and wanted to create their own -- a watered down version that would have been easier to execute. This became a loud and raucous bone of contention on more than one occasion. Fortunately, in the end they stayed with the strategy we provided to them and the work resulted in the creation of two TV commercials which notched the highest persuasiveness scores in the history of The Coca-Cola Company, but getting to that point was a long, painful experience.

Agree To Spending Before It's Spent

Caution is the watchword when it comes to protecting your marketing development budget. Agencies love to tell you that they're going to do this or that and need your verbal approval. What they pitch usually sounds great -- but they don't mention the price tag until the project is completed. If this happens, you might as well just do a wire transfer of all money in your marketing account to theirs. By not locking down a price, you've given them a blank check to spend your money like a drunken sailor in Las Vegas!

I learned this lesson the hard way. When my team was developing the concept for a theme park in downtown Atlanta during the '96 Olympic Games to be called "Coca-Cola Olympic City", we contracted with an agency to develop conceptual ideas of what would be in the park and to create artist renderings for a presentation to Coke's senior management and the Board of Directors. We believed that an 8-person team from their shop was working on the project. No price tag was ever confirmed, because when we began the project we weren't sure of everything we would need from the agency. Thirty days later we received a bill for $750,000 and I nearly had a heart attack. The itemization showed over 60 people inside their shop working full time on our project!

> ### *Marketing Truth*
>
> *Make the agency provide written estimates of everything they are going to do BEFORE they do it, then question every single line to understand exactly what it entails. Question every detail. You'll save thousands of dollars on each job by finding and shaking out the fluff.*

Getting The Best Work Out Of Your Agency

It is wonderful and rewarding when your agency delivers a campaign that not only looks good, but also drives the sales needle! There are several things to keep in mind when dealing with an agency that will foster an environment for developing great work:

Give Them The Freedom To Explore

Creative people need their space. They need to feel free to open their minds to the cosmos and make connections from wide and varied stimulus. Remember, agency creative's are not like you and me. They walk to the beat of a different drummer, and the key to their success is in making brilliant connections that you and I could never dream up in our lifetimes.

Many marketing people make the mistake of telling the agency how the finished campaign should look. Usually the comment can seem very innocent when the client is chatting with the account manager on the phone. But what happens afterward is stifling. By making a seemingly innocuous statement, you paint a vision of what the agency believes you want them to create. This is a surefire way to mess up a campaign's creative development. When the information shuffle is completed, it typically has been translated into what sounds like a dictum by the time it reaches the creative team -- leaving them feeling undercut -- killing motivation and curtailing independent creative thought. The creative's don't give you their best work, and just crank out what they think you, the client, wants.

The better way to manage the agency is to give them a clear, succinct brand positioning strategy -- one that has a clearly focused target audience, strong consumer benefits and rational "reasons why" -- and let them go! Encourage them to get out of the box, to do something great, and tell them nothing more than you're expecting incredible work. Give them an energy booster. This will inspire the team to give you their best. By encouraging them to be free, they will feel unrestrained, allowing their brains to function and do the job they are best at doing.

To demonstrate what I mean, I want you to pretend you are an agency creative for just a moment. You're being asked to write me a children's song that encourages kids to embrace everyone in the world -- all ethnic persuasions -- in peace, happiness and harmony. That is your assignment. I know you can do it, and that when you're done, it will be great!

Now think about how you would begin this process. The assignment is very open-ended, so you feel like you have the room to create the song almost any way you choose. The assignment has empowered you to use creative license. It can be any kind of tune you want -- bouncy, slow, happy, jazzy, simple, and orchestral -- as long as it turns out to be a children's song that delivers the message. You can choose any words, create any chorus. The only limitation is your own imagination.

Now try the assignment from a different perspective. I'm asking you to write me a children's song that encourages kids to embrace everyone in the world -- all ethnic persuasions -- in peace, happiness & harmony. I know you can do it, and that when you get it done, it will be great! Oh, and by the way, if I had to describe to you what our goal would be, I'd like you to make it a great tune like Disney's "It's A Small World" -- you know what I mean:

It's a world of laughter a world of tears.

It's a world of joy and a world of fear.

It's a place we can play and be happy today,

It's a Small World After - All.

Now how do you feel about tackling this assignment? It's likely that right now the creative part of your brain has probably shut down. You can do nothing but play back "It's A Small World" in your head. Go ahead; try to hum a new tune!

This is the dilemma the agency creative team faces when clients, no matter how innocently, offer creative suggestions. The direction curtails creative processes and inhibits free association, forcing their minds to think in restricted channels. You can't get the best creative ideas if you work this way!

Give The Agency Adequate Time To Develop Concepts & Ideas

Rome was not built in a day, and most great ad campaigns take a while to develop into greatness. Most incredible ideas don't pop into your head fully formed and ready for execution. The same is true of creative executions. You begin with a seed of an idea, you let it take root and grow, you tweak it, you add to it, you subtract from it, and every once in a while it suddenly explodes into something beautiful you never expected.

Then again, sometimes you get what you think is a great idea one day and by tomorrow you've figured out that it stinks. The same holds true for the creative process within agencies. If you try to make the agency deliver on too-short timing, you increase the chance that you'll get half-baked ideas. Don't try to rush greatness. Most good campaigns take 6 to 8 months of development.

Provide Stimulus & Inspiration

It's not often that someone sitting at a desk in an office with phones ringing and distractions all around develops great new ideas. Inspiration comes from seeing a sunset, walking on the beach, exploring, and probing, watching and hearing new things.

If you want your creative team to give you inspired work, you must provide inspiration. Take them on a tour of the manufacturing facility. Take them into the fields where crops are grown. Go stand in stores and watch consumers shop. Have some focus groups with consumers who use your product, with consumers who DON'T use your product, and especially with consumers who are using your competitor's product!

Involving your creative team in competitive research is incredibly valuable. You don't want the creative team to just see your own happy consumers. They also need to see unhappy consumers, indifferent consumers, passionately opposed consumers. You and they will learn much more by listening to people who don't use your product or don't like your product than you will from those who do. Don't shield your warts and shortcomings -- let the creative's see everything, feel everything, touch everything, smell everything and probe everything.

Setting Ground Rules For Creative Critique

Creative review meetings to evaluate your agency's work should be conducted with as much decorum and care as a traditional Japanese tea ceremony. Bear in mind that when the agency is coming in to present the work, all of it has been reviewed within the agency several times before you get the chance to see it. The creative team has its egos attached to the effort. Be careful to offer fair, honest and timely feedback, yet in a way that fuels idea building and not idea bashing. You as a client have several rules of behavior to follow that can help create this environment.

First, before the presentation, you need to establish a pecking order within your marketing team and a clear understanding of rights when it comes to making comments. The majority of the team should be restricted to exclusively making comments of a strategic nature -- is the work on-or-off strategy -- and discussing which concepts better communicate the strategic positioning. Only the one or two most senior people in the room should have "creative critique" rights. You don't need everyone in the room trying to be an art director.

Marketing Truth

When critiquing the advertising agency creative presentations, the first comment should always be a strategic evaluation of whether or not the concept delivers the brand positioning strategy – target audience, benefit, and reason why. This is a great training exercise for junior marketing people to develop their strategic evaluations skills.

I cannot over-stress the importance of limiting junior people to commenting strictly on strategic evaluation. I learned this lesson the hard way in my first creative meeting at P&G, which happened to be a new TV campaign for Citrus Hill Orange Juice. I was only about 4 weeks into the job. My brand manager had failed to inform me of the rules of decorum, and so when the agency concluded its creative presentation and the category manager turned to me and asked "Eric, what do you think?" I immediately replied "It looks like a Tropicana commercial I saw on TV last night. They've got a woman in a plaid shirt walking through an orange grove, just like this ad". When I finished, there room turned ice cold, and if looks could kill, I would have been carried out on a stretcher. I broke the cardinal rule of a junior person -- I insulted the agency's creativity -- and the incident affected my relationship with that agency for the duration of my stay at P&G.

Offer Honest, Open & Timely Feedback

When you have seen all of the work that the agency has presented, give them your gut reaction right there on the spot. Don't wait and let it settle. Your gut reaction is probably the right reaction. Tell them which concepts worked for you and which did not -- again, strategically first, and creatively second. If there are hints of great ideas in some concepts but their execution just doesn't work, encourage the agency to take a look at it again and see if it can be revised to make it better. Developing a great campaign that really works usually requires several iterations. And often the seed of the best idea is buried in one of those early presentations, and only after several rounds of work does it blossom into the core concept.

The Right Place at the Right Time

Once you have a great advertising campaign ready to go, you have to figure out where to place it. Media planners are probably the most under-appreciated, under-paid and least understood members of the advertising agency team. While the Account Supervisors and Creative's are busy jetting to clients and making impressive presentations, the media planners sit in their humble cubicles crunching numbers and sending faxes. Don't make the mistake of taking them for granted.

Media planners are the whizzes that determine how, when and where to place your brilliant advertising. A good planner will save you thousands of dollars and do a great job of reaching your core consumer. They might even recommend innovative strategies to maximize your consumer impressions, like providing editorial PR material at the same time you buy a print ad to double your exposure in a key magazine.

Beware media planners who offer you a straight formula of national consumer impressions, costs and day parts. Essentially, these types of planners are paying retail for off-the-rack ad placement. A talented planner will have ideas for beating the system, taking advantage of an under-valued show, or creatively tagging your spots to tap into your MDF funds.

You may never have an opportunity to speak with your media planner if you don't specifically ask, since many agencies simply forward their proposed schedules through their Account Executive. Let yours know how much you value the media planner, and ask to include him or her in your placement discussions. When you express interest and encouragement in the process, you'll probably be pleased and surprised at how energetically your media planner will respond.

Advertising That Works

Great advertising is innovative, creative, unique, and convincing. When all of the elements come together, most campaigns become greater than they could have ever been imagined at the beginning when just a few strategic words where scribbled on a page. The work that many agencies turn out is truly inspiring, and the art of making great advertising is one that must be constantly nourished to get consistently great results.

Advertising That Doesn't Deliver

Advertising can be delightful, surprising, memorable, touching and humorous. . . and *still* not sell the product. Why? Sometimes a muddled or indecisive brand positioning statement is at fault. Other times the creative concept and execution of the campaign fails to convince consumers of the product's benefits. Some commercials create a sensational mood and memorable image, but don't connect them to the product. Regardless of the specific reason, every day I see millions of dollars wasted on advertising that doesn't work. The money may as well have been flushed down a toilet.

How can I be so sure? Because after examining hundreds of hours of TV commercials, thousands of print and billboard campaigns and studying consumer response to this mountain of information -- through a combination of purchase intent, persuasiveness feedback, sales figures and qualitative analysis -- I've found a series of common errors that consistently arise in faltering campaigns. These blunders, committed time and again, either leave the consumer cold and disinterested in the product or, at their worst, actually create a consumer aversion to the brand.

Although great advertising can be breathtaking, developing an effective advertising campaign is not an art. It is the result of strategic discipline, rigorous research, and a clear understanding of the relevant and meaningful benefits that make your product appealing to consumers. Only upon this solid foundation does "art" -- the actual creative endeavor of making the advertising -- begin to take shape. Companies and their advertising agencies must be watchful that the creative executions deliver strong, clear messages that compel the consumer to action and set their product apart as being different, better and special in the mind of the consumer.

The Power of the Rings

My analysis of the foils and foibles of advertising began during an extensive advertising review of all Olympic-themed ads by major sponsors of the Olympic Games through the years. I climbed on a plane and flew to the IOC headquarters in Lausanne, Switzerland to tour the IOC Museum and review their collection of sponsor advertising which they had collected since the 1932 Games. When I reviewed campaigns from dozens of companies over several decades, I was shocked to see that many of the executions appeared almost identical and could be interchanged between brands or products without anyone noticing. Dozens of companies had produced a spot with a runner sprinting to the finish line, raising arms in victory, with the voice-over "Go for the Gold – McDonald's, or Chevron, or Bank of America, or…anyone.

The core problem was that the advertising failed to create a relevant connection between the company or brand and the Olympics. Usually the campaigns depicted athletes in beautiful action shots with stunning photography. The brand logo was layered in with some copy about effort, endurance, being the best, or going for the gold.

Does that ring a bell? Do any Olympic-themed advertising campaigns stick out in your mind as brilliant executions, offering a clear understanding of why that particular brand is associated with the Games? Chances are, even though the 10 worldwide Olympic sponsors have all been using the Olympics as a primary advertising vehicle for the past 20 or so years, you can't remember more than two or three of these brands -- and what does that tell you about the effective spending of their $50 million sponsorship fees? Do I hear a flushing sound?

VISA is one of the few companies that have made good use of its sponsorship dollars because its campaigns make a clear and logical connection between the brand and the Games. You probably remember VISA's "at the Olympic Games, you can't buy tickets with American Express" campaign with the memorable tag line " VISA -- we're everywhere you want us to be." The sponsorship is believable and consumer-relevant, which places it far ahead of the competitive sponsor crowd. Better still, it flaunts the cache' of Olympic sponsorship to reinforce the practical benefits of VISA over its key competition.

The Coca-Cola ad campaign -- "For The Fans" -- also hits the mark with consumers. The underlying strategic premise -- that Coca-Cola refreshes the fans of the Olympic Games -- is believable and relevant. Athletes aren't depicted drinking Coke; fans are. All promotions, advertising and collateral material contain the tag lines: "Cheering Is Thirsty Work" or "Refreshing The Olympic Spirit". The campaign earned the highest persuasiveness and awareness scores among Olympic sponsors and launched the brand to record sales figures.

Expanding The Study

After reviewing the learning from the Olympic ad study, I wondered if perhaps many of the "sins" committed by the Olympic sponsors were as pervasive in other types of advertising. My team conducted another study evaluating advertising campaigns from virtually every consumer category; fashion, packaged goods, restaurants, automobiles, and airlines -- you name it, we took a look at it. And here's what we saw: the very same blunders that had tripped up the Olympic sponsors were crippling the campaigns of brands in virtually every category we reviewed!

These errors were so consistently devastating to a campaign, and so negatively affected consumer behavior, that I dubbed them "The Six Deadly Sins of Advertising."

The Six Deadly Sins of Advertising

I know what you're thinking: aren't there *seven* deadly sins? Yes, but in advertising, unlike in religion, lust is not a sin; it's a virtue. Sex is used to sell everything from cars to chewing gum, and it does a mighty fine job of motivating consumers. So let the libidos run wild while we concentrate on the other six sins, still as lethal as ever.

Sin #1: Pride

Like the tragic Greek youth Narcissus, many companies adore their own image. They like to see their name and logo in conspicuous places. Bigger is better; lights are sensational. They don't feel they need to tell consumers anything about their product; they assume size matters more than message.

Well, those giant billboards *are* impressive, aren't they? But let me ask you a simple question: What is PNC? What do they sell? What is EnergySolutions? What do they sell? Most consumers have no idea, but each of these companies paid a boatload of money to put their names on major league stadium venues so they could stand back and congratulate themselves. If you're not going to bother communicating with consumers, why pay top dollar for a consumer vehicle?

It should not come as any surprise that consumers ignore such empty advertising, because it doesn't communicate anything to them. Consumers pay attention when advertising relates to their lives, touches a cord, lets them in on the joke, and offers interesting information. They pay no more attention to the giant logo signs scattered around sports arenas -- or on highway billboards -- than they do to the license plates in the parking lot.

To illustrate the problem, I conducted a study a few years ago that measured consumer recall of advertising inside sports arenas. Consumers leaving the facility were initially asked to write down the names of the advertisers with signage inside the building ("unaided recall"). Then they were shown an extensive list of advertisers names (including all the advertisers inside the building, and several others who were not) and asked to mark those they believed were advertising inside ("aided recall"). Even with this nudge to the memory, fewer than 10% of the consumers could name more than 5 advertisers out of the total 50 companies and brands advertising inside the arena. Not coincidentally, most of the signs were narcissistic in nature, bearing only a company name or logo. Consumers were blocking them out.

Marketing Truth

> *Never produce advertising that only states your brand or company name. Always have a relevant consumer message linked with your name and that reinforces your brand positioning statement.*

The cure for Pride is simple: link the brand name with a message. It doesn't have to be a long message. Instead of a sign that just says "Coca-Cola"; it should say "Coca-Cola Refreshes". What is the difference? The latter communicates the core brand positioning that is reinforced with the hundreds of other encounters a consumer has with the brand on a weekly basis. Instead of posting a sign that merely says "Budweiser"; the brand should aim for "Budweiser, King of Beers", or add the Budweiser Clydesdale horses or other advertising icon to the logo. These simple elements don't require much space, and they help to reinforce the Budweiser brand identity.

These small differences have an enormous impact on consumer recall. In our stadium study, the few brands that carried a message with their name were much more frequently remembered than those that did not.

Sin #2: Gluttony

Some brands gorge themselves on pretty pictures and affecting imagery without giving any consideration to whether those images provide any real sustenance for the brand. They don't bother to link those fabulous -- and expensive -- images to their product in a way that will lead to health and growth for their business.

"Wow, those images are brave and powerful and successful, just like us! What a great symbol for our business," the executives shout. Well, boys, maybe *you* can make that connection, but your consumers won't. And besides, maybe they don't particularly need an airline that's all that; they might just want to fly to Chicago.

Unfortunately, many products in our day-to-day life continue to perpetrate this sin. It's bad enough when perfume ads feature naked people in strange settings, but that's at least defensible; although the ads have absolutely nothing to do with the product, they do play to that mysterious consumer desire to believe that top designers, whose names are on the perfume, are bizarre and visionary. But what possible rationale could justify using random imagery for family-oriented household products like waffles?

Eggo ran a TV ad that featured a mad professor who clones himself into a dozen or so versions and then fights with his many alter egos over a single Eggo waffle. The advertising isn't funny or compelling, the concept is tired, and the product is incidental. Even the setting is unappetizing -- a laboratory -- and the commercial contains no ancillary products like milk, juice or toast that help me envision the product as breakfast -- or even as food! I suppose if I am ever cloned I'll relate to this commercial, but until then, it will never persuade me to add Eggo waffles to my shopping list.

Marketing Truth

Never use imagery in your advertising that does not relevantly link and support your brand image, personality, or its usage occasion. Always develop advertising in which the consumer can "insert" his or herself into the picture to envision the relevance to their life. If you succeed in getting consumers to visualize themselves in your advertising, you win!

Don't get me wrong -- I'm not saying fantasy doesn't work. Fantasy works well as an advertising hook, particularly when it invites consumers to jump into the picture and join in the fun. A powerful way to convince consumers to buy your product is to make them believe that when they use it, it transports them to another place -- one that is more fun and interesting than the mundane and everyday world in which they live. Have you ever sprayed Dow Bathroom Cleaner into your sink and then visualized the "Scrubbing Bubbles" racing around battling your sink scum? Or visualized having "Money Coming Out the Wazzoo" from your E-Trade account? Or fantasized about being at the beach when sipping a Corona beer? Fantasy is OK as long as it is grounded in the reality of what the product does or how it makes you feel. We all know that the Scrubbing Bubbles don't really exist, but they are much more fun to think about than cleaning a dirty toilet.

Sin #3: Envy

Envious brands are so consumed with a competitor's success that they imitate an existing campaign instead of carving out their own unique identity. Earlier in this chapter I related the story of how Citrus Hill Orange Juice created a TV spot that looked suspiciously similar to advertising that Tropicana was airing. The new Citrus Hill ad featured a woman with shoulder length brown hair, wearing a plaid shirt, walking through an orange grove, picking an orange, and concluded with her standing next to her young daughter by an old pickup truck loaded with orange crates.

Tropicana was already airing a commercial featuring a woman with shoulder length brown hair, wearing a plaid shirt, walking through an orange grove, picking an orange, and then standing next to an old pickup truck. The difference is obvious, right? The Citrus Hill lady was with her daughter, not alone, and *their* truck was loaded with orange crates! The advertising agency assured us that these "key" differences set us apart and reinforced our brand image.

Guess what? Consumers couldn't tell the difference. While the agency and the Citrus Hill brand team had convinced themselves that their ad was nothing like the Tropicana ad, in reality, consumers saw the Citrus Hill ad and assumed it was for Tropicana.

Beer brands are so consumed with envy, it's surprising the only green beer you see is on St. Patrick's Day. Just how many advertisements have you watched in the past month that shows attractive young people standing around partying with a bottle of beer in their hand? Or how about attractive guy and girl bantering over a beer at a trendy bar? I'll bet you can remember which ads are for which brands, right? Yeah, right. Maybe that's why "The World's Most Interesting Man" was such a hit; at least you could tell him apart from the suds studs and beer babes that usually populate their commercials.

Marketing Truth

Never produce advertising that looks anything like something that your competitor is currently running or has run in the past. Always ensure that your campaign is different, better and special, making your product a hero, convincing consumers of the unique benefit your brand offers and why they should consciously choose to purchase your product.

Sin #4: Greed

Some marketers are so greedy for profit they'll say almost anything to sell their product, even if their product claims are so outrageous they cannot be believed.

I'm sure you've seen the commercials for exercise equipment that promise to turn your body into the king or queen of Muscle Beach with just 15 minute-a-day workouts. You believe it, right? I'm sure Arnold Schwarzenegger was devastated when he learned that after all those years of torturous effort, he could have built the same body by buying one of those Bow-Flex machines!

I'll bet Arnold was equally surprised to learn how beneficial a Snickers candy bar could be as part of his training routine. Imagine, all those meals of steamed vegetables and fish, then one day he happens across a Snickers ad featuring world class athletes pausing mid-workout to nibble a Snickers bar -- how refreshing! Do you think he would believe the scenario? Not for one minute. And consumers didn't believe it, either. I have a hard time thinking that even the most loyal Snickers corporate employee, wiping chocolate from his lips as he reviewed the storyboards, saw anything true or real in this advertising campaign. He probably just thought it was a nifty way to associate Snickers with big name athletes. It wasn't a good bluff, and it didn't sell product.

Occasionally the promise of a dishonest campaign is so tantalizing that it does persuade consumers to buy the product, only to be disappointed. This might be a short–term strategy for immoral marketing companies that don't want repeat business, but it generally spells death for the brand within 6 months. It's also susceptible to lawsuits.

Have you ever gone to a restaurant, seen a great advertisement for a meal (with a pretty picture of what you'll get), ordered it and been disappointed that the food in their advertising looked a whole lot better than what was served on your plate? I know I've been duped a few times. Wendy's committed this sin when they introduced "Dave's Big N Juicy" burgers to replace the Old Fashioned Burger that had graced their menu for decades. The PR campaign wrapped around the change told of Wendy's exec's crisscrossing the country for over two years, stopping at dives, hamburger shacks and drive-ins all over the USA in search of the perfect burger. That this extensive research resulted in the creation of this wonderful new signature burger. The PR had me going. On the day of its release I rushed to Wendy's to try out this mouth-watering new sensation. To my disappointment, I was served the same "Old Fashioned" Hamburger with a crinkled pickle, red onion, and different bun. Tasted exactly the same as the Old Fashioned, only it now cost fifty-cents more. Fool me once…I haven't been back to Wendy's since.

Consumers live by the old adage, "If it looks too good to be true, it probably is". They don't fall for the con jobs very often.

> **_Marketing Truth_**
>
> *Never oversell your product benefits by stretching the truth. Never develop advertising that puts your brand in a position that consumers will find hard-to-believe. Always communicate clear, meaningful consumer benefits, backed up with a rational and believable reason why.*

Sin #5: Sloth

Slothful companies don't invest the work and energy required to connect their product in a relevant way to the consumer. They try to be trendy when they are not. Levi-Strauss is a major sinner in the sloth category. In an attempt to reclaim the "coolness" of wearing Levi's among the teen segment, they borrow a series of cutting edge advertising techniques that work for other products, and apply them randomly in Levi's ads. The result; a series of nonsensical spots, such as one featuring a guy driving through a car wash with the windows down or teens sitting around Denny's talking about nothing. Levi's didn't bother to figure out why those trendy-looking commercials worked for other teen-oriented brands; they simply jumped on the trend, and fell flat on their faces.

Sin #6: Wrath

It's easy to understand how so many companies get caught up in angry advertising. Either they emerge from consumer research saying, "Wow, consumers really *hate* that problem!" (whether it be dishwasher spots or slow bank lines) or they themselves work up such a lather about a particularly loathsome competitor; their venom spills over into their advertising.

But angry advertising doesn't work. The average consumer must hear a message approximately seven times before he or she absorbs it, and few people can tolerate an abrasive ad through more than a few repetitions. More importantly, the brand itself becomes associated with a strong negative emotion -- it's that *angry* brand -- and who wants to be affiliated with that? It's a lesson many politicians have learned the hard way during furious mud-slinging campaigns that backfired when voters just got sick of the whole ugly mess.

There Is No "Right Way"

There is no magic formula or "right way" to create good advertising. But there are thousands upon thousands of advertising case studies to help you to learn what has worked and what hasn't.

Marketing Truth

Here is the biggest truth in this entire book. Advertising is entertainment. Yes, entertainment. It is not a sin to advertise to consumers. All they ask is that you make your advertising entertaining and enjoyable to see! Whether we are selling computer chips or phone apps or ice, we are in the entertainment business and need to make our advertising position our product as the hero and be entertaining!

The Six Deadly Sins of Advertising are just a few things that can help raise your awareness of what not to do. They can perhaps save you the anguish of developing campaigns that won't do the job. Just avoiding these mistakes is still no guarantee of success, but they can help reduce the chance of failure.

The best advertising will always push the edges of creativity, developing ways of presenting your product that captivate and inspire consumers, and most of all, make your product the hero. Pushing to the edge means that sometimes you'll go too far and fall off the cliff. That's OK too, because a carefully considered failure provides a learning tool for next time. The saying goes "Tis better to have loved and lost than never to have loved at all". It's also better to have pushed the edges of creativity and gone too far than to never have tried to get out of the box -- miring yourself in mediocrity. Michael Eisner, the former Chairman of the Board at Disney Studios has a favorite saying "Average is Awful". Take his advice. Go ahead, take a chance, and do something great!

Eric D Schulz

Chapter Thirteen

Website and Search Engine Optimization

What is the only advertising that works 24 hours a day, seven days a week, and 365 days a year? It's your website. Just like the city that never sleeps, your website is always available to promote your products and services to consumers. In the Internet age, websites act as digital storefronts for businesses, enabling entrepreneurs, small businesses, and corporations alike to advertise and sell around the clock and around the world. Just like a traditional storefront, a website will often provide the first impression to potential clients, and an attractive and professional site can draw in viewers and turn them into customers.

The web has leveled the playing field for entrepreneurs and small businesses competing for exposure on a world stage, and a great website can give you a much needed advantage over your competitors. The website of a one-person entrepreneur working out of a home office can effectively compete with mega-corporations. It's all about creating that first impression. Your site is the most important marketing tool you have at your disposal, and how you build it and figure out how to get people to it are some of the biggest marketing challenges you face.

Web Design Gotta-Do's

Website design costs can vary from almost nothing to hundreds of thousands of dollars, and to be honest, price has nothing at all to do with how good a site is – what differentiates the good from the bad is STRATEGY. Building the perfect website isn't as easy as plugging a few images into a template and sticking it on the Internet. There is one essential need in website design:

> *Marketing Truth*
>
> **YOUR WEBSITE HAS TO LOOK PROFESSIONAL**! *Your customers expect your website to be aesthetically pleasing with a professional looking facade. Anything less makes your online*

business looks unreliably small. Research has shown that 52% of web-users will not return to a website if it has poor aesthetics.

Look at the website for Apple: www.apple.com. It is one of the best examples of what a website should look like. Clean, functional, easy to navigate, not a lot of words. They showcase their products, making each a hero, and tell you what differentiates them.

Your website can be as casual or formal as you wish, but you need to design your website according to your target audience. If you're selling homemade quilts, for example, you probably won't want loud music playing in the background or flashy, animated text. You'd likely want soft colors and links to photos of each quilt pattern, and a story about where and how your handcrafted quilts are made.

There is a lot to think about when designing a website. There's graphics and images, content, colors, videos, and everything else about the site to take into consideration. On one hand you may want to attract the 40-50 year old crowd, but you definitely don't want to alienate your 20-30 year olds either. For most website owners the process of cutting through the clutter to get to the solutions that make sense for your web design is simple: **know your ideal customer.**

You see, once you know who your ideal customer is, you'll have a clear understanding of what they want and what they don't. Once you have this clarity, it will help reveal the right choice of colors, images, and overall message.

Content Management

Now all you need to do is target your message at these key points:

Your Customer's Emotions

The truth about consumers is that they buy for emotional reasons. They buy what they want and then they find rational reasons to justify the purchase. Make sure that your headlines and content are packed with benefits. Have you ever heard someone talking about the purchase of his or her new sports car? They will run off a list of **features** like the amazing suspension, or the super-dual-cooled engine that lets them run at higher RPMs for longer. But that's not really why they bought the car. The fact is the car is exciting to drive! They love the feel of the way it hugs turns, and they love the way other people look at them! **Benefits** evoke emotion in your customers.

Your Customer's Subconscious

As much as 95% of your customer's thinking is subconscious. Much of that thinking is taken up by making judgments about our surroundings. It takes only 1/20th of a second for site visitors to form a judgment about your website or product. Make sure the opinion they form is a positive one because it will last throughout their entire experience with your site. Make sure that your branding is solid, that your site looks professional, and **include plenty of trust indicators** –yes, even if you're not selling online. Testimonials, association logos, and number of years in business will all send the right message to your customer's subconscious.

Your Customer's Budget

All you need to know about your customer's budget is this:

> *<u>Marketing Truth</u>*
>
> *Most consumers are willing to pay a 20-25% price premium for their favorite brand before they'd switch to a competitor.*

In other words, don't focus on cost. Focus on value and benefits.

In your own experience, can you remember buying a brand name product because you trusted that it would out-perform the generic brand? When it comes to your customers, their emotions, beliefs and subconscious are going to drive their purchase more than their budget will. If your website looks more like a premium brand than a low-cost alternative, you'll be utilizing the same strategies that marketers of Fortune 500 companies use every day.

Permission Marketing

One of the critical elements of your home page content is convincing the visitor to participate in permission marketing. Create easily clickable links to "like" you on Facebook, "follow you" on Twitter and sign up for an email subscription. This is the ultimate win in website success. Now you can share your content with them anytime it is ready. Use the official "Twitter follow" button and "Facebook like" button (which you should link to your Facebook page URL, not the website address). They have made it almost too easy to follow you! With one click, if they are logged in to Facebook and Twitter, they can follow you.

Is Your Website Driving New Customers – or Driving Them Away?

New visitors to a website spend less than 10 seconds deciding whether or not they will be able to find what they are seeking on your site. Just like with packaging, your website needs to scream like a carnival barker the benefits your products and service provide, and how they are different, better and special. Here are several suggestions for effectively managing your content:

#1 - Provide Value

Customer-focused, relevant website content is essential. People search the web with questions. They have come to your site for answers. Make it easy. How can you solve their problem? What should they do next to find out more? Condense your value down to a few sentences or paragraphs in laymen's terms and you'll turn web visitors to customers. People like to know whom they are doing business with. Testimonials, reviews, press, licenses, awards, and even years in business, or years of experience can let your customers know that you can be trusted with their business. Bios and photos of you and your team can also give the website a personal touch.

#2 – Headlines

A typical website visitor spends an average of less than a minute on any given web page. Web users skim and prefer easily digestible bits of content. Endless paragraphs of text will only make their eyes glaze over. At first, display small, juicy headlined tidbits or a high level overview presented in such a way that they want to read more. Then allow them to drill down to more detail.

#3 - Show the Way

The best websites allow people to know where they are and where they need to go next at all times. A visitor to your website should be no more than a couple clicks away from the content they seek. Make navigation links intuitive, and even redundant if necessary by displaying them both in the main navigation menu and in the footer navigation. Replace any nondescript "click here" links with action words like "Download the 10 Keys to Branding" here.

#4 - Know the Competition

What differentiates you from the competition? Quality, selection, price, personalized service and customization are among many factors that can distinguish your business from competitors. Let your customers know how they will be treated and how you do business.

Spend some time surfing the web and taking note of elements you like and don't like in general on websites - style, navigation, content. Then take a look at your competitors' websites. What works? What doesn't? Review these trends and think about what your own website can emulate and what it can do even better to make it the best user experience possible.

#5 - Build Trust

Your website is an extension of your business and your brand. Now more than ever, consumers are turning to the web first for information on products and services they are interested in. What is your website saying about you? Show visitors how you stand out from the competition with case studies of how you helped a client, photos of your recent work, or testimonials from satisfied customers. Alternatively, show before and after photos of your projects or services. Downloadable guides, sales/marketing materials, or even video tutorials can also show how you can address a problem for your clients.

#6 – Update Frequently

There is nothing worse than checking out a company's website and finding the most recent update is two years old. If you are going to date stamp news and content updates make sure they are updated regularly. Keep the site content fresh to increase the quality and volume of your visitors.

#7 - Analyze Success

Measuring the effectiveness of your website and online marketing initiatives is an important barometer for any business and, with tools like Google Analytics, it has never been easier. Creating customized landing pages tailored to a specific campaign can assist you in tracking leads and channeling money to those efforts that yield the greatest results.

#8 - Provide quick-reference FAQs

This might be the easiest source of content. What information could help customers make more informed decisions about your products or services? If you find yourself answering the same questions repeatedly, consider including the answers on your website. This will save you the time and effort of answering these questions in person or on the phone.

#9 - Give a call to action

Increasing the number of visitors to your website isn't the end goal. Maybe you want them to make an appointment, call or visit the store, join a mailing list, or connect via social media. Make it clear what you want them to do next and include incentives to act now with discounts, giveaways, or limited time offers.

Content is extremely important to the success of your website and online marketing. The key is to focus on the needs of your customers. People search the web with questions, and they've come to your site for the answers. Provide information that is relevant and valuable and you can't go wrong.

Search Engine Optimization (SEO)

You want to stand out from the competition. On the web, this may seem a daunting challenge when a search for any imaginable business or service yields hundreds of thousands, if not millions, of results. So how do you get your website to the top of the list?

While "build it and they will come" may have worked for Kevin Costner in the movie *Field of Dreams*, it is not a recipe for website success. How will potential clients find you once your website is up and running? What will they type into a search engine when they are looking for your product or service? Relevant keywords contained within your website content, links, and code are all factors that influence your search engine ranking and moving your website to the top of the list where it will be seen and visited.

Search Engine Optimization, or SEO is the process of improving the quality and volume of traffic to your website from search engines such as Google, Yahoo, and MSN. Your company does not have to be the biggest or best to catapult to the top of the search engine rankings; your website just has to be built using a combination of strategies to catch the search engine's attention.

As you would assume, the earlier a site appears in the search results list, the more visitors it will receive. When performing your own web searches, how often do you click past the first page of listings, or even look past the first few results? Research shows that searchers actually select the top two listings on the results page more than 50 percent of the time.

More visitors to your website translate to more potential customers. And these web searchers are the kind of visitors you want: 60 percent of local web searches are done with the intent to make a purchase, and 80 percent of the people performing a local search will call or visit the store.

So, people are looking for you online, ready to purchase your products and services. Make it easier for them to find you with these 5 steps to Search Engine Optimization.

#1 - Identify Profitable Keyword Phrases

Put yourself in the mind of the consumer. What words would a potential customer type into a search engine when they are looking to buy your services? The first and most important step in Search Engine Optimization is knowing what potential clients are looking for. Typically, the more specific, the better. For example, a search for "dentist" in Google returns an overwhelming 40 million results. "Baltimore cosmetic dentist" narrows the field by 99 percent.

#2 - Optimize Site Architecture

Now is the time to go behind the scenes of your website to include those targeted keywords into the underlying HTML code that your site is built on. At a minimum, tags within the code, including the page title and description, can all be customized to match what your audience may be searching for. Using the above example, "Cosmetic dentist in Baltimore offering cosmetic, implant and neuromuscular dentistry services" would be a better title for a page within the site than simply "Services."

#3 - Tailor Content

Keywords should be included in the viewable content of the page as well. Provide valuable, relevant and updated information to users and you'll be rewarded by both search engines and visitors who will keep steady traffic coming to your site. Answers to frequently asked questions about cosmetic dentistry would be ideal for a site catering to people interested in these services.

#4 - Create Links to Your Site

Inbound links to your site from other websites act as validation to search engines, so the quality and quantity of these links are important. Search engine algorithms take into account a multitude of factors when ranking the billions of web pages across the Internet universe. A link from a New York Times article mentioning your business counts significantly more for your site's ranking than a link from your friend's personal web page.

A few hours a week should be devoted to creating these inbound links from relevant sources such as industry message boards, forums, and directories. If your time is limited, consider contracting your web designer for this purpose. The ideal scenario is to have links with keywords in the link text itself that match up with the keywords now on your web page. Press releases can be used for this purpose. A press release describing the innovative new procedure used by Dr. Smith, an experienced "cosmetic dentist in Baltimore," using these same words as a link to the page previously optimized would be perfect. At this point, the search engine is likely convinced of the content on this page and will display it more prominently than a non-optimized site when a user searches the web for those keywords.

#5 - Analyze Success

Obviously, some keywords will have much higher competition than others. Localizing your keywords to a geographic area and targeting more specific terms is generally advisable. Google AdWords provides a keyword tool that allows you to view the popularity of particular keyword phrases and offers additional similar keywords that you may want to consider. By keeping an eye on what keywords are driving traffic to your site, you will be better prepared to focus your efforts on what produces the greatest results.

Search Engine Optimization is a continuous process. By following and repeating these steps, or hiring somebody to do it for you, you'll have a long-term solution that drives an increase in the quality and volume of traffic to your site at a fraction of the cost typically spent on traditional marketing channels. That is a return on investment that anybody can agree with!

Integrating Your Website with Your Marketing Plan

So how can you make your website work in unison with your paid advertising and your social media? The brand media management models many national advertisers and larger and more sophisticated local clients are adopting have evolved rapidly over the past few years. No longer is media planning compartmentalized into the traditional buckets of Print, Electronic Media (TV & Radio), and Out-of-Home. The *new model is Paid, Owned, and Earned Media*. You website affords you the opportunity to in effect, become your own media company, and how you will use it with both traditional media and social media in this new model is changing.

There is angst in ad land over the complexity of media. Ad planners wring their hands, bemoaning the proliferation of media channels and the unpredictable ways in which "consumers" jump from TV to Facebook to text messages to Google to foursquare to iPods…and so on.

Out of the chaos in the media world and the complexity of infinite digital channels, a new way of looking at media is emerging that is simple, useful and strategic:

Paid media (the advertising you BUY) jumpstarts owned media (the things you OWN or CREATE, like your website, videos, etc.).

Your Owned Media sustains the chatter you create in social media and PR.

There are a plethora of benefits to approaching media this way; the most important are these two:

1. No matter what new media channels the geniuses invent tomorrow, this logical set of strategic categories doesn't change; and

2. The end result of using media this way is the creation of a permanent marketplace advantage for a business: Total cost of marketing ultimately goes way down because expensive media buys are less necessary. Credibility goes way up because ordinary people are talking up the brand

to their friends and online connections, which have a far greater impact on purchase behavior than anything a brand could ever do or say on its own.

Roughly eight years ago, it became clear that traditional media (outdoor, newspapers, magazines, TV, music and so on) and traditional advertising tools (billboards, TV spots, print ads, radio spots and so on) were on a collision course. For example, in the television world, new technology - Digital Video Recorders (DVR's) - began passing control over advertising from the media companies to the audience. The day is rapidly approaching when no one can force people to watch ads. So the ads will have to go away or become something else.

Marketing Truth

It has become accepted that advertising needs to add value to people's lives or it will be ignored. It has to be useful and valuable, entertaining or informative or both.

Everyone supposedly began to understand, in other words, that brands have to be media companies, but almost no one knew how to do that or what it really might mean. A terrific example of this is the Smartwater media campaign, begun by posting a video entitled "Jennifer Aniston Sex Tape". If you are going to generate some viral marketing interest, that's a great way to do so. The video is funny, informative, and entertaining, and since its debut on March 7, 2011, has received over 9.7 million online views. Smartwater is very smart.

FIRST, PAID MEDIA: What exactly is paid media? It's any form of advertising where brands pay the media owner to insert the brand's message. Central to this exchange is the idea that the media owner has gathered an audience that the brand wants to address. That's why the brand is willing to pay.

Examples of paid, include TV spots, print ads, billboards, paid search, online banners, promoted tweets and so on.

The truth about paid media: Paid media works, but only so long as the money spigot is turned on and gushing. Stop spending and paid media stops working with little or no residual benefit. Put another way, the meter is always running and no matter how far you ride, you never own the taxi.

One exception to this is embedded paid media. Chevrolet for example has embedded its cars into the new "Hawaii Five-O" TV series and in the "Transformers" movies, with virtually every vehicle shown in each episode is a Chevrolet. These episodes will have a long shelf life with online viewing and television reruns / syndication, which could extend the reach of this paid media for years.

NEXT, OWNED MEDIA: Owned media is real, engaging media that is created and owned by a brand or company (that's YOU) and primarily housed on the web. That sounds simple enough, but it requires great skill to execute. Brands now create and own all kinds of media. First and foremost is their website, Facebook pages, Twitter feeds and blogs. For many larger brands with deeper pockets, it can also include Films, TV shows, webisodes, magazines, books and so on. Owned media is what everyone is talking about when they say, "Brands must be media companies."

The truth about owned media: It is relatively expensive to create great content, but when the spending is over the media can keep working indefinitely. In the case of owned media, the brand's spending is really investing; the brand is creating a valuable asset with a more or less unlimited useful life. Audience generation usually requires paid media to get it started, especially if anyone's in a hurry to get noticed, which everyone usually is.

FINALLY, EARNED SOCIAL MEDIA & PR: Earned media is positive brand messaging that's produced and spread by unpaid (at least not paid by the advertiser) influencers. This group includes bloggers and tweeters, journalists and media reporters, Facebook updaters - anyone large or small, amateur or professional, who finds your brand content worth sharing with others, is creating earned media. Earned media is routinely focused on spreading content that an advertiser created (see "Owned Media" above).

This makes owned media the center of all attention because it is or should be <u>the object of paid media</u> and <u>the subject of earned social</u>

media. The purest variety of earned media, of course, involves content that is both created and spread by brand advocates on their own – think Diet Coke and Mentos for example.

The truth about earned media: ***Earned media, when it happens, is the best form of advertising on Earth***. Not only does it spread brand messages at no additional cost, it also carries more credibility and has greater impact on purchase decisions (according to global survey evidence from Nielsen) than anything the brand can ever say about itself. But it is impossible to control and very hard to generate completely free marketing from a brand's fans. ***Generally, you need <u>a paid campaign to get it going</u> and <u>owned media to keep it going</u>***.

Paid media, more and more, is all about generating an audience for owned media. Go-Daddy.com is the king of this. They use paid media to drive viewers online to their owned media. The titillating and funny videos featuring hot women like Danica Patrick & Jillian Michaels (the OWNED media) generate viral web-talk (earned media). Paid media's greatest virtue is that it gets attention and it's fast. But it works best if it's getting attention for something specific–if it's pointing people to a piece of content that can deepen their knowledge, understanding and emotional connection to the advertiser's brand. So the first new rule of paid–whether it's a billboard, TV spot or banner ad or search–is that it should point to a really good, genuinely engaging, audience-pleasing piece of owned content.

Owned media is about telling the brand's story in great depth and infinite variety. This is the kind of media that connects the advertiser's brand to the audience's lives. Like all great media, it's got to be deeply engaging, informative, and entertaining. But that's just table stakes in the owned media game, because the content also must embody the brand and accomplish the brand's business goals. Fueled by a smart paid campaign to generate audience, owned media needs to be search optimized so it can be easily found and it must be spread across digital and traditional channels where its audience spends time. When all this is done properly, there is nothing more powerful than owned media, which has the unique ability to gather and grow communities of brand fans.

It used to be that owned media was pretty much restricted to a brand's web site. In today's world of distributed digital content, owned media needs to be strategically spread all over the internet – on Facebook, Twitter, forums, blogs and more - on the digital and traditional channels where its intended audience is most like to encounter it.

Advertisers looking for earned media have only one choice: a really well executed owned media strategy. Owned media, deployed so it is easily shared and commented on, is the sole reliable sustainer of earned media. Every marketer, of course, has the option of praying or waiting for lightning to strike. But only by creating a piece of attractive owned media can advertisers set off a predictable round of conversation and pass-along that has the potential to spread brand stories and messages almost endlessly through the ranks of their audience.

Paid, owned and earned–the present and future structure of media–only work together in integrated, content-focused programs.

Chapter Fourteen

<u>Social Media</u>

The one thing that writing a chapter on social media assures is that by the time it's finished, some of the information will be obsolete. Social media changes on a daily basis. One minute you've got Facebook as the hot new girl; the next its Twitter, then it's on to Pinterest. Over the past five years, marketing managers and CEO's have all been jumping on the bandwagon of social media. Why? It's free advertising (or so they think). They believe if they set up a Facebook page and hire a couple young kids to tweet for them, they can cut money from the advertising budget.

Unfortunately, executives are now learning it's not quite that simple. And, social media IS NOT ADVERTISING. It is a conversation channel. A recent study of Chief Marketing Officers at Fortune 100 companies showed 69% admit they don't know how to effectively use social media as a marketing tool. So, let me ask you this. If sixty-nine percent of CMO's at top Fortune companies don't know how to effectively use social media to market products, how likely is it that ANYBODY knows how to do it right? Is everyone just fumbling around in the dark looking for the light switch? Yes, many are doing just that. And lots of people are out there stealing money running "Social Media Marketing Conferences", schlepping themselves off as experts when they too don't really know what they are doing. They show examples of campaigns that have worked for certain companies in certain industries that are well positioned to use social media and try to tell everyone they too can do it. Well, they can't. Some brands, products, and services aren't a great fit for social media, as we'll see as we move through this chapter.

What Is Social Media?

Social media includes web-based and mobile-based technologies that are used to turn communication into interactive dialogue among organizations, communities, and individuals. Social media technologies take on many different forms including magazines, internet forums, blogs and micro blogs (e.g., Twitter) content communities (e.g., YouTube), social networking sites (e.g., Facebook), virtual game worlds (e.g., Skyrim), and virtual social worlds (e.g. Second Life). Technologies include: blogs, picture-sharing, video blogs (vlogs), wall-postings, email, text messaging / instant messaging, music sharing, crowd sourcing, and voice over internet (VoIP), to name a few. Many of these social media services can be integrated via social media aggregation platforms. Social media network websites include sites like Facebook, Twitter, Bebo and MySpace.

Let's start by taking a look at the big social media players and recent research findings.

Facebook

Facebook has over 901 million users worldwide. An average Facebook user has 130 friends, likes 80 pages, and spends 7.5 hours on the site per month. In the USA, 79% of those ages 14 and over have an account. But the sparkle of Facebook is losing its luster. Are you spending less time on Facebook? If so, you're not alone. A June 2012 survey of Facebook users found that 34 percent of them spend less time on the site than they did six months ago. Why the cold-shoulder? Those among the 34 percent described Facebook as "boring," "not relevant," or "not useful."

Only 20 percent said they now spend more time on the social network, while almost half spend around the same amount of time. Among the more than 1,000 Americans surveyed, 21 percent said that they have no Facebook account.

A full 40 percent of all Facebook users visit the site every day. The most active ones are those 18 to 34 years old-- 60 percent of them hop onto the site each day. And the least active are those 55 years and older--only 29 percent of them hit the site on a daily basis.

Is Facebook in danger of going the way of MySpace? Possibly. As your friends continue posting irrelevant photos and blabber, more users will slip away. But perhaps of equal concern to Facebook may be the brush-off being received by advertisers using the site to reach consumers. Eighty percent of social network users say that Facebook is their preferred social network for connecting with brands. However, a strong majority of 80 percent of the Facebook user respondents also say they've never bought a product or service as a result of ads or comments on the site. Now that's a problem. General Motors recently pulled a $10 million advertising budget from Facebook, saying the advertising wasn't working. So, if Facebook isn't something that marketers can effectively use as a marketing tool, is social media really a marketing tool at all?

Twitter

Twitter now has 140 million active users producing 400 million tweets daily. It has become the most efficient global information network on the planet. Twitter is still the enigma of the social networking fraternity with its usefulness questioned by a lot of people. In classifying the content of tweets, an April 2012 study found 40.1% of all tweets were "pointless babble", 37.6% "conversational", 8.7% "had pass-along value", 5.9% were "self promotion", and 3.6% "news". Interestingly, 89% of Twitter users regularly tweet about TV shows they are watching. Twitter users skew female (54%), with 45% of all users in the 18-34 age bracket. Its simplicity is still its main attraction along with its immediacy.

Research shows that the main reason people re-tweet is due to interesting content. One million accounts are added to Twitter every day. The top 3 countries on Twitter are the USA at 107 million, Brazil at 33 million and Japan with nearly 30 million. The busiest event in Twitter's history was a "Castle in the Sky" TV screening, with 25,088 tweets per second (previous record was the last minutes of the 2012 Super Bowl with 10,245 tweets per second).

In addition to TV viewers, many sports fans find tweeting during games an enjoyable way to share the experience with others both in the stadium and watching at home.

Twitter is seeing success in the mobile space. The platform is perfect for "on the fly" commentary. Its ad platform is inherently suited to mobile, and the company is seeing a growing share of ad revenues from its mobile platform. Thirty-four percent of marketers claim they have generated leads using Twitter.

LinkedIn

LinkedIn has been around since 2003, but, over the past couple years, it has seen tremendous growth that has catapulted it to success and driven it to become an essential tool for business growth. The most powerful aspect of LinkedIn is that it is an organic way to network with people who you might never have the opportunity to meet in any other scenario. Whether you are a job seeker, a business owner looking to make connections with other businesses, or a recruiter, everyone can benefit from joining.

LinkedIn has become <u>the</u> searchable talent pool for recruiters, and an essential place to be if you are job seeking. Forty-one percent of people use LinkedIn for marketing, 70% for job hunting, and 80% for talent recruitment. There are over 150 million LinkedIn users. If you aren't on the professional social network, you are missing out on networking opportunities that have never been seen before. LinkedIn shows you how many connections are available, whom you could be introduced to, and how your business can grow from merely having an active profile. Executives from every single Fortune 500 company are currently on LinkedIn; 50% of LinkedIn users are key decision makers in business. This offers an immediate opportunity to realistically make connections to these executives. What used to require event networking and cold email marketing can now be done in an organic and natural way.

Because LinkedIn users upload their resumes that include company worked for, job titles, skills, and academic background in addition to other data, it can be used as a highly targeted advertising choice for those seeking certain business intelligence, such as business schools recruiting for their graduate programs (target undergraduate degree past five years; working in vicinity, working in certain jobs, for instance, HR professionals, etc.)

YouTube

YouTube is the web's second largest search engine behind Google. YouTube gets millions of visits each week, and accounts for nearly 10% of total internet traffic. It's one of the most recognized brands on the web. In 2012, the site celebrated its seventh birthday and announced that it has surpassed 2 billion views per day. Seventy-eight percent of YouTube traffic comes from outside the USA. Every minute, 48 hours of new video is uploaded to the site. There are 490 million registered users of YouTube, who spend on average 15 minutes per day watching videos and racking up an estimated 92 billion page views each month. You Tube is most popular among teens ages 12-17 and young adults ages 18-35.

As a marketing tool, YouTube has the unique ability to communicate via video rather than merely words and photos, and is especially good when videos are entertaining to the point where viewers want to tell others about it, sharing it so that it "goes viral". The most watched video is Lady Gaga's "Bad Romance", which has been viewed 250 million times.

Many marketers are finding success using YouTube as a place to post videos that answer customer service questions, or promote their products more in-depth than can be done in a typical :30 second TV ad. The average length of a YouTube video is 2 minutes, 39 seconds.

Pinterest

One social site has captured the attention of the masses recently... and it is not called Facebook or Twitter. Sure, the number of users is clearly not as high as what you'd find on those two behemoths, but Pinterest is gaining traction, especially with the female demographic (72% of users, primarily between the ages of 25-54).

Pinterest is a pin-board-style social photo sharing website that allows users to create and manage theme-based image collections such as events, interests, hobbies, and more. Users can browse other pinboards for inspiration, 're-pin' images to their own collections and/or 'like' photos.

Pinterest's mission is to "connect everyone in the world through the 'things' they find interesting" via a global platform of inspiration and idea sharing. Pinterest allows its users to share 'pins' on both Twitter and Facebook, which allows users to share and interact with a broad community. Pinterest caters to those looking for recipes, room décor, and do-it-yourself crafts. Top ten audience interests include fashion design and collections; music, art and memorabilia; vineyards and wine; and crafts. Top brands on

Pinterest include Better Homes and Gardens, Whole Foods, and Bergdorf Goodman.

The site launched as a closed beta test in March 2010. On August 16, 2011, *Time* magazine listed Pinterest in its "50 Best Websites of 2011" article. In December 2011, the site became one of the top 10 largest social network services with 11 million total visits per week. In January 2012 comScore reported the site had 11.7 million unique users, making it the fastest site in history to break through the 10 million unique visitor mark. American users of the social network spend an average of 1 hour and 17 minutes on the site, well ahead of Twitter (36 minutes), LinkedIn (17 minutes) and Google+ (6 minutes). Pinterest is projected to account for 40% of all social media driven purchases in 2012.

It's All About Entertainment

Social media is an entertainment outlet, pure and simple. People aren't going to social media to enhance their education – unless the education they are seeking is what Ashton Kutcher is up to this afternoon! Seventy-six percent of adults say they use social media as entertainment; 73% as a creative outlet; 54% for gaming, 47% for how-to information; and 39% for following celebrities.

The Meaning of "Like"

So what does it really mean when a consumer says they "like" your brand on Facebook? Only 50% of users say my "like" constitutes permission to market to me on Facebook. Yes, you read that right. ONLY 50% SAY IT'S OK NOW TO MARKET TO ME! What my like means is that I want a deal! They expect access to exclusive content, events or sales. They expect discounts or promotions through Facebook.

How Often Do Consumers Want To Hear From Companies?

Of Facebook users that indicated it was OK to send marketing messages, the vast majority said it was permissible to hear from brands **once a week or once a month** – zero percent said it was OK to send me stuff daily, let alone multiple times a day!

Purchase Advice Is What They Need

In June 2011, 29% of social network users went online to seek purchase advice. What consumers want to use social media for is to be able to find and read consumer feedback (71%), learn about products and services (64%), get coupons and promotional discounts (64%), and have the ability to leave feedback (59%).

Things that impact purchase intent are user-generated product reviews (59%), online Q&A areas (42%), and community forums (conversations between customers) 26%.

Social Media is Great For Contests and Giveaways

The one niche where social media has found undeniable success is its effective ability to give things away. My first experience came one afternoon in 2009 when I had taken a handful of tickets to an NBA game to a local university where I was speaking to a class on sports marketing. My plan was to give every student a pair of tickets to the upcoming game. After distributing the tickets, I still had about 100 extra tickets, and since we were having a hard time selling tickets to the game anyway, I decided to see if we could get rid of them via our social network.

I called my social media manager and asked him to use three social media channels – Facebook, Twitter, and Text-Messaging – to send out a message that "Jazz guy is sitting in the Brick Oven Restaurant with free tickets to tomorrow night's game. Available now until they are gone!"

Exactly three minutes and 20 seconds later, the first fan arrived to claim her tickets. Within 20 minutes all of them were gone, and fans were still streaming into the restaurant. I could have easily given away 100 more – and all off of one single post to Facebook, a tweet and a text message.

Social Media is Perfect for "Things We Like To Talk About"

If you look to water cooler conversations and catalog the topics of discussion – movies, TV shows, sports teams, foods / restaurants, entertainment, local news and events, hobbies – all of these areas are perfect fits with using social media. Why? *Because we already have conversations about them!*

Conversely, I've never had a conversation at the water cooler about laundry detergent, feminine hygiene, prescription medications, makeup, or hundreds of other topics. So why do all these different consumer products and services that fall into these areas seem so focused with making a splash with social media? Answer, they shouldn't be.

Marketing Truth

Not all communication channels are right for all products and services, and if people <u>organically</u> don't have conversations about your product, product category or service, you probably don't need to be focused on a social media strategy.

The Perfect Business Segments for Social Media

There are certain industries that are perfectly positioned to effectively use social media -- restaurants, fast food chains, and retail stores. Industries with **disappearing inventory** – sports tickets, airline seats, movie theatres, restaurants – where they need a butt in the seat fast or else it is worthless – those are perfect areas to use social media. Need to stimulate purchases? Need some customers now? Tweet and post a **time-sensitive instant offer** of "first five customers to show this tweet get a free burger".

Sports teams can use social media effectively to disseminate **breaking news**, information and special offers. TV / Radio station absolutely can use social media to **attract eyes and ears**. Watch this show for a chance to win X. Listen at 4 p.m. to win Y. A local TV station in Utah used Facebook giveaway contests so effectively to drive it's 10 p.m. newscast that it was able to rise from a perennial #2 position to #1 in the market and continues to build their ratings / share advantage on the back of their effective use of "watch and win" contests nightly within their newscast that are exclusively executed via social media.

Email Marketing / Texting

Email marketing / text messaging / instant messaging fall into the social media space, but they are a different animal than social networks and sites. Email marketing allows you to send real advertising to customers. Texting lets you talk in real time to your customer. The problem lies in developing a list of folks who will opt-in to receiving your emails and text messages.

I have found that consumer promotions are the best way to develop an email / texting list quickly and cheaply. Run a contest that has great interest to consumers, and have the method of entry be via email (send an email to contest@wow.com), or via text message (text "contest" to 74332). When I was running the marketing for an NBA team, we grew our email list from 7,000 addresses to over 250,000 addresses in 18 months and our texting database from zero to over 75,000 mobile numbers through consumer promotions. Once you have built a significant number of customers you can reach directly via email and text, this DOES give you the flexibility to cut advertising dollars.

The Right Way To Use Social Media: Timely, Relevant, And Actionable

There really is a simple rule for effectively using social media and it's this -- your messages must be TIMELY, RELEVANT, and ACTIONABLE. If they don't meet at least two out of these three criteria, don't do it!

Many companies have invested in having people dedicated to social media, and therefore figure that if I've got this person, they better be posting on Facebook and Twitter 17 times a day! And therein lies the problem. If you are doing this, you're spamming. Grit your teeth, and hold yourself back. Look at every message -- is it TIMELY, RELEVANT, and ACTIONABLE?

As my momma always said, if you don't have anything nice to say, don't say anything at all. If you are the marketing manager for Tide, what information can you give to me that is timely, relevant, and actionable?

The bad publicity the brand received over children mistaking the new Tide Pods for candy is something that falls into timely, relevant and actionable. Yes, absolutely, respond to that issue. But if you're Cheer detergent, what in the world could you possibly have to say that is timely, relevant and actionable, one that would start a conversation? I seriously doubt that there is anything. If you don't have anything worthwhile to say, stay quiet until you do have something.

Social media CAN be a powerful marketing tool if you use it correctly. Unfortunately, most companies are just using it for spamming out useless information. If what you have to say isn't timely, relevant and actionable, stop doing it.

Chapter Fifteen

Trade Promotions

- In business and marketing, "trade" refers to the relationship between manufacturers and retailers.

- **Trade Promotion** refers to marketing activities that are executed at retail between these two partners.

- Trade Promotion is a marketing technique aimed at increasing sales of products in retail stores based on special pricing, display fixtures, product demonstrations, value-added bonuses, no-obligation gifts, and more.

Twenty years ago, the rules at retail were pretty simple. All you had to do to earn a feature and display inside a retail chain was to pull together some sort of generic promotion or offer a price reduction. Retailers appreciated the investment you were making in your business and were happy to reciprocate. The brand sales team could usually walk into a store, show the manager a copy of the Sunday coupon scheduled for the weekend paper, and viola, walk out with a commitment for a large product display.

Of course, it didn't hurt to be friendly with store manager. And what could be friendlier than to swap a few jokes, and then slip him some tickets to a ballgame or a free cd player you just happened to carrying along. In return, he'd place a sizable order for your product and build a conspicuous display on a front-aisle end cap. It didn't cost the salesperson anything -- those tickets were on the corporate account -- and the store manager had to come up with several displays every week anyway. The good old boy system worked this way for many, many years.

Today, you have about the same chance of finding a store where these arcane tactics will work as you do of having a Good Humor Ice Cream truck parked in your driveway on a hot summer afternoon. The rules have changed, and marketers are struggling to understand exactly how to cope with these changes.

Blame It On the Accounting MBA's

Those darned accountants are at the heart of the confusion. After decades of looking the other way, the bean counters at corporate headquarters for the large retail chains finally took notice of just how much money some companies where willing to throw around at the store level to buy shelf space and end-aisle displays. Legend has it that the store manager at the largest volume grocery store in Los Angeles owned a 24 ft. boat, backyard swimming pool, a Jeep Cherokee, a Porsche 924, vacationed twice a year in Hawaii, and sat courtside at Lakers games -- all courtesy of corporate sales people in exchange for the in-store marketing favors he'd granted.

Like all good business school grads chanting the mantra "maximize shareholder value", the number crunchers changed the system to channel cash to the corporate bottom line instead of allowing it to be lavished on store and department managers. A smart move on their part, but boy, did it mess up the selling tactics of the corporate sales teams and put a damper on the lifestyles of the rich and famous that many store managers were living. Many brands were so accustomed to the Wild West mentality at retail, they completely lost their footing when corporate standardization set in.

The Robinson - Patman Act

Congress also had something to do with the way Trade marketing evolved by passing the Robinson - Patman Act, which states that manufacturers must treat all retailers equally. This law was created because corporate sales teams were taking advantage of the 80/20 rule, which means you invest 80% of your resources against those 20% of accounts that provide the most volume. Virtually all spending at retail -- from displays and contests to those tantalizing freebies -- was focused on the few largest accounts, with little or no attention given to smaller chains & independent stores. The smaller stores complained that they could not compete in this biased environment, and they were right.

Today, the Robinson-Patman Act ensures that no account can claim favored status. Consumer product companies must provide the same rewards, incentives and displays to every retailer. The little guys still have a tough time, since "the same" rewards are offered in proportion to the number of cases a retailer orders. In other words, although the marketing company offers a promotion or display to everyone who orders 25 cases of product during the promotional period, they know full well the small retailers may never be able to satisfy the case requirement. But these promotions follow the letter, if not the spirit, of the Robinson-Patman law.

Marketing Development Funds

Nothing captures people's attention like cold hard cash, and no incentive program is more alluring than money. Marketing Development Funds (MDF's) are cash rewards earned by retailers in return for their orders and sales. These funds accrue for each brand independently. For example, if Vons in Southern California sells 15,000 cases of Heinz Ketchup and the MDF is .35 cents per case, Vons would accrue an MDF fund of $5,250 on Heinz Ketchup (15,000 cases x .35 cents / case = $5,250.) In addition, if Vons sold 4,000 cases of Heinz 57 Sauce and the MDF is .50 cents per case, it would accrue an MDF of $2,000 (4,000 cases x .50 cents / case = $2,000) for Heinz 57 Sauce. Keep in mind, these MDF funds are in addition to the profit margin the retailer already receives on each sale.

MDF dollars do have strings attached. Various consumer products companies have different rules about how the money can be used, but it is usually connected to funding marketing activities within the chain for the specific brand on which they were earned. For example, with its $5,250 MDF fund on Heinz Ketchup, Vons might choose to fund a Heinz Ketchup coupon in its mailer, pay for an ad feature in the chain's weekly specials circular, fund a price reduction, buy an end–aisle display for a week, or participate in a proprietary marketing program offered by the retailer (like a "summer barbecue" promotion or sampling program). MDF typically cannot be combined between brands without the company's approval.

How often are MDF incentives used? Is each and every price reduction, end-aisle display or ad in the weekly specials circular paid for by the brand out of the MDF funds? Generally, yes. There are no free rides.

Displays, Price Reductions and Feature Ad's

Why would a brand pay so much money to get a little bit of marketing activity in the store, like an ad or a display? Why not save the money and just sell your product off the shelf? Because despite the high cost, marketing programs are ultimately quite profitable. Every year companies evaluate the effectiveness of in-store displays, price reductions and ad features in moving product. The results are impressive. Display and feature activity can increase a brand's weekly sales by 4 to 13 times the average volume.

Average Impact On Sales (Grocery Store Channel)

Normal Everyday Shelf Display	1x
Off-Shelf Display Only	4x
Feature Only*	7x
Feature* & Display	13x

* Assumes a meaningful advertised price reduction

The Results of In-Store Marketing

To understand the ramifications of in-store marketing activity, let's run the numbers for a typical brand so you can see how it works. Suppose that you are a sales rep for Franco-American Spaghetti. Assume the following pricing:

Franco-American Spaghetti: (12 cans per case)

Cost To Produce:	$3.12
Price Sold To Retailer:	$6.60
Price Sold To Consumer:	$9.48

You decide to create a program with Safeway in the Northern Virginia area, which has 70 stores in the advertising region. In a typical week with normal placement in the canned goods aisle, Safeway sells around 10 cases of Franco-American Spaghetti per store, at the everyday price of 79 cents per can.

You'd like to explore the options of buying a display only, a feature only, and a display / feature combo. For the feature, you'd like to reduce the retail price down to .59 cents to the consumer.

The prices for a week of marketing activities within the 70 Safeway stores in this region are as follows:

End cap Display:	$7,000
Feature in Weekly Circular:	$5,000
Feature & Display:	$12,000
Price Reductions:	Negotiable

To persuade Safeway to agree to run the feature price at .59 cents in their ad, you've agreed to offer a $1.00 per case price reduction financed through your MDF funds. Display & feature activity is paid out of the MDF as well.

Let's look at the hypothetical financials to understand the impact of marketing activity from the brand point-of-view.

Franco-American Spaghetti Impact On Sales --70 Safeway Stores

	Normal Everyday	Display Only	Feature Only*	Feature* & Display
	1x	4x	7x	13x
Case Sales	700	2,800	4,900	9,100
Gross Dollars:	$4,620	$18,480	$32,340	$60,060
Less Cost:	$2,184	$8,736	$15,288	$28,392
Less MDF:	$0	$7,000	$5,000	$12,000
Less Price MDF:	$0	$0	$4,900	$9,100

Net Brand Profit:	$2,436	$2,744	$7,152	$10,568
Profit Margin:	52.72%	14.84%	22.11%	17.59%

If the brand does nothing and continues selling on average 10 cases per store, the brand profit for the week is $2,436. You can see that just purchasing a display will not improve bottom line profitability. Despite moving 4 times the number of cases, it will only produce $308 more profit. Both Feature Only ($7,152) and Feature / Display ($10,568) significantly improve the brand profitability and sales volume for the week. A feature improves profitability by 293%, and a feature display combo provides a 433% profit lift!

Now look at the same scenario from the financial perspective of Safeway:

Safeway Financials

	Normal Everyday	Display Only	Feature Only*	Feature* & Display
	1x	4x	7x	13x
Case Sales	700	2,800	4,900	9,100
Gross Dollars:	$3,363	$26,544	$34,692	$64,428
Less Cost:	$4,620	$18,480	$32,340	$60,060
Plus MDF:	$0	$7,000	$5,000	$12,000
Plus Price MDF:	$0	$0	$4,900	$9,100
Net Safeway Profit:	$2,016	$15,604	$12,252	$25,468
Net Margin:	30.37%	44.90%	27.47%	29.77%

Notice how Safeway protects its net margin regardless of what the brand does by charging for the display and feature activities. Even though the consumer thinks Safeway is a swell store for offering a great deal on Franco-American Spaghetti, the brand is actually paying for the price reduction and other marketing activities through its MDF accrual.

When brands perform in-store marketing, everybody wins! The consumer gets a great low price, the brand gets a significant boost in its weekly profits, and Safeway gets a healthy addition to its bottom line as well.

The Different Types of In-Store Promotions:

The types of in-store trade promotions that can be executed are:

- **In-store displays**
- **Temporary Price Reductions (TPR)**
- **Coupons**
- **Contest and sweepstakes**
- **Rebates**
- **Premiums**
- **Sampling**

Proprietary Retailer Programs

The retail business is becoming increasingly competitive, and retailers are acutely interested in building their own consumer base. That's why you see so much advertising for grocery, mass and convenience stores these days. Retailers have also learned their lesson from the consumer products companies; they know how well consumer promotions can work to generate sales and consumer loyalty. Most major retailers execute several storewide promotions each year that they hope will entice consumers to shop. These are often holiday-oriented sales, checkout coupons, on-shelf instant coupons, "club card" continuity programs, proprietary signage & shopping cart ads.

Retailers are eager for their vendors to support these promotions, not only to create a bigger splash at the store level, but also to fund their very execution. Let's take a look at a few of the retailer promotions and analyze how they might, or might not, work for you.

Checkout Coupons

Checkout coupons are often offered through a company called Catalina Marketing or directly through the retailer. The attractiveness of these coupons is that they are "directed" coupons that are generated depending upon what the consumer buys in the grocery store, printed at the checkout stand and handed to consumers with their change and receipt.

Most of the time brands use this tactic as a competitive counterattack. For example, Pampers might fund a checkout coupon to give to every consumer who makes a Huggies purchase. "Directed" couponing seems like a clever way of targeting your couponing at the competitor's consumer, instead of funding a general coupon that will probably by redeemed primarily by consumers who already use your product.

Unfortunately, coupons delivered at checkout are usually pretty dumb investments. Think of it this way: every time a consumer buys a product, it takes them out of the market to buy from that product category until the item they just purchased is used up. This is what's often referred to as "purchase cycle".

As a marketer, your job is to try to figure out when a consumer is most likely to make a purchase in your product category, and then hit them with your marketing efforts just _before_ they buy. Good timing will dramatically increase your chances of making a sale. Checkout coupons hit the consumer with a purchase incentive immediately after they've just bought the product, at the furthest possible point from another product purchase!

Direct Mail "Smart" Coupons

A much more effective means of targeting consumers with "smart" coupons is to tie in with the Club cards that many large retailers now offer. These cards are ingenious. Every time a consumer goes to the store and the clerk swipes their card, it stores that consumer's entire history of purchases in their mainframe computer. The store now knows exactly what products a specific consumer buys -- the brands, the sizes, and the flavors -- and knows precisely when she bought them!

Now you have an incredible opportunity to target consumers with coupons at just about the right time in their purchase cycle. For example, if you are the brand manager for Tide, and you know that the typical box of detergent lasts 27 days in a household, you can send a Tide "smart coupon" through direct mail to all consumers who bought a competitive laundry detergent 20-24 days ago. The loyal Tide consumers are none the wiser (they don't get anything in their mail), and you've got the targeted opportunity to steal away competitor's customers at the point where they will be going to the store to get more detergent. This is by far a "smarter" way to use coupons!

In-Store Instant Coupons

In-store instant coupons are usually displayed right next to your product on the store shelf, or attached to each product package. The coupon dispenser is usually bright red with an LED flashing light to draw attention to it. These coupons often do work to stimulate product sales and steal business away from your competitors, particularly in a price-sensitive category.

So why don't you see thousands of these coupon dispensers in stores? The primary reason isn't effectiveness, but rather the expense of coupon's redemption and where the cost is borne within the corporation.

Coupon redemption's are paid by the brand-marketing budget at corporate headquarters, not out of the retailer's MDF. So while the corporate sales force and the retailer LOVE instant coupons because they generate sales, brand teams HATE instant coupons because they chews away at the national marketing budget, leaving the retailer MDF fund intact and in fact helping to build that war chest with every product sold (and that money is managed by the sales team and the retailer, not the by brand marketing team).

Why do the brand teams hate in-store instant coupons with such a passion? Because in-store instant coupons have a 90% redemption rate! The feeling within the brand groups is that these coupons steal away profits by landing in the hands of loyal consumers who would have been happy to pay full price, in addition to those new users who you may be converting from competition. This risk of couponing your loyal customer is especially steep if you are already the category leader.

For perspective, look at it this way. When a corporate brand team puts a coupon in the Sunday newspaper, the redemption rate is usually around 2%. So a brand team can print up 40 million coupons for the newspaper, and only around 800,000 of them actually get used. If you do the math on a .20-cent coupon that means the brand team pays about $160,000 for this national activity.

Now look at what happens when you do in-store, instant couponing. Think of our Franco-American Spaghetti example again, and let's say the brand team wants to generate the same amount of volume as it would with a feature / display combo in those Safeway stores, which means selling about 130 cases each. The coupons will offer the same discount as the feature -- .20 cents off. To generate the required sales means that about 1,600 coupons must be placed in each of the Safeway stores. Over the 70 stores, this would amount to 112,000 coupons. At a 90% redemption rate, the cost of the coupons would be about $22,000.

Compare this to the national coupon, which covered the whole country for a cost of $160,000. This in-store coupon only covered 70 stores at about 1/8 the cost of the national effort. There are about 5,000 large grocery stores in the United States. If you tried to execute an in-store couponing promotion in all of them, the cost would be an astronomical $1.57 million on the redeemed coupons!

If you compare the cost of the coupon redemption ($22,000) with the cost of the feature / display activity calculated in the earlier example ($21,100) it's pretty much a wash, but the critical issue is knowing out of which bucket of money the funds are coming. Feature/display promotions are paid out of the retailers MDF accrual fund. Coupons are paid at corporate headquarters. Since corporate has the "yea / nay" vote over how their brand marketing dollars are spent, it's a battle to get the OK to move ahead with this activity. That's why you don't see more in-store instant coupons!

> ### *Marketing Truth*
>
> *Only use in-store coupons if you are the #3 brand or lower in the competitive market share race. Only then is it likely that more new users are being converted than your regular purchasers using it and getting an unexpected deal.*

Shopping Carts & Proprietary Signage

Just about every retailer who has shopping carts will offer you the chance to buy advertising on them. Unfortunately, while this seems like it would be a great way to get your message delivered to the consumer at the right time, it usually doesn't work very well. Most consumers don't pay attention to cart ads. As soon as they step inside the store, their eyes are bombarded with stimulation from the thousands of products displayed on the shelves that are screaming for their attention. Consumers are looking everywhere but at their cart.

Another in-store tactic you might see is the scrolling electronic message boards. Brands usually buy this program to coincide with features to draw consumer attention to the special price. These electronic billboards can be very effective if they are located in the aisle in which the product is sold. The same goes for tiled floor signs. They are usually placed in close proximity to the product on the shelf. If the tiles carry a relevant brand message or highlight feature activity, they too can positively influence consumer purchase.

> ### *Marketing Truth*
>
> *Use in-store signage ONLY in support of feature activity and consumer promotions. Do not just put your brand name / logo on the sign!*

Beating The System

With the Robinson-Patman Act restricting what you can offer retailers, and retailers themselves ever more focused on sending cash to the bottom line, it is getting tough for brands to execute retail trade promotions that stand out from the crowd. But there are ways of beating the system and developing unique, volume-driving promotions that can separate your in-store marketing efforts from the sea of sameness. You just have to be creative and think a little differently than everyone else.

Brands that execute national consumer promotions do not receive much assistance from retailers in showcasing their offers. That's because national promotions are offered to every retailer, so the consumer offer is the same in each retail outlet. Retail chains are competitive, and want to differentiate themselves from one another. They are most interested in providing the consumer with reasons to shop at their store, instead of at the market down the street. As a result, you probably won't get much support for your big national promotions -- what they really want are account-specific promotions paid out of your MDF funds.

Account-Specific Promotions

You can beat the system with proprietary, account-specific promotions that can be executed within the parameters of Robinson - Patman. As long as the activity is exclusively funded by MDF dollars, your promotions are considered fair and legal.

The sales manager at Disney Home Video who managed the relationship with Target stores was a genius in account-specific promotions. Faced with the challenge of stimulating sales after a record-breaking year at the chain, he was hungry for a big idea to drive consumer purchases to even higher levels.

Consumer research indicated that when retail stores played Disney's children's videos on in-store TV monitors, sales rocketed, even when the videos were offered at full-price. Moms walking by the TV playing the video would grab one from the nearby display as an impulse purchase for their kids.

That gave the manager his big idea -- to create a portable TV cart that not only showed the Disney movie, but merchandised a few dozen copies of the video as well. He had the Disney creative services team put together a prototype cart, took it to Minneapolis for a presentation, and Target management loved it. The video cart was attractive and entertaining, and made Target seem special for having it. They used accrued MDF funds to purchase a video cart for every store, giving Disney a proprietary in-store promotion to stimulate consumer purchase of their videos. Walk into any Target store and you'll see this cart playing Disney videos, usually in close proximity to the front door or checkout stands.

Tagged Media

Retailers love for brands to run advertising that directs consumers to their stores. Often as part of account-specific promotions, the brand will agree to purchase local TV and radio commercials that include mention of the retailer. This mention is technically called "tagged media". For a typical TV spot, the brand will communicate its own message in 20 seconds and leave the last 10 seconds for a "tag" -- a commercial for the retailer. For :60 second radio spots, it is usually a :40 second brand / :20 second retailer split or a :30 second brand / :30 second retailer division. Again, this is legal if MDF funds are used to pay for the activity.

Offering Unique Point-Of-Sale Materials

Another way to beat the system and get the retail trade to execute an in-store marketing activity for you is to produce awesome point of sale material that the retailer wants badly.

Again, Disney is the king of this tactic. They leverage the imagery of their classics characters to develop incredibly beautiful pieces of in-store display material that is often too incredible to pass on. The retailers use MDF funds to purchase the POS, and Disney ends up "owning" the look of the store, with Lion King's or Toy Story characters everywhere. This is a very effective tactic for the big "classic" video releases. You'll see the same strategy from Budweiser and Pepsi around Super Bowl time, and from Coors and Pepsi at Halloween.

Carving Out Proprietary Shelf Space

One of the fears facing all brand marketers is losing shelf space to a competitor. Just like the Mexican American War, if you lose the first battle, it's tough to reclaim your territory any time soon.

As a means of "owning" shelf space, some brands have developed proprietary shelf units that they "sell" to the stores using MDF dollars. When the shelf units are installed, they effectively eliminate the threat of competitive infiltration. Most retailers won't mix and match competitive product in another brand's display unit, since it ruins the look of the shelf and generally appears messy.

McCormick's Spice is a master of this tactic. Go into any store and you'll see a rack fully stocked with the brand's offerings. They effectively own their shelf space and are impervious to competitive attack!

Campbell's Soup has more recently rolled out a new merchandising gravity-feed rack for its soups, giving it not only premium signage in-store but the ability to make their display look "full" at all times. Coca-Cola also understands the critical value of real estate. Coke controls space by offering coolers, vending machines and fountain dispensers to retailers that are designed to house only Coca-Cola product and keep "The Blue Devil" Pepsi at bay.

Third-Party Promotions

Many brands beat the system by developing third party promotions that "just happen" to also include a retail partner.

The way it works is simple. A promotion company approaches your brand with an idea for sponsoring a promotion. They tell you that they've got a major retailer involved as the title sponsor, and that if you participate as a sub-sponsor, the retailer will give you in-store marketing activity, typically display or features. Your brand signs the contract with the promotion company, the retailer signs the contract with the promotion company, and you've effectively circumvented Robinson - Patman!

I witnessed first-hand how third-party promotions work when I was in Cincinnati working for Procter & Gamble. The Utah Jazz and Boston Celtics were coming to town to play an NBA exhibition game. A marketing promotion company cut a deal with the local Kroger supermarket chain to be the title sponsor of the event. Kroger received the sponsorship for free from the promotion company, in exchange for agreeing to allow the promoters to sign on 6 consumer product brands as co-sponsors and committing feature / display activity for each of the co-sponsoring brands in each of the 90 Kroger stores in the Cincinnati area.

The brands each paid the marketing promotion company a participation fee, and Kroger ran a full-page newspaper ad for the brands in addition to large in-store displays featuring all 6 products. Because no money was exchanged between the brand and Kroger, the promotion was immune from Robinson-Patman.

Marketing Truth

> *TV stations and radio stations are great at developing third-party promotions. When you have the triumvirate of a media partner, retail outlet, and consumer brands, you have an extremely powerful marketing combination!*

Remember how I cautioned you against using promotion agencies to develop your consumer promotions? The rule doesn't always apply to the trade side of the equation. You don't necessarily need to offer the trade something unique, different and special as you do with the consumer; you simply have to give them what they want, which is often funding for their own promotional programs. If you are managing a small or medium-size brand that rarely gets attention from retailers for executing in-store marketing activity, by all means pursue third party promotions. They can often slip you in the back door.

New Products -- Slotting Allowances

When introducing a new product to retailers, many stores require the manufacturer to pay what is called a "slotting allowance" in order to get the new product into their store. Since new products have no MDF accrued from case sales, the retail chain's corporate offices charge this fee to place the product on a trial basis. These fees are usually quite high, in the $10,000 to $25,000 range *per item depending* upon the store chain. Most companies struggle with the expense of placing a new product, which is one reason why new items are often introduced gradually, market by market, as their sales show promise. For perspective, if each of the top 50 grocery chains in the USA charged on average a $20,000 slotting fee, that's $1 million dollars to just get one new product on store shelves! That's a tremendous gamble for an unproven product.

You may be thinking – "Why are the stores so greedy?" There's more to it than making a quick buck. Remember, stores are primarily interested in how much profit they can produce per square inch of shelf space. In order to put a new product in, something else has to come out, and the new product must quickly prove that it can generate the kind of sales that justify its place on the shelf. Stores charge these slotting allowances to make sure that their profits for that shelf space are covered in the event that the new product fails to sell.

Retailers have no choice but to be this persnickety about letting new products into their stores. They've been burned before. In the past 10 years, manufacturers have bombarded them with new offerings at an alarming rate. This year it is expected that over 40,000 new products will be introduced -- for perspective, that's about 200 new products introduced each and every business day! If the stores accepted every new product produced, they would have no room for your favorite brands.

When retailers take in a new product, they usually give it 45 days to prove itself, or out it goes. If the new product loses its shelf space, there is no refund of the slotting fees, and if the manufacturer wants to get the product back into stores to give it another try, they must again pay the fee.

Considering that 8 out of every 10 new products fail, slotting allowances are the only means retailers have of protecting their bottom line. The hefty fee also forces the manufacturers to take a long, hard look at their new products to make sure that they are worth the investment, with meaningful consumer appeal that will produce sufficient sales to sustain distribution.

Circumventing Slotting Fees

So you're stuck with paying slotting fees . . .that is, unless you know how to play the trade-marketing game. Developing unique and proprietary marketing initiatives to offer the retailer can sometimes entice him to reduce the slotting allowance to about $200 -- the actual cost for setting up the new UPC in the computer check-out system.

One brilliant execution I've recently seen was executed by Welch's Grapes, who was attempting to get into the store their new line of fresh grapes in the fresh fruits and vegetables section of the store. Welch's partnered with the grocery chain to build the World's Largest Grape Display", and advertised this gargantuan effort in their weekly sales ads. Customers flocked to the store to see the giant display, with most taking home three or four pounds of delicious Welch's Grapes!

Many Coca-Cola bottlers effectively use the inducement of "Torchbearers" in the bi-annual Olympic Torch Relay as a means of leveraging retailers for incremental shelf space. They offer a retailer the opportunity to select one of their customers to carry the Olympic Flame, in return for waiving slotting allowances on new soft drink flavors. It works like a charm. Other ways to use this tactic are to offer high-value items to the chain -- Ski-Doo's, motorcycles, or camping equipment -- for in-store raffles. Retailers love these proprietary in-store activities!

Marketing Truth

To win at trade promotions, you must create ways for your product to gain more in-store marketing activities than your competitors on a calendar basis. It's all a numbers game. If you can get more frequent in-store activity than they do, you will win!

If you can effectively master the art of working with the Trade, you'll be ahead in the game. Take a bold approach to wooing your trade partners. Make your company the most original, interesting and just plain fun organization that your buyer deals with in his busy week. Take some risks, and offer him opportunities he's never heard before, even if he hates the first five or ten you try. Remember, you always miss 100% of the shots you don't take. Trade relationships are too valuable not to make the effort.

Eric D Schulz

Chapter Sixteen

<u>Consumer Promotions</u>

Walk into any supermarket, drugstore, mass merchant, convenience store or local car wash and you'll soon be dizzy from the onslaught of consumer promotions. Enter here to win a cruise, get a free month membership at the local Gold's Gym, redeem an instant coupon, buy one and get one free! Chances are, you're so accustomed to the promotional hoopla where you shop, you hardly notice anymore. You're not alone. Although virtually every brand in the market executes consumer promotions, presumably with the intention of boosting sales and attracting consumers, very few do anything that consumer's notice. And fewer still create promotions that are truly great.

There is a good reason why so many consumer promotions fall flat. The primary culprit is short-term thinking by the marketing team. Most generally view consumer promotions as a way to get a quick volume bump and never consider the possible long-term implications. In fact, promotions are often so under-appreciated that promotion planning, development and execution are delegated to the most junior staff members. After all, how much expertise does it require to drop a coupon, organize a sweepstakes, or coordinate a mailing? Anyone could do it, right? Right. That's why everyone does, and also why these promotions usually don't work. But a well-executed consumer promotion, one that has been developed with care and thought, can serve as a catapult for your business. Sure, it'll create a bump in sales, but its impact won't stop there. A great promotion creates brand personality, carves out competitive advantage *and* drives sales, with results that endure long past the promotional window.

Creating Promotions On Strategy

Like every other piece of the marketing mix, consumer promotions must be focused on the brand positioning strategy. This means that the ABC's of Strategic Positioning -- addressing a target **A**udience, strongly stating the consumer **B**enefit of the brand, and calling out the **C**ompelling reasons why your brand delivers this benefit better than anyone else -- are the cornerstones upon which the idea must be built.

Let's assume, for example, you are selling bubble bath to an audience of women 25-40. Your benefit is providing a relaxing oasis in her busy day, and your compelling "reason why" is tingling bubbles and unique relaxing scents. Before you start to wonder, "should I drop a coupon, or should I build a display?" you should be thinking, "how do I communicate my core benefit -- a relaxing oasis -- in a promotion?" Next you ask, "what are the best channels to reach my audience," and finally, "is there a way to reinforce my reasons why -- tingle and fragrance?"

Once you've focused on your strategy, the next step is to take a good analytical look at your competition. Catalog the consumer promotions that have been executed by your brand and by other competitors to search for strategies that have worked and identify patterns for success. Along the way, you'll also begin to recognize the trappings of failure.

The Four Plagues of Consumer Promotion

One way to learn to do things right is simply to avoid doing them wrong. The following Four Plagues of Consumer Promotion are guarantees of mediocrity, if not disaster. Avoid them at all cost.

Been There, Done That

Many brands have an overwhelming compulsion to "do what we did last year". After all, it's safe, it's familiar, and it doesn't require much mental energy. If your business improved by 2% last year with promotion "X", you can predict that if you do it again this year you'll see a 1.5% to 2% lift. You won't earn any medals for valor, but you don't risk total failure either.

This is the worst virus any marketing person can become infected with -- and it's contagious. At McDonald's how many times have we seen the 'Monopoly" game? It was cute and interesting the first time around, but after twenty times, does anyone care anymore?

Many Procter & Gamble brands teams are also infected with this disease. The promotion plans of P&G brands are numbingly predictable. Put a Sunday newspaper coupon on the same week as last year, put another in the Publisher's Clearing House envelopes during January and July. For the big excitement, throw in an on-pack promotion or sweepstakes once a year.

Been There, Done That doesn't set in each time a promotion is repeated. Every once in a while a promotion is so compelling, unusual or otherwise remarkable it bears repeating. Sometimes you <u>can</u> get away with a repeat promotion and be effective, but you can bet it won't be as successful the second or third time around.

Sleeping Sickness

The second affliction that besets many consumer promotions is the dreaded Sleeping Sickness. This ailment is characterized by brand promotions that are lame or so tiresome they put consumers to sleep.

Couponing is a prime carrier of Sleeping Sickness. Newspaper coupons are boring, and redemption percentages are at an all-time low -- yet companies continue to place them. The TV show "Extreme Couponing" has driven some renewed interest, as have some of the coupon websites that have popped up like coupons.com, couponmom.com and others. But heavy users of coupons are a tiny market. The vast majority of shoppers don't use them at all.

Copycat consumer sweepstakes are another symptom of Sleeping Sickness, despite the deafening sound of snoring that accompanies them. How many hundreds of brands have offered grand-prize trips to Walt Disney World in the past 20 years? Not only is the trip an over-used prize, the promotion almost always fails to support the brand's positioning statement and core consumer benefit. Ditto for the hundreds of brands who have given away a car, TV, or other electronics equipment. Yawn. Consumers are sleepy and so are sales.

Trinkets & Trashitis

The most prevalent promotional ailment is Trinkets & Trashitis. This malady offers some piece of merchandise (often referred to as a "premium") to the consumer in return for purchasing product. Usually the premium is a cheaply made imported plastic doodad, which might be exciting if you're a seven-year old kid but probably won't impress anyone else. Marketing teams love premiums because they misguidedly think they can "self-liquidate" the items -- sell them to the consumer at a small price, usually the price the brand paid -- to recoup dollars and balance the promotion budget. That way the promotion costs them nothing, which looks great on paper for senior management. This type of promotion is usually presented as "Buy 3 boxes of product X and send in $1.99 (plus shipping and handling) to get this wonderful trinket of trash, overstated as a $10.00 value."

Folgers suffered a doozie of a Trinkets & Trashitis promotion shortly after I arrived at P&G. A relatively new hire in the brand team had the bright idea of offering sets of napkin rings to consumers to stimulate multiple purchases of Instant Folgers Coffee. His thinking was simple. At the time, Instant Folgers Coffee was running an advertising campaign entitled "Good Enough For America's Finest Restaurants". The television ads would take hidden cameras into fine dining restaurants, and they would swap out the coffee being served with instant Folgers coffee and show the responses. It was an effective campaign that drove Folgers sales.

The young marketing buck figured "Hey, all fine restaurants use napkin rings, so let's offer consumers the chance to get a set of napkin rings for their home." He somehow convinced management that millions of women were simply chafing for new napkin rings and would be willing to purchase a set for $2.99 when they bought their Folgers instant coffee. Then he placed his order for the rings, (which the marketing team later came to find out nearly doubled the national annual production of napkin rings.) Consumers ignored the promotion, and the brand team is still sitting on nearly a million rings in their warehouse. Need some napkin rings? Call Folgers. I think they can hook you up.

Unfortunately, one of the brands on my watch contracted this illness as well. In an attempt to stimulate sales of Disney's Sing-Along Songs videos, my team developed two cute little Sing-Along microphones featuring Mickey Mouse and Ariel, The Little Mermaid. The brand team's plan was to create a box that contained both a Sing-Along Songs video and a plastic microphone, charging about $2.00 more than the cost for the video alone -- a $14.99 suggested retail price (versus $12.99 for the video alone). Senior management fell in love with our adorable microphones just as we had hoped, and just as we were getting ready to present the new items to our sales force, the Head of Disney Home Video arbitrarily raised the suggested price to $17.99 -- over protests of the brand team, I might add. Consumers didn't bite. They knew the cheap plastic microphone wasn't worth $5.00, no matter how cute it was. Right now, approximately 1.5 million of those darling little gems are stashed somewhere in Disney's warehouse if anyone is interested!

But don't feel too sorry for our microphones; they certainly aren't lonely. If you checked the warehouses at most major companies, you'd find millions upon millions of dollars worth of trinkets and trash produced for unsuccessful promotions just sitting around collecting dust until somebody can figure out what to do with them. Nobody ever will. Who wants to dig up stuff that didn't work before and have his or her name attached to a second failed attempt? It's better forgotten and buried in a warehouse. Hear no evil, see no evil, and speak no evil.

Oddsitis

Las Vegas bookies are the inspiration of the final infirmity in the Four Plagues of Consumer Promotion. The disease Oddsitis is one that marketing teams commit when they misguidedly believe that if they offer high odds of winning some kind of prize in their sweepstakes, consumers will automatically respond.

Soft drink brands are common victims of this disorder. You can almost always find a brand on the store shelf touting "1 in 12 Wins" or "1 in 6 Wins" with an under-the-cap promotion.

Unfortunately, offering what consumers perceive to be "high" odds of winning creates an expectation of winning every time. When the consumer loses he thinks, "hey, why didn't I win? I think that 1-in-6 odds is a bunch of bull." But high odds also work against the brand even when the consumer wins! Since he is already expecting to win, a low-level prize is a fizzle instead of a bang.

> ### *Marketing Truth*
>
> *The four plagues of consumer promotions are sure-fire bombs that neither captivate consumers nor move the sales needle significantly. Avoid them at all costs!*

Elements Of Promotions That Work

Just as we have discovered patterns of promotional strategies that consistently don't seem to work very well, we also see a distinct set of core ideas that seem to invariably be associated with all great promotions.

Publisher's Clearing House Prize Patrol Giveaway is a promotion that illustrates all the elements of success. You've got to hand it to them; the uniqueness of their offering -- giving away millions of dollars live on TV from your front door -- is an intriguing consumer hook that never gets old. Everybody wants to win a million dollars on TV in front of their neighbors and the whole wide world. I know I keep a lookout in my driveway for the Prize Patrol van every time they go on the air to give away the money -- and I bet you do too!

What is it about this promotion that keeps me glued to my window -- and my mailbox? If you break it down to its elemental features, you'll find a terrific blueprint for success. First and foremost, the Prize Patrol is successful because it allows the consumer to fantasize about seeing his or herself win. The prize is compelling and the spokespeople are credible; nobody doubts that there actually is a big winner. In fact, their mailings show you photos and dollar winnings of several past winners.... Michael Oaks of Petersboro, Tennessee, Freida Franks of Boise, Idaho, and so on and so on. Regular folks, just like you and me, all past winners of Publishers Clearing House. And with every mailing, each more personalized and tantalizing than the last, the consumer is strongly led down the rosy path to believe that the big winner has every likelihood of being you!

The promotion also has incredible momentum. Consumers receive early mailings for registration (registration occurs automatically with a purchase), and then continually advance through "stages" over several months. Naturally, each of these progressive stages includes a strong incentive to make yet another purchase. Sure, by law you can enter the sweepstakes without buying anything, but non-purchase entries must be mailed in a plain white envelope with a measly 3x5 card inside, instead of being rushed to Clearinghouse Headquarters in an Exciting "Winning Number Enclosed!" envelope with colorful bonus prize stickers. No one with any secret hope of winning would trust his entry to the plain white envelope!

As the giveaway date draws near, TV advertising announces the time of the next "live" giveaway. Concurrently, the consumer receives in the mail a "finalist" package, telling him that he is so close to winning, PCH must have his permission to televise the award moment from his front door (and by the way, wouldn't you like to mail in one more purchase with your permission slip?). The mailing requests an alternate address where the consumer might be if he knows he won't be home at the time of the giveaway. They ask him to select the form of payment in which he'd like to receive his award (Ten Million Lump Sum? One million a year for ten years? $500,000 a year for 20 years?) He signs publicity release forms (and probably makes another purchase; what's $4.99 when you're a shoe-in for millions?) The finalist's package asks your preferred airline for travelling to New York City for the press conference; your preferred Manhattan hotel; and which Broadway shows would you like us to get you tickets for while you are here in New York City? The finalist's package is a stroke of pure genius. After going through all the paperwork, it seems a sure bet that the Prize Patrol is coming your way!

Although the contest only has a single prize -- the Grand Prize -- it is extremely successful. The reason is clear: Publishers Clearing House knows the three ingredients of greatness that every successful consumer product promotion has in common:

The Three Ingredients of Greatness in Consumer Promotions

1. The contest offers a unique, desirable prize that ONLY YOU CAN OFFER.
2. They make you believe you have a good chance (or at least a fair chance) of winning.
3. They make it easy to enter.

You don't have to give away a million dollars in order to create an effective consumer promotion that includes the Three Ingredients of Greatness. Miller Beer executed a terrific promotion that drove sales with a unique and memorable "scratch n' sniff" promotion. While the vehicle of scratch n' sniff has been around forever, the way Miller executed the promotion was brilliant. The scents were all strange smells, not the usual perfume and cologne. For example, if you were to smell "beef", you'd win a half-side of frozen beef; if you smelled "suntan lotion" you'd win a trip to go hang out at the next Sports Illustrated Swimsuit photo shoot.

This promotion was perfect. It hit a bulls-eye with males ages 18-34 and supported Miller Beer's strategic brand positioning benefit of "unexpected fun". The promotion was unique and different, unlike anything ever executed before. It was easy to play, and everyone got a weird scratch scent with purchase, so each consumer believed he had a good chance to win.

When I was at the Utah Jazz, I executed a series of consumer promotions to help grow ticket sales and build our email and text-messaging databases. Before the promotions began, the Jazz had slipped to 20th in league attendance. We had an email database of only 7,000 addresses, and no texting database at all. I offered a monthly promotion with great prizes that ONLY the Utah Jazz could offer – the chance to win a new SportCourt installed in your yard, and to have NBA All-Star Deron Williams come over to play you one-on-one! Another offered fans the chance to attend an exclusive dinner with Jazz star Kyle Korver, where they would arrive by limousine and dine privately with Kyle. Another gave fans the chance to "work" at a home game and perform jobs like Team President (sitting with the team owner at courtside), working as a team ball boy (handing players towels during timeouts), or managing the Dance Team (what 18 year old guy doesn't want to do that all night long?) Another offered the chance to have Jazz players and coaches' come to your house for dinner. How cool was it for the family that had Jerry Sloan drop by for dinner, or for the family that hosted Andrei Kirilenko and his wife?

Over four years of promotions, we grew the email database to over 250,000 contacts, and the text-messaging database to over 75,000 mobile phones. This then gave us a great way to market directly to Jazz fans and save on traditional media costs…an added bonus. Oh yeah, and we sold out 54 consecutive home games and grew our season ticket base from

7,000 fans to an NBA leading 15,000 fans during the same period. Consumer promotions work!

Creating Brand Personality With Promotions

Most consumer products do not have a brand personality, although they certainly should. Those that do can create tremendous competitive advantage for themselves through consumer promotions.

Consumer promotions are a terrific way to involve consumers with your brand and develop a rapport. Like any relationship, the key to winning consumer friendships is the same as getting friends in school - to develop an engaging personality. Associating with your brand should make people feel good about themselves and their choices.

Oscar Meyer Hot Dogs is one brand that has developed a winning brand personality using an imaginative promotional vehicle - the Oscar Meyer Wienermobile. This giant traveling hot dog on wheels is a sight to behold when it comes to your neighborhood grocery store.

My first encounter with the Wienermobile was in 1963 at the ripe old age of six. I was living in San Bernadino, California, and my Mom took me to our local Vons Supermarket when I saw a sign on the door promoting a Saturday appearance by the Wienermobile.

I was so excited I almost wet myself. As Saturday arrived, I leapt from bed at 6 a.m., rushed to wake up my parents, needing to get to Vons for the Wienermobile appearance. Oh, it was scheduled for 1 p.m. I was ready though. At 12:30 we left for the store and got a prime position by where the Wienermobile would be parked. As 1 p.m. approached, I looked out on Baseline Avenue and saw the Wienermobile turn the corner and head into the parking lot. My heart jumped into my throat as the giant hot dog on wheels approached. A little man wearing a white suit and a big chef's hat jumped out of the Wienermobile, and led us all in song:

"Oh I wish I were an Oscar Meyer Wiener,

That is what I'd truly like to be-e-e,

Cause if I were an Oscar Meyer Wiener,

Everyone would be in love with me!"

He then gave me one of my childhoods' most prized possessions – a wiener whistle that looked just like an Oscar Meyer Hot Dog. When a kid goes home after seeing the Wienermobile and having his big moment on stage singing the Oscar Meyer wiener song, do you think that Mom can serve anything other than an Oscar Meyer Wiener ever again? Not a chance. All other hot dog brands may now leave the building.

Even though it has been fifty years since my Wienermobile encounter, my mother to this day will only buy Oscar Meyer Hot Dogs, and on summer holidays when I go home for a barbeque, she makes sure each time to point out that we have Oscar Meyer Hot Dogs for grilling.

How many other consumer promotions can you name that have successfully created a fifty-year staying power? And, yes, Oscar Meyer is STILL using the Wienermobile as its key brand promotion tool. In fact, at the time of this writing, the brand is running a consumer promotion promoted on the front of Oscar Meyer Wiener packages offering consumers the chance to have the Wienermobile come to their house! (Yes, I've entered!)

Goodyear Tires has developed a brand personality through its fleet of Goodyear Blimps. How can a thing that just hovers in the air have a personality? The brand has crafted its persona by becoming synonymous with "Big Event" -- if it's happening, the Blimp will be there. You know that you are at a special event (hence, YOU'RE pretty special) if the blimp has made an appearance. These airships have become a part of Americana. The company drives sales by offering rides on the famous airship with the purchase of a set of new Goodyear Tires. Who wouldn't want to hang out and be seen with the blimp? It's cool. Kind of like sitting courtside at a Lakers game with Jack Nicholson.

Borrowing A Personality

In high school, there are some kids who are popular because they captain the football team, are a cheerleader, or they're incredibly good-looking. Then there are kids who are popular because they're best buddies with the football captain or they date the cheerleader or that really good-looking girl, and maybe they sort of look and act the same way.

If a brand has a hard time establishing its own personality, it can employ the same strategy that worked in high school; it can become desirable by association.

Brands associated with American Idol have successfully leveraged the popularity of this program to borrow personality. Coca-Cola has "cups" in front of all the judges; it also has the "Coca-Cola Red Room" where contestants wait in the wings. Ford leverages American Idol by having the contestants make a special "Ford Commercial" every week.

Travelocity has leveraged the television show "The Amazing Race" to enhance its brand personality, by offering unique Travelocity trips to the winners of each "leg" of the race and showing their Travelocity lawn Gnome at each exotic locale.

Continuity Promotions

Continuity promotions -- ones that require a series of purchases -- are tricky, but they can be highly effective and well worth the trouble. Airlines are the kings of continuity promotions with their "Frequent Flyer" programs. Before "frequent flyers," consumers had no incentive other than price to differentiate between carriers. They'd shop for their desired destination and choose the lowest rate. But the Frequent Flyer programs compelled consumers to develop loyalties to airlines. Suddenly, consumers were earning credits toward travel when they used their credit cards, purchased a full tank of gas or stayed at a hotel -- activities they would have performed anyway. Awards were adjusted to create the belief that free tickets were attainable -- *if* consumers concentrated their efforts on one airline. This shrewd promotion allowed the big carriers to escape the low-fare race to some extent and develop a loyal consumer base.

You'll often find continuity programs in fast food chains such as Taco Bell and McDonald's that offer game pieces that must be collected during several consecutive visits in order to win. These promotions work especially well in this venue because the typical fast food consumer eats out several times each week. Continuity promotions provide an incentive for the consumer to return to the same restaurant during the promotional period, instead of "eating around."

In fact, nearly any product or service that consumers use frequently, or actively seek out alternative products, can benefit from continuity promotions. Radio stations run them all the time, using their top shows to advertising promotions that will be announced later in the afternoon, when consumers are less likely to listen – "Get the Secret Word at 7 a.m., then listen again at 5 p.m. today and when you hear the Secret Word, be the ninth caller to win." Even banks have joined the continuity game, offering special services like "personal bankers" to encourage consumers to satisfy all their banking needs in one location, instead of shopping around at the many aggressive credit unions, securities brokers and mortgage companies that have cropped up. They know that if they make loan applications and IRA planning easy, they have a better chance of keeping you close to home.

Proprietary Promotions

Another way to capture competitive advantage is to offer the consumer something highly desirable that she can ONLY get through your brand. These are often contractually tied in with sponsorships. During a recent Super Bowl, Papa John's Pizza offered a great promotion where depending upon the outcome of the opening coin flip to start the game, consumers could win a free pizza and two-liter of Pepsi. Chevrolet leveraged social media and proprietary apps with the Super Bowl to give away vehicles during the game to fans that were interacting online.

ABC Network ran a great promotion with their show "Revenge", offering a summer trip to the Hamptons (where the show is set). The only way to enter the contest was to watch the show and go into a special social media site where fans discussed the show in real-time during the broadcast.

Walmart offered consumers the chance to with a trip to the Hollywood Premiere of the second installment of "The Hunger Games" by offering a contest where if a consumer pre-ordered the DVD of "The Hunger Games" through the walmart.com website, they earned an entry into the Hollywood trip contest. All of these are great examples of proprietary promotions tied to sponsorships.

Other Types of Consumer Promotions:

There are many other types of consumer promotions that have been developed and executed over the years by different companies. Here's a short list of different types of promotions and when they might be useful:

Cash back Offers: Need to react fast? Cash back offers are a great way to maximize sales in the short term.

On-Pack Premiums: Attach a sample of your product to another top-selling product. Encourages trial and increased consumption.

Collect & Win: Increase purchase frequency with a reward only redeemable by collecting enough barcodes, stamps or coupons.

Instant Win: drive sales of items with immediate consumption.

Product Sampling: The classic "try-it, you'll like it" approach is a tried and true method for overcoming reluctance to buy a new brand.

Bonus Offers: Buy One, Get One Free can give you an edge in the market.

Multipacks: Packaging multiple products into one easy to select pack (preferably discounted) can quickly add volume to sales figures.

Trial Size: Encourage consumers to give it a try with a low-cost, one use package.

Buy Now, Pay Later: Deferred payments are a successful way to generate sales, especially for higher priced items.

Interest Free Financing: a successful way to generate sales, especially for higher-priced items like automobiles.

Scratch N' Win: instant-win redeemable prizes are especially effective.

Cause Helper: Fundraise for a charitable cause and actively help your community and help your brand.

Community Builders: Helping in your local community to build your brand.

Loyalty Programs: Reward customers for long-term loyalty and multiple purchases.

Surprise Sweetener: Surprise your customers with a reward they receive only after they've purchased. (A Surprise inside every box).

Special Events: Consider treating your loyal brand users with a sneak peek preview or invite them to a special sale or event they have to qualify for.

Open House / Plant Tours: These can be a much-welcomed way of promoting your brand values.

World Records: Set a world's record to draw attention and drive brand sales.

Promotions That Are Half-Right

There's almost nothing I hate more than to see a "pretty good" promotion that could easily have been an extraordinary promotion if only the marketing team had observed the Three Ingredients of Greatness.

AT&T Mobile is a good example. Each year during the NBA Finals, AT&T executes a promotion that selects a single consumer to shoot baskets during halftime at one of the NBA Finals games for a chance to win $2 million dollars. The promotion is called "The AT&T $2 Million Dollar Shootout". Registration is simple: the consumer just calls a number shown on the TV screen during commercials.

AT&T successfully addresses two of The Three Ingredients of Greatness™ (unique and desirable prize, easy to enter), but fails to make you believe you have a chance to win and that YOU will be selected. They've got it two-thirds right, and it's a good promotion. But it's not GREAT.

How could they improve the promotion to be GREAT? Several ideas come to mind. What if AT&T borrowed some of the techniques perfected by Publishers Clearing House (remember, it's OK to steal ideas!) and created a mailing that would go out to each person who registered by phone that included:

--A set of official rules for the shootout.

--An itinerary of the NBA Finals (potential dates).

--A notification to the contestant that if selected they will receive a videotape of the event from AT&T. No need to worry about setting up their Flip Recorder.

--3-point shooting tips from the NBA All-Star Game's 3-point champion.

--Bonus entry for being an AT&T customer

Then, as the NBA Playoffs progressed, send a second mailing that included materials that made them feel even closer to the jackpot, including:

-- A registration form for their preferred flight arrangements / preferred airline / preferred hotel to stay in at the Finals.

-- Publicity release forms and advertising release forms.

-- A request for the name of the contestant's bank.

-- A request for the preferred method of delivering the money that's won (direct deposit, certified check, etc.).

-- A reminder that every customer of AT&T Mobile gets bonus entries.

Instead of the current method of selecting and notifying the winning contestant -- in which AT&T holds a drawing and then calls the winner on the phone to notify them, and the public has no clue who won until the person walks out on the court to shoot -- AT&T should make the selection itself a highly anticipated and talked about "event". How? Hold the drawing to select the winner, but keep the person's identity secret for a week. Through a series of TV spots airing nightly during the NBA Playoff games, slowly reveal the chosen contestant.

Start by showing a US map, highlighting the REGION of the USA the winner lives in. The next night, highlight THREE States, stating that the winner lives in one of these states. The next night, highlight the STATE of the contestant. Then highlight TEN cities in the State. Then THREE cities. Then THE CITY, and finally reveal the winner with a celebration event in that City that airs during the Playoff Game Halftime show. Over a one-week period (seven days), the promotion would send consumers into a tizzy thinking they had won -- or that they may know the person who has won if it's not their state / city!

That's how AT&T could make it a GREAT promotion instead of one that's merely pretty good.

The Octopus Planning Matrix

Let's assume you've done absolutely everything right. You've focused on your strategy, you've researched the competitive environment, and you've come up with a brilliant idea that incorporates The Three Ingredients of Greatness and makes your product a hero!

Don't stop there. Once you've got your hands on a really dynamite promotion idea, your challenge is to give it the biggest bang possible. That means exploiting every conceivable means of extending its reach and effectiveness. The only way you can be sure you're maximizing the power of your promotion is to analyze its possibilities in the *Octopus Planning Matrix*.

The matrix is so named because when laid out on paper it resembles the form of an octopus. It begins with your core idea, the "head" of the matrix, and then creates extensions, or "legs," which can support the core idea in a variety of channels and stretch its reach among retailers, the media, and consumers.

The best way to illustrate the idea is to develop a hypothetical promotion using the Octopus Planning Matrix. Let's imagine for a moment that we are developing the promotion concept for M&M's Chocolate Candies. We first need to know what the brand positioning strategy is, so let's create one:

> *For target consumers' ages 5-24, M&M's Chocolate Candies are sweet and delicious treats that colorfully brighten your day! That's because M&M's multi-colored candy coated chocolates (both in plain and peanut variety) are fun to eat and provide a playful pick-me-up!*

The consumer benefit the brand wants to communicate is that M&M's "colorfully brightens your day". This is the core strategy that all brand promotions must support. The qualities that support the "colorful brightening" benefit are "fun" and "playfulness".

The next challenge is to dream up a promotion concept that meets the criteria in The Three Ingredients of Greatness -- the promotion must be unique, unlike anything else around, and something ONLY M&M's could offer; it makes M&M's the HERO; it must make consumers believe that they have a good shot at winning; and it must be easy to enter. Of course, it also must stimulate sales, so let's assume that we need to execute the basic promotion via the packages of M&M's candies, and that we're planning our promotion for the key Easter holiday period, when retailers are most likely to display and feature candy product.

In real life, the marketing team would probably go off to brainstorm and hire several promotion agencies to try to develop an idea for them, playing the odds that with enough people working on it, somebody will come up with a usable idea. But we'll jump ahead and assume that we've got a plan that everybody likes.

The promotion will be called, "M&M's Great Color Caper". The premise of the promotion is that a renegade bunny, a mischievous cousin of the Easter Bunny, broke into the M&M plant and mixed 5 new "wild" colors of M&M's under the cover of darkness, then dumped over 100 million of these colorful counterfeits into the packaging processors. M&M's is collecting all the evidence to bring that bad bunny that perpetrated this preposterous predicament to justice. The bunny has left behind incriminating evidence; paw prints on the wrappers. M&M's is posting a reward of $1 million dollars for consumers who collects paw prints in each of the five bogus colors and sends them in to the M&M Candy Detectives – our favorite talking M&M's -- Red and Yellow.

First of all, notice that The Three Ingredients of Greatness are all addressed: the promotion is fun & unique; it allows ALL consumers to think that they have a good shot at winning (since every wrapper contains paw prints); and it's easy to play the game. The product is the hero. Furthermore, every consumer receives wild new colors mixed in her candies, which reinforces the fun and playful tone of the brand, and the renegade bunny character can become a central display figure at retail.

With the Renegade Bunny as the core promotional idea, we are now ready to begin extending the promotion through the Octopus Planning Matrix:

M&M's Candy Octopus Planning Matrix

```
                          The Great M&M's Color Caper
         ┌────────────────┬─────────────┬──────────────┐
      Packaging       Point of Sale     Media        PR Events
      ┌────┴────┐          │              │              │
  New Colors  Promotional  In Store    TV, Radio,    Press Releases
   (MFG)      Package      Display     Print Campaign
              Design          │              │              │
                         Promotional    Internet Web    Radio Station
                         Signage        Site            Giveaways & Contests
                                            │              │
                                       Rosie O'Donnell  M&M Mountain
                                       Show Promotion   Central Park, NYC
```

For each box within the planning matrix, you must develop a specific plan of execution to cover all your bases. For example, under packaging, you have two things to worry about -- developing new art for the packages that communicates the promotion (and the colored paw prints inside), and working with manufacturing to develop and mix the new colored M&M's into the promotional packages. Under PR, you'd develop press events, promotions for radio stations, and create a major event to rally attention to the promotion -- like maybe sending the Renegade Bunny out for Store Appearances or Fugitive Sightings (with rewards for the consumers who spot him).

For retail Trade promotions, perhaps you would create "footprints" floor stickers that could be placed in retailers to reinforce that the renegade bunny had been there.

Notice how everything in this plan supports the strategic positioning statement for the brand. The new wild colors highlight the benefit, "colorfully brightens your day". The concept is fun and can be executed with energy and creativity at retail. This is how you create GREAT consumer promotions!

Marketing Truth

Top companies develop consumer promotion plans that extend far from just the retail store environment. They use the promotion as a means to create radio station tie-ins, stage PR events, rally employees and develop unique promotional opportunities with the retail trade.

Using Promotion Agencies To Do Your Thinking

Many big companies off-load their promotion ideation to "promotion agencies". This is a terrible mistake. Most agencies simply develop an array of promotion concepts, and then they serve as carpetbaggers and pack them up and shop them around to dozens upon dozens of companies. NEVER buy a ready-made off-the-shelf promotion. It will violate the first of The Three Ingredients of Greatness -- to have a unique and captivating idea. Lady Gaga never shops off the rack, and neither should you. Chances are, your competitors could show up at retail with the same idea. *Don't let your promotion agency do your thinking for you.*

Not that promotion agencies don't have value. They do, but the best way to use them is to involve them in the brainstorming process and once you get the great idea, let them help you execute it. That's when agencies are the most valuable -- in execution.

Take It To The Promised Land

If I could communicate only one idea about consumer promotions it would be -- <u>avoid the sea of sameness</u>. Your goal should be to explore uncharted territory, to create something unique and special that breaks through the clutter and captures consumer attention, and most importantly – MAKES YOUR PRODUCT A HERO.

If you want an idea that will just give you a one or two percent lift, just offer the trade a price discount and save the time and energy of everyone in your organization. <u>Life is too short to work on 1% to 2% ideas</u>. Consumer promotions can be 10% solutions if you get out of the box and do something great! Go ahead and think like The Man From LaMancha -- dream the impossible dream. You'll be surprised where it takes you.

Chapter Seventeen

<u>Public Relations</u>

PR professionals are lobbyists in the truest sense, spending most of their day on the phone coaxing newspapers, TV stations, radio stations and other members of the media and trade press to talk or write about their company. A PR pro at work is a study in helpful cheerfulness. But underneath the chatty veneer, the expensive coifs and the designer suits beats the heart of a warrior.

Like a modern day cavalry, PR professionals ride to the rescue in times of trouble to defend the honor and good name of their employer. The moment unflattering news about the company hits the Internet, they saddle up and wage a bloody campaign against the perpetrator, defending their company with vigor and valor. Once the emergency is passed, they lay down their weapons and shift back into promotional mode, canvassing the media world with uplifting and inspiring newsworthy data while awaiting the next corporate crisis.

One Voice To The Media

The most vital function of the PR department, during times of war and times of peace, is to provide a single, consistent voice to the outside world. They make sure that everything the press (and ultimately consumers) hear and see about your company and brands are accurate and conform to the corporate image and individual brand strategies. The press and consumers are easily confused by too many "voices" speaking on behalf of the company. At the best companies, only PR interfaces with the media.

Many marketing people think they are the best spokespeople for their brands. In fact, they may be. But unless the PR department asks you to do an interview, marketers should market, and PR people should work the **press!**

<u>**Marketing Truth**</u>

Marketing managers should never speak to the press without first being asked by the PR department to do so, and the, coached on what to say. PR professionals are accustomed to daily dealings with the media. A good PR person can protect marketers from making gaffes that will come back to haunt them.

Coke senior management takes its media dealings VERY seriously. Every employee who *may be* approached by the media to act as a spokesperson for the Company is required to attend a full-day "media training" seminar to acquire the proper media interviewing skills. The training is a small bit of insurance to help protect Coke's pristine corporate image.

The One-Man PR Department

Obviously, if you're a small shop or entrepreneur, you may need to assume the PR functions yourself. How defensive do you need to be when dealing with the local press? Not very. The media is unlikely to invest time and effort in researching your company, or writing a negative article, unless you are already an established player with high name recognition. If they grant you any notice at all, they'll probably use exactly what you give them, so write that press release carefully!

The actual mechanics of Public Relations are complicated and can be tedious, from compiling extensive contact lists for the daily, weekly and monthly publications (backing out each press release date to correspond with their lead times) to tracking stories and planning future placements. We won't discuss the details here, but the following strategies will work for you whether you're the biggest fish in the pond with a bustling department of PR professionals, or a free-swimming guppy making your first foray into PR waters.

The Three Types of Public Relations

Corporate promotion and crisis management are perhaps the most visible tasks handled by a PR department, but there is actually much more to their jobs. There are three different and distinct types of public relations efforts, each with different goals, objectives and tactics employed to accomplish their respective chores. These different PR functions are:

CORPORATE PR -- handles the day-to-day operations of the company -- corporate announcements and company news, executive appointment and promotions, earnings reports, development of the annual shareholders reports, organizing corporate meetings, publishing company newsletters, and other official communications. They are experts at making everyone feel warm, fuzzy, uplifted and motivated about the direction of the company and the caliber of its employees.

DEFENSIVE PR -- is focused on defending the company against attack. It springs into action at the first signs of trouble or when a negative story concerning the company hits the wires. These pros are experts at crisis management and in diffusing tough situations.

MARKETING PR -- proactively develop programs and initiatives to support brand marketing efforts. This is an integral part of the annual business plan for each brand. These efforts are vital to gaining "free publicity" about the company's products.

Most PR people handle the tasks of defensive and corporate PR flawlessly, because this is where they get the sharpest corporate focus and, therefore, the most training. But if you use your PR department only as trouble-shooters and overlook its potential as a marketing tool, you've just squandered marketing value.

Marketing Truth

A great marketing PR initiative can add significant value in free publicity to augment paid marketing support. Top companies dedicate resources to do nothing but develop and execute PR efforts in support of their brands.

Marketing Disguised as PR

Public Relations departments typically use two traditional methods to spread their gospel: the press release and the press conference.

The first weapon of choice for most pros is the "press release". Each week, the corporate PR department writes pages filled with fantastic newsy tidbits and distribute this merrily positioned and carefully worded information to employees, the press and key influencers. If you read enough press releases and newsletters from the same company, you start to believe that perhaps this enterprise is the best run business ever conceived. Many PR professionals are so gifted at writing copy, they can make the announcement of a mere building addition sound like an effort that will generate hundreds of thousands of jobs, inject millions of dollars into the local economy, and return Keiko the whale to his heartbroken orca family.

The second implement of war used to advance the corporate agenda is "the press conference". Since press conferences require members of the press to actually leave their place of business to attend the event, this tactic is usually reserved for really big news. If a company doesn't have a newsworthy story, no one will attend.

Frequently, corporations spend big money to host a press conference that is really a marketing event in disguise. The most extravagant I've participated in was the announcement of Coca-Cola's sponsorship of the Sydney, Australia 2000 Summer Olympic Games. The event was held inside the famous Opera House overlooking the breathtaking Sydney Harbor in the spring of 1996.

To create the mood and ambiance, Coke shipped a $100,000 Corporate Olympic Sponsorship display from its headquarters in Atlanta and reconstructed it inside the Opera House for the 2-hour session, which was attended by approximately 40 members of the press and 5 television crews. The event began with a skydiver leaping from a plane high above Sydney Harbor, unfurling a giant Coca-Cola / Sydney 2000 flag which fluttered magnificently over the water as the skydiver descended to land on the mooring surrounding the Opera House. He then stepped into the crow's nest of a giant crane that lifted him six stories and allowed him to jump out onto the balcony of the Opera House, delivering the flag into the hands of the Prime Minister of Australia.

After the traditional speeches featuring the Prime Minister, the Head of the Sydney Olympic Organizing Committee, the Mayor of Sydney, and Coke's Vice-President of Worldwide Sports, a special pen appeared that had a miniature secret agent like camera mounted in the tip. A projection screen descended from the ceiling, and as the contracts were signed with the special pen, the press watched the signatures forming on the big screen. OOOH! Once the final contract was signed, fireworks were launched over the harbor, four F-18 fighter planes from the Australian Royal Air Force buzzed the Opera House, and two thousand red and white Coca-Cola helium-filled balloons were released into the sky. It was quite a show, and it worked. The press event was the lead story on all Australian newscasts and the front-page headline story in all newspapers the following day -- and it made Coke look terrific!

Disney staged the largest PR / marketing event in history with its New York Central Park premiere of "Pocahontas". More than 500,000 people filled the park to watch the movie opening. Before the event "exclusive" stories and sneak previews were featured on programs such as Entertainment Tonight, Access Hollywood and Inside Edition. Coverage of the opening made newscasts worldwide that night and even though the cost to Disney was rumored to be well over $2 million to stage the event, the value of the free media coverage Disney obtained exceeded that amount ten-fold.

The Marketing PR Model

Most corporate PR efforts fail at the starting block. Many companies mistakenly assume that PR is no more than an application of The Three P's -- keep *plugging* away, *pestering* and *plastering* the media with information, and sooner or later you'll see your name in print. Wrong. The media doesn't want quantity, they want *quality*. Give them something that they can get excited about and they will use it. It's that simple really. If you offer nothing more than a standard press release with the same boring information that everyone else puts out, 99 times out of 100 it will find its way to the garbage can without being read. City desk editors are bombarded with press releases. They want to see something interesting and different -- they want news!

Marketing Truth

PR is driven by the power of the great, creative idea. Develop a PR plan that is innovative and interesting to the media, and then package it well!

Instead of churning out sound-alike press releases, spend your time and energy dreaming up ideas that are different, better and special and develop a tantalizing "hook" for the press to latch on to.

PR Hollywood Style

Movie studios are the masters of the PR domain. Granted, their product category is unique, but they know how to work the press like a bunch of trained poodles, and regular everyday products can take a lesson from studying how they do it.

The PR campaign for any major movie begins before the film is in the can -- sometimes, before a single frame is shot. Every step along the way is trumpeted as a major news event, from purchasing the rights to a hot novel to signing the first major star. As production begins, the studio will often hire its own crew to shoot a behind-the-scenes "Making Of" documentary, to air on a major network or cable station several weeks before the movie's release. They scan dailies to find enough action, excitement and star close-ups to produce a trailer – often a full year before the movie's scheduled release; these are the "Coming Next Summer" teasers that often run in theaters while editors are still madly working on the movie. Finally, they'll invite entertainment press to the set for "exclusive" interviews with the stars and sneak peeks and at spectacular costumes or special effects. All of this PR for a film that hasn't even wrapped!

Two or three weeks before the movie's opening, the studio will host a press junket with its major stars. This is a national tour, often including satellite interviews, designed to give the most important members of the media personal access to the actors. Sometimes, they'll only be allotted fifteen minutes apiece with the stars, but it's enough to allow the journalist to report, "When I sat down exclusively with George Clooney this afternoon, he seemed. . ." In between screenings and interviews, the media is wined, dined, courted and invited to elaborate (and expensive) Hollywood-style parties to impress upon them both the scale of the movie and their indebtedness to the studio. Often, these press junkets will overlap with a major film festival, like Cannes or Sundance, where all the big players march out their upcoming movies and big stars in a furious competition for attention and ink.

Next come the private screening for the press, which in addition to the expected film critic crowd, included invitations to virtually anyone in the media who might have something positive to say about the film. Conversely, if the studio thinks the film's final version is weaker than expected, they'll refuse to provide advance screenings to avoid negative reviews. Today, simply omitting the screenings becomes its own news and cause for negative PR.

Finally, the opening week PR blitz hits. By now, consumers have seen all the advertising and are wondering, when the heck does this movie open, anyway? On opening week, they'll know. For example, take a look at the premiere-week PR for Snow White and the Huntsman. Charlize Theron made the rounds to a flurry of talk shows including Ellen DeGeneres, The Tonight Show, Jimmy Fallon, Live! With Kelly, and morning shows including The Today Show, CBS This Morning, and Good Morning America. She granted live interviews on local radio stations in every major market. She also taped several segments for Entertainment Tonight and Access Hollywood, which would run as a series throughout the week.

Sound like a lot of press? That was only Charlize's part of the effort. While she was making the "first tier" rounds of media, co-stars Kristen Stewart and Peter Ferdinando were traveling similar circuits to quadruple the exposure on programs like David Letterman and Jimmy Kimmel.

Why all this frantic activity just for opening week? If the movie is good, won't the news spread over the course of its run? Yes, but opening weekend can often ring up 50% of the film's total gross dollars, and announcing the film's performance at the box-office ("#1 this weekend!")

generates momentum for the weeks that follow. If a film is a real gem or wildly popular, like "The Hunger Games", box office performance will remain strong for weeks and months to come. But most movies have a short shelf life and need to make their money up-front, and like any other new product introduction, it helps to make a bang from the start. Distributors will be more likely to commit to a longer run if the film performs well at opening.

Publicity promotion is part of the stars' contracts when they agree to be in the film, but the PR department at the studio is responsible to make sure it happens and to plan how. Actors understand that as exhausting as promoting a movie can be, it's essential to create consumer excitement and "sell" the film. That's why even actors who think of themselves as *artists,* and who no longer need to sell their box office appeal, will still make the rounds for a project they care about.

Marketing Truth

PR campaigns should develop momentum, with a beginning, middle and "blitz" climax. Overlap your efforts so consumers receive new, and slightly different, news about your product from many different media sources.

The Folgers Coffee PR Campaign at Miami (Ohio) University

A while back, the people at Folgers were spending a lot of time worrying about the future of coffee. Coffee houses were in their infancy, and coffee had fallen out of fashion with young consumers. At the age when people traditionally began a lifelong coffee love affair -- sometime during the college years -- they were instead choosing soft drinks, even for a morning pick-me-up. The coffee consumer base was aging and no new drinkers were emerging to take their place, leaving Folgers with a declining category that was projected to atrophy to 40% of its 1991 size in just a little more than 20 years.

Desperate times call for desperate measures, so the company sent me directly to the heart of the matter. I found myself back in school, on the campus of Miami (Ohio) University to determine whether we could change the way students felt about coffee. We wanted to test whether the right PR plan, combined with advertising, could affect their attitudes and entice college students to begin drinking coffee.

The campaign was entitled "Jump Start Your Brain" with Folgers, repositioning the brand as a fun and stimulating pick-me-up. Phase one offered free coffee to students as they lugged their books past 45 different "coffee stations" on campus. The stations were restocked twice each day with freshly brewed 5-gallon containers of Folgers.

Next, we infiltrated campus activities. At hockey and basketball games, we gave all fans a piece of paper to fold into a paper airplane for the Folgers Coffee "Miami to Miami for Spring Break" Paper Airplane Toss between periods and at basketball's half time. All students got the chance to fly their planes at targets on the ice and playing floor to win free airline tickets to Miami Beach for the upcoming Spring Break.

The piece of paper the students were given to make into a "plane" was filled with coffee "fun facts", strategic messages which the students read while they held onto their planes for the hour or so from the time they arrived at the until the Airplane Toss was held. The vehicle was an incredibly effective communication tool. In follow-up research we found that nearly 60% of the students on-campus knew the "Folgers fun facts". Great -- the first hurdle was behind us; we'd communicated our brand strategy and equated the product with on-campus fun.

Now, to get the students to really drink the stuff. To do that, we hosted the "FOLGERS COFFEE FREE MIDNIGHT MOVIE" on Saturday nights at a local theater. Admission was free by drinking a cup of Folgers at the door of the theater. If a student didn't want to drink the coffee, he could pay $4.00 for admission. The theater was packed with students every Saturday and hundreds more had to be turned away. We never collected a single dollar at the door; everyone drank coffee! Even the students who were turned away from a sell-out were happy; they milled around outside drinking coffee and chatting with friends for a few hours.

Notice the elements of the PR plan. They were FUN yet RELEVANT to the Folgers brand. The paper airplane toss communicated strategic messages about Folgers coffee, the movie theater promotion accomplished product sampling in a unique way. Best of all, the PR stunts were cheap! We cut a deal with TWA to provide the "Miami to Miami" airplane tickets for free in exchange for advertising exposure on the airplanes (this too was a great promotion for TWA as the medium was relevant to their brand), and the movie theater buy-out cost us a grand total of $250.00!

Developing A PR Plan

There are only two things required to create a great PR plan. The first step is <u>deciding what it is you strategically want to communicate</u>. To illustrate, I'll walk you through an example. Lisa Clements, a friend of mine who used to be the Marketing Director of the San Francisco Zoo, created a PR plan in which she developed 4 key strategic messages to communicate to the media and ultimately consumers through the year. Each message would be communicated via an event, one each quarter. For example, her "spring" strategy was *"to communicate that the Zoo is deeply involved with captive breeding programs for endangered species"*.

The second step in the process is <u>to develop a fun and interesting way of positioning the strategy to the media, giving them a unique newsworthy "hook"</u>. While the strategic message *"communicate that the Zoo is deeply involved with captive breeding programs for endangered species"* seemed boring, Lisa put an incredibly interesting twist on the way she presented the program to the media. She worked with the zookeepers and created San Francisco Zoo's "Sex Tour". It was a tour held on Valentine's Day for adults only, showcasing the different sexual strategies and unusual appendages of various endangered species, from bears and giraffes to insects and snakes. The program was incredibly successful, attracting huge amounts of national media coverage and sellout tours! It is still the zoo's most effective fundraiser, now in its fifteenth year! Look in any newspaper around Valentine's Day and you'll see several zoos throughout the country that have adopted this promotion.

Marketing Truth

A great PR plan reinforces some aspect of the brand positioning strategy – the benefits, the "reason why", or the brand personality – in a unique and interesting way.

FUN is the Magic Ingredient

Life for most adults is very boring and routine. They get up and read the paper over breakfast, go to work, eat lunch, come home from work, eat dinner, play with the kids, watch the same TV shows regularly, then go to bed.

Everyone is looking for a little excitement, something that looks fun and interesting to offer a break from the everyday routine. That's the opportunity PR offers to consumer product marketers. Give the media and consumers some fun! Figure out a way to offer up something that is unique and interesting to get the media excited -- if you do, you'll get all the coverage you want and more. GREAT IDEAS are all that drive PR.

When we were developing the PR plan for the re-release of Winnie the Pooh videos, we wanted to send our press kit in some sort of package that differentiated us from everyone else, and would remind the recipient of how adorable and irresistible Pooh really is. We decided to pack our materials inside a Pooh Cookie Jar. The press loved it. They cranked out literally hundreds of articles in magazines and newspapers about our Pooh videos and the appeal of the Pooh character. The Today Show proudly displayed their jar on their coffee table while the hosts talked about the new video releases. This simple and fun idea generated millions of dollars' worth of free media exposure.

PR on Small Budgets

For many small businesses, there isn't a budget for PR events. That's OK. You can still play the game – and well!

A small preschool in my hometown has one of the best PR strategies I've ever seen. They use PR to bring new families with young children to see their facility.

During the summer, they hold a "Touch A Tractor" event. The preschool owner goes around town and gets the local construction companies to all bring a tractor or two to their parking lot on a Saturday morning for kids to crawl around on. The police bring a patrol car; the fire department brings an engine; a local racecar driver brings his car over. The lot is filled with cool tractors, cars, trucks and hundreds of kids and parents attend the free event (which they use to fill their summer programs).

During the fall, the preschool creates a "Kid-Friendly Haunted House" inside the school that is free to community. Again, hundreds of families with young kid's line up every night to bring their youngsters through, and the event secures enrollments and waiting lists for their school-year programs.

A local grocer recently staged a great PR event in their parking lot. They got several of the brands they carried to create games and food sampling in the parking lot and throughout the store. The parking lot was jammed; the store was elbow-to-elbow with shoppers! Great PR!

Like the song says "All I want to do is have some fun. I've got a feelin' I'm not the only one". Have some fun -- develop a GREAT PR plan for your product by dreaming up some fun, creative ideas! Just remember three words -- It's got to be <u>Different</u>, <u>Better</u> and <u>Special</u>.

Chapter Eighteen

Partnerships & Alliances

Strategic alliances are a kissin' cousin to sports sponsorships, minus the huge sponsorship fees. Like sports sponsorships, alliances are formal partnerships between your product and highly visible properties such as charities or non-profit organizations, blockbuster movie releases, concert tours, television programs or special events. The right partnership can help your brand to capture a unique position in the consumer mindset and differentiate your product from competition, which explains their high popularity.

Alliances usually fall into one of two camps, either *cause-related marketing* -- campaigns created as fund-raisers for charities and non-profit organizations such as Special Olympics, Save The Rainforests, Feed The Homeless, Help Find A Cure For the Disease Du Jour -- or *popularity marketing*, borrowing the imagery, personality and notoriety of a hot property to apply to your brand. Popularity properties are most often blockbuster movies, major concert tours like Taylor Swift, Katy Perry, or The Rolling Stones; top-rated TV programs or special events such as The Academy Awards.

Cause Related Marketing

Charities and non-profit organizations are the usual partners in cause related alliances. Although alliances can, and should, have many different promotions and PR efforts attached (refer to the Octopus Planning Matrix in Consumer Promotions), this type of alliance is usually executed at the store level as "Buy my product and we'll donate 'x' cents to the cause for each purchase you make".

From the consumer's point of view these promotions are a terrific deal. All she has to do is buy a product that was probably already on her shopping list (although she may need to switch to a different brand) and suddenly she is elevated from the status of a mere shopper to a social benefactor. She walks away from her purchase feeling good about her product selection, and about the quality brand that "cares."

Now put on the hat of a marketing manager. Why do YOU think brands hook up with charities and non-profits? If your answer is to be good corporate citizens and to generate funds for needy organizations, you're about half right. Yes, good citizenry is a part of the reason why they do it, and they obviously benefit from positioning themselves as The Lone Ranger fighting for the greater good of needy causes (unlike those other faceless greedy corporations). But good works, or even a good reputation, is almost never the primary motivator. Most brands adhere to the old notion that charity begins at home, and every tie-in, charitable or no, is measured for its ability to stimulate sales and increase profits. The brand manager bets on the consumers' attachment to the charity or cause to compel them to purchase the product.

The value of the donation to the non-profit or charity is usually minuscule compared to the brand's profit on each extra product sale, so if the tie-in can generate any extra sales at all, the company banks a handsome incremental profit <u>and</u> looks like the good guy by giving to charity; the classic win-win situation! For this reason, cause-related campaigns are that rare marketing tactic with a low-risk and high potential reward.

Let's run the break-even numbers of a hypothetical brand to see how a typical donation arrangement works out financially. Assume that in a normal week Brand X sells 100 units of product.

Consumer Offer: Brand X will donate 10 cents from every product purchase to the Save the Whales Foundation.

Retailer Cost:	$3.49
Brand Cost-to-Produce:	$2.19
Brand Profit:	$1.31

Breakeven Analysis	Units	Profit	Donation
Normal Sales	100	$131.00	$0
Sales w/ Donation	108	$130.68	$10.80

The break-even point for the brand is a mere 8% increase in product sales! For every incremental sale above 8%, the brand posts higher profit numbers than it would during a typical week. To put it in perspective, assume that the cause-related marketing campaign generates a 25% increase in sales for the week. After deducting for the donation, which would equal $12.50, the brand profits would soar to $151.25 --an increase of 15.5%!

Even if consumers don't respond to the tie-in by purchasing extra product, the campaign is a low-risk proposition. The worst thing that can happen is nothing at all -- sales remain flat -- in which case weekly profits would slip by a mere $10.00 (a profitability decrease of only 9%). Even in this worst-case scenario, the brand benefits by wearing the good citizen white hat, which at the end of the day is probably worth the $10.00 in lower profits.

More importantly, the brand knows that most retailers will also want to enjoy the halo effect of associating with a compelling charity or cause. A good cause-related alliance may earn free or discounted displays, feature ads or other in-store marketing support. You already know how much that type of activity is worth, both in saved costs and incremental sales.

Procter & Gamble brands all participate in cause-related marketing each year through their corporate relationship with Special Olympics. Twice each year you receive in your home a Sunday newspaper supplement stuffed full of coupons from a wide variety of Procter & Gamble products -- Tide detergent, Bounty paper towels, Sure deodorant, Folgers coffee, Hawaiian Punch fruit drink, Mr. Clean cleaner and more. The ad, which arrives in homes on the Sunday between Christmas Day and New Years Day, pledges support to Special Olympics for every P&G product purchase. But you probably haven't noticed the fine print of the offer, where P&G protects its upside from the promotion by setting a "cap" for the total donation -- in other words, once product sales generate enough donations to reach the maximum contribution, all incremental sales line P&G's coffers with no donation to the charity.

The Procter & Gamble sales force uses the fundraising component for Special Olympics and the massive couponing effort to persuade the grocery trade to offer price breaks for in-store displays and feature ads. P&G supplies retailers with handsome promotional signage using Special Olympics logos and imagery. As a result, P&G virtually owns in-store activity at grocery stores for the first few weeks each January. The promotion is so powerfully entrenched in the retail promotional schedule that competitors generally throw up their hands and concede these weeks to Procter & Gamble, steering their marketing efforts to other times of the year. This "charitable" campaign is one of the most profitable in P&G's worldwide effort.

Aha! Just another example of corporate greed masquerading as the good guy, right? Not exactly. Charities also love these promotions because they actually do provide money in the tens of thousands of dollars and free publicity for the cause. Most charities could not function without corporate partners.

Cause-Related Marketing

Some brands, including *Ben & Jerry's Ice Cream* and *Newman's Own* don't merely execute cause-related promotions; they have institutionalized cause-related marketing as part of their brand positioning strategy. Their commitment to charity conveys to the consumer that their brand is not a heartless and soul-less mega corporate greed and profit machine, but rather a nurturing corporate citizen that cares about the less fortunate and is dedicated to earning money for good causes. Some of the hype is true. In the case of the Newman brands, 100% of net profits are donated to charity.

In the post Gordon Gecko era when the corporate mantra "Greed is Good" was no longer as conspicuously chanted, many companies have felt pressure both from outside groups and stockholders to "give back" to their communities and use a portion their profits for the benefit of special charities or the underprivileged. Creating a brand positioning strategy with a cause-related marketing component is a great way to strategically differentiate your brand from competition and demonstrate to that your company has a long-term commitment to helping others.

Marketing Truth

When executing a cause-related marketing campaign, commit the plan to the long-term for annual executions. These are the rare promotions that DO bear repetition – in fact, they benefit from it. Consumers need to see the campaign executed over and over to make a solid connection between your brand and the charity / non-profit. If you execute hit-n-run cause related efforts, you miss the opportunity to elevate your brand's image and reap the long-term benefits and feel-good from the charitable association.

The NBA and Cause-Related Marketing

Charles Barkley may not accept the job of role model, but NBA Commissioner David Stern realized the power of the sports hero image in reinventing the image of the league several years ago. In fact, he integrated cause-related marketing into the heart of the NBA identity.

Think back to the pre-Larry Bird and Magic Johnson NBA of the mid-1970's. The league was in peril. Most of its notoriety and publicity involved its players' brushes with the law. Rumors swirled of rampant drug abuse. Television stations rarely covered the games. The NBA Finals were so poorly regarded as a sports property that CBS televised the games on tape-delay beginning at 11:30 p.m.

At about the same time that Bird and Magic entered the league, Stern took over for former Commissioner Larry O'Brien. Stern used the "Showtime" excitement of Magic and the Lakers along with the good 'ol country boy image of Bird and the hardworking Celtics as cornerstones upon which to build a new and improved NBA. Soon games were earning live television coverage again. During each telecast, Stern ran a public service announcement showcasing the "NBA Cares" initiative, featuring a star NBA player preaching about drugs, child abuse, reading, staying in school and other key messages related to families and youth. Season after season, these low key, intimate portraits of the players and their good Samaritan efforts continually reinforces the many ways that the league and its players donate both their time and money to worthy causes.

Over several seasons, the image of NBA players changed from a bunch of over-sized and over-paid thugs to a group of warm, concerned activists committed to helping in their communities. The campaign continues to this day. Turn on any NBA game and you'll see these "NBA Cares" public service announcements.

What makes the campaign work is that it's more than just the occasional stirring ad. The league has made a commitment, and asks for a commitment from its players, to actively participate in community service programs. In addition to its far-flung charitable affiliations, the NBA developed its own proprietary "Stay In School" program, awarding children that live in the area surrounding the annual NBA All-Star Game the opportunity to attend a celebration event featuring top music entertainers and NBA stars during All-Star Weekend. The children earn the right to attend the "Stay In School" event only if they rack up perfect attendance during the school year. The results are amazing. Kids are so highly motivated by this promotion that 98% of kids in the area qualify, filling the arena with over 20,000 screaming school children each year.

Creating Your Own Charity or Cause

In an episode of the popular, now-defunct television series "Seinfeld," the character George Costanza (actor Jason Alexander) received a Christmas card from his employer stating that in lieu of a year-end bonus check, a cash donation had been made in George's name to a local homeless shelter. George was livid; he had been counting on the bonus check. Then he hit on a brilliant idea. He'd print up Christmas cards for all of his friends and co-workers noting that this year in lieu of a gift, he had made a cash donation in their name to "The Human Fund". Of course, there was no such thing as "The Human Fund". The only donation George was making was to his own checkbook, and inevitably he was caught in his lie and humiliated.

The episode contained some nuggets of truth. At times companies, like George, invent their own "causes" instead of tying-in with an existing charity or non-profit organization. Usually these efforts are developed to fill a real void in the community, like the Ronald McDonald Children's Charities. This legitimate and worthy program was created to help families cope with the unique issues faced when their young children require extended hospital care. The company builds Ronald McDonald Houses close to the hospital for families to stay in, and offers assistance with paying the huge medical bills. In filling this important need, McDonald's also created a tremendously powerful and proprietary charity for the McDonald's Corporation.

But sometimes, companies create non-profit organizations strictly for marketing purposes. The brand group at Procter & Gamble responsible for the introduction of Citrus Hill Plus Calcium Orange Juice founded and paid for a medical organization to promote the benefits of calcium-laced orange juice for women. The official-looking endorsement logo was proudly featured on the side of every carton of Citrus Hill calcium fortified juice.

Ringling Brothers & Barnum and Bailey Circus promote the heartwarming fact that it supports the non-profit Center For Elephant Conservation in Florida. In fact, the Center is not an independent conservation organization, but is wholly owned by Ringling Bros. While the facility does in fact breed elephants and houses the largest herd of Asian elephants in captivity, the Conservatory is not run for completely selfless reasons. It serves as a location to train elephants for the circus and to "retire" performing elephants that are too old to remain on the road.

Is there a rule of thumb that you can use in determining how to select a cause-related organization? Of course; it's one of the secrets of the game!

> ### *Marketing Truth*
>
> *When it comes to charities & non-profits, IMAGE IS EVERYTHING!*
>
> *It doesn't really matter what cause you choose to support. It only matters how you demonstrate the connection. You must use powerful and compelling images.*

Think of the commercials that show starving children in third-world countries. Why are they effective in generating donations? Because the images of these destitute kids are disturbing to us in our comfortable middle-class homes and neighborhoods. Why is the Multiple Sclerosis Telethon able to generate millions of dollars each year? Because the program is laced with images of young children struggling with the crippling effects of the disease. The telethon intertwines hope for a cure with the devastation caused by the disease, driving the viewer to do the only thing he can think of to help; pick up the phone and pledge a contribution.

Product Placement: Hooray For Hollywood

Every day in LA, young men and women step off the bus from small town USA in search of Hollywood dreams. All their lives they've aspired to be movie stars. They've heard the success stories -- how Sandra Bullock was working as a secretary before landing her starring role in *Speed*. They know that it only takes one break and they can start picking out a spot for their star on the Hollywood Walk of Fame.

Many marketing managers share the dreams of these young actors. They believe that to separate their brand from the competitive pack, they should hitch their wagon and go to Hollywood. They know it only takes one measly break to make their brand a star. One lucky placement, and they could be the next Reese's Pieces.

The Legend of Reese's Pieces

ET, The Extra-Terrestrial did more than simply break every existing theatrical record; it also reinvented the rules of product placement marketing. In case your memory is a little rusty, I'll remind you that one of the many charming quirks of Steven Spielberg's lovable alien was a newly acquired love of Reese's Pieces candies. His enthusiasm was contagious. As soon as the movie hit theaters, kids began clamoring for the peanut butter and chocolate morsels. Stores couldn't keep them in stock. Every last bag disappeared as soon as shipments arrived. But here's the real surprise. Spielberg's team originally went to M&M's for product, but they turned them down. Running out of time, the producers ran to the store, bought some Reece's Pieces, and filming continued.

The sudden interest caught Reese's management by surprise, and they scrambled to adjust production schedules to make more candy. The movie exposure put the brand on the map. Before the alien started chomping away, Reese's Pieces was a guppy in the candy ocean. Overnight it became a whale. To this day the brand enjoys halo effects with consumers from that promotional tie-in over a two decades later.

The Product Placement Casino

Unfortunately, it's not always that easy to make it in Hollywood. Just as 99% of young actors end up waiting tables in restaurants instead of acting, most product placements don't generate much publicity for the brand. Yet knowing that the deck is stacked against them doesn't stop many brands from continuing to shell out big bucks to put their products in movies and TV shows. Each brand manager believes that the next product placement they make will be another "Reese's Pieces" success story -- ensuring their personal marketing legacy for time and eternity.

The truth of the matter is product placement in movies is a crapshoot. You have to roll 7's twice to come up a winner. The first and most problematic gamble is the bet that the movie will be a success at the box office. Despite all the hype and star power, some movies just flat out stink. There isn't any way to predict a clunker. Just about any movie looks good on paper and in the trailers that promote the film. Yet few generate over $100 million in box office sales, the minimum standard by which a film can be classified a huge success.

The second gamble relating to movie placement is how much exposure your brand will actually receive in the final edit, and in what context. When the studio pitches a film, it describes how your product will be used and by what star. The studio pitchmen lead you to believe that the movie's most climatic moment involves the lead star dramatically clutching a bottle of Coca-Cola, gulping gratefully and remarking "Wow, Coke in a glass bottle. It always tastes better in glass".

But pitchmen don't make the films. It's always the director's discretion to shoot the scene any way he or she sees fit. Most of the time, what you've been pitched and sold isn't exactly what shows up in the film. And even if the scene runs as planned, more often than not the scene blows right by and doesn't affect consumers in any meaningful way.

Theatrical Release Promotions

Given these high risks, it is far too chancy to create a promotion concept around a *movie product placement*. However, many brands, often fast-food chains, have found avenues for creating promotions tied to a movie's *theatrical release*.

Movie tie-ins cost big bucks. The studios view the partnerships as free advertising for their film, so they demand millions of dollars of advertising commitments behind all promotional partnerships. Thankfully, it's easy to know what to do when approached with a theatrical movie opportunity. It's one of the secrets of the game:

Marketing Truth

There are three words to remember when afforded the opportunity to promote your brand or product with the theatrical release of a movie: Don't Do It!

Notice the emphasis is on theatrical release. If you want to win in Hollywood, the surest way is to wait for the DVD / Blu-ray release. By the time a film comes to home video, you have all the information you need in hand to make an informed decision -- box office dollar totals, demographic information, sales projections, licensed products success and more. I know it's not as exciting as a big screen premiere, but video tie-ins are far less risky and far more predictable than theatrical promotions. You can be pretty sure you'll get what you pay for with a video promotion. There's no guarantee with theatrical.

TV Show Product Placement

Integrating consumer products or retailers into TV show content is becoming a huge business. Given the proliferation of Digital Video Recorders and their ability to skip commercials, many brands are now finding success by integrating their products into the TV Show content.

Coca-Cola and Ford both have successfully used "American Idol" with Coke's "Red Room" and Ford's weekly TV commercial that features all the young singers. Travelocity effectively uses "The Amazing Race" to showcase its lawn gnome and gives free trips to winners of each leg of the competition. Dozens of home-makeover shows leverage product placement, from appliances to doors to windows. All of these are much more effective ways to get your product noticed and not forgotten in a: 30 second TV ad.

Consumers like TV promotions! Almost 50% of Twitter users tweet about the TV show they are watching. ABC Network in May 2012 introduced a new social media site just for the ABC drama "Revenge", which was used to give away a trip to the Hamptons for the summer.

Marketing Truth

To successfully leverage a TV alliance, create a Watch N Win game linked to game pieces found on your product packaging to drive sales!

Special event TV programs such as *The Miss USA Pageant, The Country Music Awards* or *The Academy Awards* are also great vehicles with which to create a partnership. Any cosmetic or personal hygiene product targeted at women would be crazy not to put together an alliance with the major beauty pageants!

Major Concert Tours

Most big name acts sell the sponsorship of their concert tours in exchange for a number of complimentary tickets to each performance, signage and "mention" on ticket stubs and during the show. The sponsor is also usually allowed the rights to use the musicians and their music in advertising. Buying into a partnership with a major act is a great way to differentiate your brand and steal the personality of the performers and the emotions of their music for your benefit. The key to success with concert tours, like major sporting events, is being vigilant to concentrate your marketing efforts outside the arena, in national advertising and promotion.

VISA did an incredible job of leveraging the Elton John USA tour a few years ago. They promoted the sponsorship in credit card statements, in a broad scale advertising campaign, and in print media. Budweiser sponsors

The Rolling Stones every time they tour the USA. Bud has created numerous ads around the band, and even use the trademark Rolling Stones "tongue" in campaigns not specifically linked to the group's tour. Budweiser tries to closely link the freewheeling fun and energy of the band within its brand personality in a number of forms of consumer communications.

A benefit of allying with musicians is the ability to hone in and specifically target the demographic appeal of the act in order to craft an effective promotional plan. For example, if you were a brand manager for a product that has a youthful cutting edge brand personality like Mountain Dew soft drink, you wouldn't want to hitch your wagon with the 70's rock group *Chicago*. However if you are managing Dockers jeans, a tie-in with *Chicago* might be right on target with baby-boomers. Musicians usually appeal to very specific demographics, allowing you to zero in with your message and hit the target with your promotion.

The most notable and meaningful differentiation in allying with musicians is the ability to use their music in your advertising. Great music can make an emotional connection and create a bridge like no other art form.

There are both good and bad side effects to sponsoring concert tours. The good is that they run for several months, allowing you to change your execution along the way to get smarter and smarter about how you promote your brand tie-in to consumers. The bad is that they run for several months -- one city at a time. Your marketing campaign becomes a series of local marketing efforts in lieu of one big national effort, increasing the manpower requirements and the cost in order to pull it off effectively.

Another major drawback to concert tours is that the consumer must buy a ticket to attend the show in order to see the majority of your marketing efforts. Even with acts that attract 20,000 fans to a performance, it's a minuscule percentage of the population in a given city, especially in major metropolitan areas like Los Angeles or New York.

Marketing Truth

If your brand is lacking a personality, borrow one from a musician and their music. If you hang around with popular acts, people will think your brand is popular too!

Getting Outside The Box

The trick when creating any strategic alliance is to build a promotion that will captivate and motivate the consumer to participate -- hopefully through the purchase of your product!

Eric D Schulz

Chapter Nineteen

Sports Sponsorships & Special Events

When I worked for Procter & Gamble, I was asked to evaluate the Hawaiian Punch brand's annual sponsorship of an NHRA Funny Car. The brand was pouring $1.5 million into the race team each year in order to maintain the sponsorship and wanted to be sure it was worth the money. I had only two questions to answer: 1) Does the sponsorship effectively target and motivate Hawaiian Punch consumers, increasing their brand preference and consumption of Hawaiian Punch; and 2) is the brand sales / marketing team effectively leveraging the sponsorship with the Trade and consumers to create advertising and promotions that sell incremental cases of product to justify the annual price tag?

Instinctively I questioned whether drag racing was a good fit for a kid's beverage brand whose target audience was moms with kids ages 2 to 12. But this was supposed to be a quantitative assessment, not a gut reaction, so I met with the manager in charge of the sponsorship to hear his rationale. To my surprise, I found him enthusiastic to the point of near ecstasy about the results. He raved about Trade Hospitality tents at each racetrack and the top-level grocery managers who annually attended the events. He pulled out studies of fans at the racetracks and their awareness of Hawaiian Punch as a car sponsor. He produced dozens of photo albums to show Hawaiian Punch signage at the different racing venues and in impressive retail displays. He proudly carpeted his desk with photos of the Hawaiian Punch Funny Car parked outside grocery stores surrounded by consumers peering into the engine and admiring the paint job.

Going into the interview I had been skeptical about a sponsorship that didn't seem to make a lot of sense; how on earth could drag racing sell more Hawaiian Punch to moms? But as I sat across the table from the manager crowing about the promotion, I wondered if perhaps I had been prejudicing my analysis by the fact that I'm personally not a drag racing fan.

I was hopeful and upbeat following the meeting, and ready to see the Funny Car promotion in action. I booked flights to a few of the cities on the NHRA racing tour, creased the brim of my Hawaiian Punch Funny Car hat and prepared to catch racing fever. But a round of store checks in the very first market quickly cooled my expectations. I was disappointed by the lack of promotional activity outside of the track facility. A few grocery stores were set up with big Hawaiian Punch product displays -- a great photo-op for the local sales rep -- but these were a scant minority of our retail customers. The remaining soft drink retailers I visited gave no indication that an NHRA event was in town or that Hawaiian Punch had anything special going on at all. I began to grow suspicious of the incredible results advertised by the sponsoring brand manager. Clearly, more investigation was required.

I went back to the office and studied case sales by month in each of the markets where the race circuit had traveled over the preceding two years. Consistently, Hawaiian Punch shipments were 20% to 50% higher in each market when the tour came through town. That was great news -- and possible evidence that the promotion was working! Unfortunately, the sales figures in the month AFTER the race told a different story. Without fail, shipments plummeted to nearly nothing, regardless of the market. Hmm. I looked at the salesmen's market reports. The reps would claim huge successes attributed to the NHRA event one month, then lament competitive activity, union strikes or even rainy weather and frog infestations as factors in killing sales the next month.

Frog infestations? Something was beginning to smell fishy. I didn't have to be Sherlock Holmes to deduce that the sales reps were sending huge shipments to the retailer stockrooms during the month of the race to make the sponsorship look good on paper. After the event, the retailers were left with an over-supply of Hawaiian Punch to sell off; they wouldn't need any more product for 4-6 weeks. That was the real reason shipments died in the post-race month.

As I continued the analysis, the hard facts all corroborated that the sponsorship didn't sell more than a few extra cases of Hawaiian Punch each year, and that virtually the entire $1.5 million sponsorship was wasted. As I had initially suspected, the drag racing tie-in didn't convince moms to buy more Hawaiian Punch. Why, then, was the brand manager so personally invested in creating the illusion that it did? Because he was an NHRA racing nut, and it was through his personal interest in drag racing that the sponsorship originally came to be. He was using the brand's money to finance his personal sports fantasy and live out his dream of being a big-time race team owner.

Welcome To Fantasy Island

Unfortunately, the motivation behind Hawaiian Punch's involvement with the NHRA sponsorship is not all that unusual. In fact, fulfilling personal agendas is perhaps the most common reason most sports sponsorships are funded. Sports properties understand the lure of the childhood dream and their sponsorship pitch often sounds like something from *Fantasy Island*: "Here we can make all of your dreams and fantasies come true". Major sports properties actively market personal dream fulfillment for their sponsoring check-writers to entice them to shell out millions upon millions of dollars for sponsorships. The sponsors gladly pay it.

For example, the NASCAR sponsoring pitch doesn't stop at consumer impressions and audience demographics. As a sponsor you get special perks, like attending racecar-driving school and perhaps taking a few practice laps around the track before a big race. NBA teams sweeten the deal by offering major sponsors the chance for photos with the star players on the court, private coach's luncheons, road trips on the team's private plane and VIP treatment at the games complete with white tablecloth dinners at a private dining room inside the stadium. NFL teams ply sponsors with sideline passes, luxury boxes, the ability to attend "closed" practices and premium parking. They even take their top sponsors to the Pro Bowl in Honolulu each January. The list of sponsor privileges associated with any sports property is long and appealing.

Becoming a major sponsor of a sports property using corporate money is a terrific way for any corporate exec to become an instant high-roller, and the sports properties are adept at making anyone with access to large corporate checkbooks feel like he is a bigwig franchise owner.

To Sponsor or Not To Sponsor?

An inside joke that circulates within Coca-Cola is a statement attributed to a senior vice president who was asked how Coke determined <u>*what*</u> and *what not* to sponsor. He stated: "We have a very simple philosophy to follow. If it moves, sponsor it. If it doesn't move, paint it red and slap a Coca-Cola logo on it."

A few years ago, that was a very close description of Coke's sports strategy. Today, even aggressive event sponsors like Coke and Budweiser have taken a step back and developed new thinking about how to best use sports sponsorships to effectively drive sales and enhance consumer brand preference.

Hundreds of corporations shell out millions of dollars each year to attach themselves to sports properties. More often than not, they end up wasting their money. Why? Because often they have purchased the sports sponsorship for the wrong reason. Let's examine some of the popular fallacies offered as rationale to buy into sponsorships.

Fallacy #1:

There is high attendance at the games, so advertising at the stadium is reaching a lot of consumers. If in-stadium advertising is the primary rationale for purchasing a sponsorship package, don't do it. The fans inside a stadium are merely a pimple on an elephant's rear end compared to the vast number of consumers in any given market that you must motivate to move the sales needle. Even if a team claims attendance of a million fans over the course of a season, the vast majority of them are the same people (season ticket holders) coming back again and again.

One popular pro franchise calculated that its 15,000 season ticket holders attended about 80% of the home games each season, so despite a total attendance figure of almost a million fans for the year, only around 250,000 different fannies actually churned the turnstiles. Typically, if you start with the season attendance figures for any sports property and divide by 3, you'll end up with the approximate number of discreet individuals who attend the games. This is the figure you should use when determining the advertising effectiveness on a cost per thousand basis. When you run the numbers, you'll quickly realize that in-stadium advertising is not cost competitive with virtually any form of standard media.

A second reason not to advertise in stadiums is the inability to communicate your brand message effectively. Usually your only signage option is a static billboard big enough for your corporate name. Boring. Consumers don't notice and they don't care to see your corporate logo. This is a completely ineffective form of advertising -- in fact, one of the Six Deadly Sins!

Fallacy #2

I'm supporting the hometown team, and consumers like companies that offer support within the community. Quick, somebody grab me a Kleenex, I think I'm getting a little choked up. Please! This sappy reasoning applies only if you live in a small college town like Logan, Utah and spend your money buying a sponsorship of the Utah State Aggies or supporting the high school gymnasium scoreboard fund. If you are entering a partnership with a big-time sports property, consumers know you're doing so for commercial reasons, not as a community rally towel. Besides, many of the teams don't have a whole lot of community spirit themselves, judging from how often they and their players move around.

Fallacy #3

My company is a winner, and by associating with winning sports properties through sponsorship packages, consumers will make the connection! Sorry, but no consumer I've ever met makes that kind of correlation. Have you ever heard anyone say, "Gosh, the so-and-so's are world champions, and that 'Bank of Bigness' is their top sponsor, so I bet they're the best bank." The only people who believe that are the managers inside the bank who popped for the sponsorship -- and are probably admiring the signage from prime sponsor seats!

Fallacy #4

Athletes work hard to achieve greatness. My company works hard to please our customers. My company and this sports property is a sponsorship match made in heaven! Sorry, but Avis has already got the line "We Try Harder" trademarked. The hard work connection is not proprietary. Everybody works hard, so unless your core brand positioning strategy is one in which effort and hard work are consumer benefits or are used as rationale in your "reason why", this line doesn't work.

Fallacy #5

I've looked at Lifestyle Data, and the consumers of my product have a high ranking in being interested in and watching this sport. I'm just going where my consumers are! Whatever they are interested in, our brand is interested in supporting. Lifestyle correlation analysis can be a great starting point for looking at potential sport sponsorships, but should not be used as the final decision maker. Just about every brand I've ever seen shows their consumers are interested in NFL football, NCAA football and basketball, and the NBA. This is a reflection of the sports interests of American society in general, not a unique insight into the minds of purchasers for Hunt's canned tomato paste.

You don't need Simmons data to know that products with a primary purchaser of women ages 18-54 will show high correlations to figure skating, gymnastics, NFL football, college football, the NBA and WNBA. But do you really think that an NFL telecast is the best place to advertise feminine hygiene products? Products with a target audience of men ages 18-54 will skew to the NFL, NBA, college football and basketball, NHL hockey, Major League Baseball and the PGA. But before you jump into an affiliation, think long and hard about how the sponsorship might support your brand positioning. It probably doesn't.

I've seen young marketers work themselves up until they are frothing at the mouth in excitement over correlations in lifestyle data. Just remember, numbers and data tell only part of the story.

Relevance and Brand Linkage

There are very good reasons to buy into sports sponsorships, but to make the decision rationally you must separate yourself from the romance of the sport and consider the property as a unique MEDIA and PROMOTIONAL VEHICLE. Sorry for bursting your bubble, but that's all a sports property is. It's just another media and promotion outlet with a few extra perks built in.

Marketing Truth

When considering whether to buy into a sports sponsorship, ask these three key questions:

> *1) Are a large percentage of my consumers interested in this sport property and can I reach them through it?*
>
> *2) Is there a relevant and rational strategic link between this sport property and my brand positioning statement?*
>
> *3) Will a sponsorship package with this sport property provide an effective and cost competitive media / promotional vehicle?*

Failure to create a relevant and meaningful link between the brand positioning strategy and the sports property is where most brands stumble coming out of the gate. A sponsorship will work effectively only if you have a clear and convincing connection.

Let me demonstrate. Pretend for a moment that you are the marketing manager for John Deere lawnmowers. Let's assume that brand positioning strategy is as follows:

Target Audience: Men ages 25-54 (Homeowners)

Benefit: A John Deere lawnmower will make you and your lawn the envy of the neighborhood.

Compelling Reason Why: That's because John Deere mowers us a patented micro-blade cutting system. Each blade of grass receives not one, but three clean and even razor sharp cuts, which ensures mowing perfection.

All marketing plans, including sports sponsorships, must support this brand positioning strategy. So let's concentrate on sports played outdoors on grass like baseball, football and soccer as potential tie-in partners.

Since virtually all lawnmowers are bought during the spring and summer months, we'll assume you are considering sponsoring Major League

Baseball or Major League Soccer. Your potential strategy for a baseball tie-in is:

Target Audience: Men ages 25-25 (Homeowners)

Benefit: Major League Baseball Teams exclusively use John Deere lawnmowers, because they know that when 50,000 of their fans are coming to the ballpark to cheer, they can trust that John Deere mowers will make the ball field look its very best.

Compelling Reason Why: That's because John Deere mowers us a patented micro-blade cutting system. Each blade of grass receives not one, but three clean and even razor sharp cuts, which ensures mowing perfection and makes major league baseball players proud to step out onto the field of play.

The baseball strategy supports the brand positioning strategy, and does it with a meaningful and relevant link to baseball -- not with the game, but with the lawn the game is played on! This strategy strikes the consumer cord, because the grass at ballparks are always mowed with beautiful straight lines that make guys sitting in the stands wish their lawns could look that good. It is a solid strategic platform from which to build a terrific sponsorship plan.

Keep your John Deere brand manager hat on for a moment longer. You just received a pitch from the Committee from the college football Fiesta Bowl to become that New Year's Day college football game title sponsor. Just think, the game could be called "The John Deere Fiesta Bowl". Lots of TV coverage. What do you think? Should you go for it? Think about it before reading on and see if you can figure out a few reasons either pro or con.

Hopefully, you can see that the right answer is . . . Don't even consider it. First, you are the marketing manager for John Deere lawnmowers, not the John Deere Company, so your job is to promote the mowers and not just the company name. Second, while the game is played in Phoenix on a grass field, it falls on January 1st, not anywhere close to the buying season for lawnmowers or any other John Deere product (Spring / Summer). If you want to win the marketing game, you must concentrate your marketing efforts when consumers are out buying product, not during the off-season. Just how successful are Christmas ornament sales in July?

It Costs A Lot More Than You Think!

After the creation of a relevant and meaningful strategic platform, the second critical task is the development of a marketing plan -- how you plan to utilize the sponsorship to affect consumers and generate sales.

The marketing plan objectives should:

1. Increase consumer brand preference;
2. Outline how the brand sales / marketing team will effectively leverage the sponsorship with the Trade and consumers to create advertising and promotions that sell incremental product units to "pay out" the sponsorship price tag.

Many companies assume the money they shell out for sponsorship rights makes up the bulk of their promotional spending. They're wrong. Here's another big secret:

Marketing Truth

To effectively use a sports sponsorship, plan to spend another $8.00 to $10.00 (for every dollar spent on the sponsorship) to create advertising, trade promotions, consumer promotions, and PR events to effectively move the sales needle and influence consumers.

This secret is the key to avoiding wasted sponsorship spending. Most companies don't budget much else beyond the sponsorship fees, so they can't effectively take advantage of the rights they've purchased. They nickel and dime the promotions on the back end, where the real sales opportunity lies.

Takin' It To The Streets

To make a sport sponsorship worth its price tag, you have to move it out of the narrow reach of the sports venue and into the big wide-open consumer marketplace. Unless your product is sold inside the arena, spending more than about 30 seconds thinking about what happens within those walls is spending too much time. What happens at the venue is pretty much inconsequential to the big picture -- it's just advertising, and limited advertising at that. What you should spend your time thinking is about how to use the sponsorship to create better packaging, bigger in-store displays, and more powerful consumer and trade promotions. That's where you make your money!

Marketing Truth

> *Develop your marketing plan BEFORE you buy a sponsorship to ensure that you will have the contractual rights to execute a plan that builds your sales.*

Once you have signed your sponsorship deal, the sports property has you cornered. They have your money and they are moving on to other checkbooks. If you don't lock down the rights you'll need to execute your big ideas <u>before</u> you ink the agreement, you'll never get the authorization to do anything new and different.

I was stuck in just that predicament with USA Basketball when I worked for Coca-Cola. Sprite had purchased a sponsorship of USA Basketball that was very restrictive in sponsor rights. For the USA Men's Dream Team, I wanted to create a promotion that would allow Sprite consumers the chance to get up-close with the team -- to "Hang With The Dream Team". My wild idea was to run consumer promotions in several countries where winners would come to the USA and be Honorary Assistant Coaches of the team -- attending a private Dream Team practice, getting pictures and autographs with the players, and then sitting on the team bench at a game, with Dream Team Head Coach Lenny Wilkins allowing the winners to select the starting lineup at the beginning of each half.

So we pitched the promotion to the NBA and USA Basketball, they of course hated the idea and said "No way". We had already signed our sponsorship deal, so they had no incentive to say yes. To them, it looked like a lot of extra work for money they already had in the bank.

I really wanted to run the promotion, so I circumvented USA Basketball and the NBA and signed Lenny Wilkins (the Head Coach of the Dream Team) to a personal services contract <u>prior</u> to his being named the Dream Team Coach, giving me the rights to execute the promotion through him. Since my contract was with Coach Wilkins and signed before he was named head coach, USA Basketball could do nothing to stop me. I changed the name of the promotion to "Hang With The Coach" and took out the part about the fans selecting the starting lineups (to appease the vehement protests of USA Basketball), but other than that, the promotion was executed as I had envisioned. It was an incredible international success involving consumers from Mexico, Australia, Germany, and Japan. Sprite volume grew by double-digits during the promotional period.

<u>Marketing Truth</u>

Don't simply accept a ready-made sponsorship package offered by the sports property; develop the package to support YOUR ideas that will drive YOUR sales. You have to tell the sports property what rights you need in your package.

Building A Comprehensive Marketing Plan

To illustrate how a comprehensive sports property marketing plan can work to achieve outstanding results, let me share with you the plan executed by Coca-Cola in support of the 1996 Summer Olympic Games. This far-reaching marketing effort was the largest campaign ever undertaken by any Company in world history, with global marketing spending of around $400 million. The sponsorship cost was $40 million, so Coca-Cola roughly spent $10.00 in marketing costs for every $1.00 paid in sponsorship fees.

It seems incomprehensible that a marketing effort this expensive could ever generate enough incremental sales volume to justify the spending, but it did. Results of the campaign were outstanding. In the eight month window in which Olympic promotions were executed, global Coca-Cola volume rose +9%, overall corporate profits rose +22%, and Coke's stock price increased +32%. How did we do it?

First, we built a solid strategic platform. The campaign was entitled "FOR THE FANS", suggesting that drinking Coca-Cola refreshed the fans of the Olympic Games and renewed their Olympic Spirit. The relevant and meaningful connection between Coca-Cola and the Olympics was between the product and the fans: "Cheering Was Thirsty Work." Drinking ice-cold, refreshing Coca-Cola would help keep the fans in good voice to cheer for their national athletes and local heroes.

This strategy positioned the brand as it should -- in the stands and in homes, refreshing everyday consumers as they enjoyed watching the Olympics. It wasn't about the athletes. The advertising and promotional materials all featured fans of the Games in realistic situations -- cheering for their athletes and enjoying the events surrounding the Olympic Games.

Since the strategy was "fan" focused, all pieces of the marketing plan needed to support the concept that Coca-Cola would refresh / enhance / add enjoyment to the Olympic experience for everyday consumers throughout the world. We hoped that when the Olympic Games were over and the flame extinguished, consumers would turn off their TV's, lean back in their barc-o-lounger chairs and say, "I really enjoyed these Olympic Games, and Coca-Cola was a big part of that." We didn't expect them to say it out loud, naturally, but that's the impression we wanted to leave.

Starting with the "for the fans" positioning, we began to search for powerful, innovative ways of extending the positioning into consumer venues, both at the Games and in their homes.

Marketing Truth

The marketing plan must include "big" ideas that can be used anywhere, but must also allow for the development of local and customer-specific customized programs.

Some of the big ideas from the corporate Olympic Marketing Group included:

> Distribution of 35 million Olympic Ticket Application Booklets in the USA via Coca-Cola product displays, resulting in an 8%

volume increase for Coca-Cola classic during May 1995. This gave all fans in the United States an equal chance to order Olympic tickets and attend the Games. It was supported with a consumer promotion on Coca-Cola 12-pack cartons offering families the chance to win Free Trips to the Olympic Games.

"Who Would You Choose To Carry The Olympic Flame", a global consumer sweepstakes to nominate fans for selection to be an official Olympic Torchbearer in the 1996 Olympic Torch Relay.

The 1996 Olympic Torch Relay, presented by Coca-Cola. This 84-day journey across the USA provided the ability for local Coca-Cola bottlers to execute grassroots marketing in the over 1,500 cities, towns and villages along the relay route. It allowed 2,500 Coca-Cola consumers the opportunity to carry the Olympic flame as it wound its way towards Olympic Stadium. Torch Relay promotions were executed in 65 foreign countries in addition to the USA.

The creation of Coca-Cola Olympic City, a $29 million dollar high-tech Olympic theme park in downtown Atlanta. This attraction let consumers feel what it was like to be an Olympic Champion, allowing them to "virtually" compete against Olympic stars. It gave fans an understanding of just what amazing feats of athleticism it takes to set Olympic records, from the long jump to sprinting. Over 650,000 consumers attended Coca-Cola Olympic City in its 100 days of operation.

Coca-Cola Radio brought 75 of the worlds most listened to radio stations to Coca-Cola Olympic City to broadcast live during the Games. Top disc-jockey's from around the globe gave their listeners back home an up-close and personal feel of what it was like to be a fan attending the Olympics, bringing home the fun from Coca-Cola Olympic City.

Coca-Cola Olympic Champions, a series of over 500 personal appearances by current and former Olympic athletes including such notables as Nadia Comaneci, Bart Conner, Pablo Morales,

Evander Holyfield, and dozens more, allowing Olympic fans the opportunity to meet and talk with these notable champions up close and personal.

The second key part of the plan was to translate these "big ideas" down to the local level. Our account managers and sales teams throughout the world created regionalized, and sometimes retailer-customized, promotional extensions that celebrated the personalities and local pride of each market. While Coca-Cola Olympic marketing campaigns were rendered in over 132 countries, no two markets executed the same plan. Each country developed a unique blueprint customized to best address the specific interests and needs of their own "Olympic Fans."

Coke marketing managers in each of the different countries could choose to tap into the "big ideas" or they could pass on them -- the choice was theirs. Each country took into account the interests and aptitudes of their fans to ensure that the plan would be captivating and those consumers would enjoy the Coca-Cola promotions. In Brazil the plan focused on soccer and volleyball; in Thailand the effort was exclusively built around the sport of boxing; in Australia, the focus was swimming and basketball.

Despite the hundreds of different promotional executions throughout the world, the "For The Fans" strategy united all countries behind one Coca-Cola theme and one Coca-Cola creative look. The flexible structure allowed each country to execute promotions in whatever way they saw fit for their fans. It worked.

Marketing Truth

Think Globally. Act Locally. Design your sponsorship program to address both a broad marketing and regionalized interests to extract the most value from your sponsorship rights.

Take Me Out To The Ballgame

Sports properties can be a wonderfully fun and incredibly effective vehicle for marketing your products to consumers, provided you find the right link between your brand and the sports property before buying your sponsorship package.

Special Events

Each year across the country, millions of families attend thousands of special events, from festivals, fairs and celebrations to conventions and sporting events -- and at each event a mob of companies are found hawking their wares. Sponsors camp out on every square inch of free space clamoring for consumer attention, waving banners, offering free samples and prizes. Yet at each of these celebrations, one company tends to dominate the scene, rising above the throng. Most of the time it's Coca-Cola. Coke's preeminence at these events is not coincidental. It is the result of years of practice, practice and more practice to get the system right.

Pre-Planning

Developing a winning special events formula begins with the pre-planning process. I know, you're probably thinking "this isn't Einstein theory, of course it starts with planning!" But what you call planning and what Coke calls planning are two very different things.

Coke begins its planning processes far in advance of the event. For example, when Salt Lake City was selected as the host city for the 2002 Winter Olympic Games in the spring of 1996, Coca-Cola's marketing department had already visited Salt Lake City to scout billboard locations -- BEFORE the bid was announced! Coke locked up all of the prime spots along the interstate highways, close to the airport, sports venues and key hotels, *six years* ahead of the Games. In 1998 their staff began working closely with the Salt Lake Organizing Committee to place Coca-Cola signage in the best locations at the sports venues, to have Coca-Cola product available at all concession areas, and to develop a means to get Coca-Cola banners in as many key locations as possible around the city -- *four years* before the Opening Ceremonies.

While the Olympics are perhaps the most planning-intensive affair on earth, other big league events like the Super Bowl, NCAA Basketball Finals, The Academy Awards, State Fairs and Spring Break also require a great deal of pre-event planning. The development process for these events typically begins as soon as the prior year's event concludes and continues for the 12-month cycle. It begins with an immediate post-mortem of this year's successes and disappointments and brainstorming for the upcoming year, followed by an extensive documentation of the event, which generally takes about two months to write. Next, event officials work with sponsors to develop the new marketing plan, and the process of execution begins in earnest.

Organization

Coca-Cola has dedicated an entire department to special events called "Presence and Signage." Its role is to assign an events specialist to every major special event to oversee both the strategic direction and the mountain of minutiae that goes along with it. The specialist develops the marketing plan, works with local bottlers in the event city and hires contractors and promotional agencies as needed to help execute the plan.

And while corporate headquarters has specialists assigned to the "big" events, each local bottler usually has several individuals within their shop who are event specialists and divide up the hundreds of local events that come into their area each year -- shindigs as small as the Pleasant Grove Strawberry Days celebration to major State Fairs and everything in between.

Coke takes special events seriously. It never wants to see a consumer drinking anything but a Coca-Cola for refreshment at any big event. Walking around a State Fair or cheering at a ballgame is thirsty work, and Coke wants every thirsty consumer to automatically reach for a Coke. This special events strategy is merely a logical extension of the brand's over-arching ubiquity strategy; Coca-Cola refreshment must always be within an arm's reach of desire.

I was at a meeting once with a senior Coke executive who had ascended the ranks from bottler sales rep to corporate vice-president. The meeting invited managers from different corporations to discuss their sponsorship of an upcoming special event and to coordinate efforts. About 200 people were in attendance. As we were settling in to start the day, an attendee from another company walked into the room holding a 32 oz. "Big Gulp" cup with "Pepsi' emblazoned on the side. The Coke executive went nuts.

His face turned bright red and he stormed out of the meeting, refusing to return until the offending cup was removed and a public apology made by the philistine. That's how serious Coke is about dominating events -- including corporate meetings!

Developing A Plan

The event plan addresses five key initiatives that enable Coke to "own" events. Does Coke play fair? Not exactly. Coke will use every tactic at its disposal to achieve its objective. Don't get me wrong, Coca-Cola doesn't do anything underhanded, illegal or immoral, but the behind-the-scenes details are carefully managed and manipulated to ensure that Coca-Cola is first in line for every perk that is available to sponsors at the event, and that Coke receives preferential sponsor treatment. Coke is the 800-pound gorilla at any special event, and it gets to sit wherever it wants.

The five-step plan begins with the development and procurement of all of the possible points of distribution Coca-Cola can have at the event for its beverages. Existing concession stands are first priority. Second is finding new locations where Coca-Cola can erect beverage stations or "hawk" product in and around the event, in effect creating new Coca-Cola concession stands. Third is contacting each and every vendor who will be at the event to ensure that they have a supply of Coca-Cola and Coca-Cola branded cups on hand, especially if they are selling food or beverages. These containers are more than just good signage; they actually drive consumption. If a consumer is hot and tired and sees someone walking around with a Coke cup, it fuels his or her desire for an icy cup of his or her own. Finally, the team searches for locations to install extra vending machines for additional product availability.

Once the quest for beverage locations is exhausted, the attention turns to the second initiative: <u>event signage</u>. Coca-Cola wants consumers to see a Coca-Cola advertisement no matter where they are at the event. If the event will have television coverage, Coke ensures that its sign can be identified in the background. Coca-Cola managers offer free signs and banners to every vendor to use at their locations (of course, the banners have Coca-Cola logos on them). They also canvass the city streets and parking lots around the venue, offering Coca-Cola signs and banners to businesses to extend the Coca-Cola presence beyond the venue boundaries.

An important note: we've already spent a great deal of time discussing why signage at events usually doesn't work to build business. Giant logos typically do nothing to impress consumers. But here's where Coke walks a fine, and brilliant, line. Coke signage is always placed in an area that is either selling the product, so that it actually directs consumers to a purchase, or in a location that represents the center of activity at the event. It is always associated with fun and refreshment -- never just a courtside billboard or incidental backdrop.

This signage strategy is further developed in the third initiative: "brand activation". This is the overall strategy for how Coca-Cola relevantly interacts with fans at the event in a way that will support the brand strategy. Remember, the brand strategy -- refreshment within an arm's reach of desire -- contains two major concepts; refreshment and availability. All brand activation efforts are designed to highlight one or both of these brand attributes.

The methods of execution can vary widely. For example, in many theme parks you'll find a Coca-Cola "Cool Zone", an area where cool mist is squirted from overhead pipes with fans blowing to cool off consumers on a hot day. Folks can step into this oasis and cool their body, buy an ice cold Coca-Cola from the bank of nearby vending machines and emerge totally refreshed, thanks to Coca-Cola. To reinforce its image of being "everywhere that's anywhere," Coke makes itself the center of attention at such major events as at the Calle Ocho Festival in Miami each year. Coke erects a huge performance stage in the middle of the action and hires top-flight Latino entertainers – Shakira, Jennifer Lopez, Santana, Marc Antony and more - to perform. Whatever form it takes, brand activation always focuses on Coke's two primary messages: refreshment and omnipresence.

Next comes hospitality & hosting, the schmoozing part of the package. This is an elaborate plan for Coca-Cola to host and provide special attention to their key customers, including account buyers, bottlers, store managers, restaurant marketing managers and anyone else who might have influence on Coke's success at retail. Coke provides for all the needs of its

VIP guests, including airfare, ground transportation, hotel accommodations, meals, entertainment and event tickets. From the moment the guests step off the plane until the moment they get back on, Coke makes sure that comfort is the catchword. Services include delivering luggage directly to the hotel room; access to special VIP lounges inside the hotel for socializing and free meals; special events for spouses, expensive gift bags . . . and the list goes on. At the event itself, special guests enjoy exclusive Coca-Cola VIP lounges and tents with air conditioning, free food and drinks and entertainment. As one Englishman commented after witnessing the lavishness of the VIP effort, "Kings and Potentates have endured shabbier treatment".

While the impression to the guests is that Coke spares no expense, in reality, every dollar is accounted for. The hospitality and hosting effort is a key component of the event plan that makes sure than every Coca-Cola sponsorship reinforces the brand image not only to the consumer, but to the trade customers as well. If retailers enjoy working with Coca-Cola, they are much more likely to favor the brand in their stores or restaurants. This isn't just theory; it's proven strategy. In the long run, the cost of the hotels and the tents and the gift bags is slim in comparison with an all-out bidding war with Pepsi for the same channels of distribution.

The final piece of the planning process is <u>competitive activity</u>, and here where the Coke team earns its reputation for ruthlessness. During the development of the marketing plan, Coca-Cola sets up a team of marketers to play devil's advocate (the devil being Pepsi) and create a guerrilla ambush plan for the event. The guerrilla team pretends that it works for Pepsi and devises a scheme to infiltrate the event and embarrass Coke. This competitive scenario is incorporated into the marketing plans to ensure that all possible attack points are neutralized before the event takes place.

During the event, Coke sets up swat teams, constantly on the move in and around the event, searching of any signs that the "blue devil" Pepsi or any other soft drink is trying to crash the party. If the swat team spots a competitive threat, even something as seemingly innocent as a lone can of competitive product on a vendor's cart, the Coke police swarm the offender with event managers to seize the offending can, remove it and destroy it. The same fate awaits any offending signage that may crop up. If the sign is posted on event property it is immediately seized. If it is off grounds, the property owner is first approached with an appeal to remove it, then offered incentives to comply. If all else fails, a giant Coca-Cola truck appears to park on the street in front of the sign. Hmm, I wonder how that happened!

Marketing Truth

An effective event-marketing plan requires attention to five key areas:

1. Points of Distribution – *where your product will be available to the public for purchase.*
2. Event Signage – *create a dominant presence*
3. Brand Activation – *creating relevant links to you brand-positioning strategy.*
4. VIP Guest Hosting – *offer special or preferential treatment to your customers.*
5. Neutralize Ambush Threats – *anticipate competitive threats and develop plans to deal with them should they pop up.*

Secrets For Standing Out In A Crowd

Over the years, Coke has managed to develop a huge arsenal of tricks and gimmicks that can cheaply and effectively affect consumers at special events. They are captured by what's known as **THE BIG BANG Theory**:

1. **Big**: Size matters most at special events. The more space you can take up, the more chance consumers will notice you. Height is critical. Try to TOWER over the event, with signage high in the air!

2. **Audacious:** You've got to do something that nobody else is doing. Go over-the-top. Have the spirit of P.T. Barnum!

3. **New**: Dream up something that nobody has ever seen before.

4. **Giggles**: Make me' laugh. They'll remember your name, and your brand, fondly if you gave them some unexpected fun.

The Big Bang Theory doesn't mean you should erect a big tent and put on a circus, but the mental models are closely linked. At most special events, people just walk on by, and you only have a short window of opportunity to "grab 'me." Like the hawkers at carnivals who beckon you to step inside and see the incredible, unbelievable human pretzel lady fold herself into a one-foot cube, you must attract the attention of the consumer to get him to stop and stay awhile.

Coke employed the Big Bang strategy brilliantly during The Olympic Torch Relay. The event unmistakably fit the definition of **BIG**; it traveled cross-country to over 1,500 cities, towns and villages on its 84-day journey. The entourage that accompanied the Olympic Flame covered a full city block, complete with motorcycle police escorts blaring their sirens to draw attention that the flame was approaching!

AUDACIOUS was an understatement. Who else but Coca-Cola would attempt to bring the Olympic Games into all of these different cities, with over 10,000 Coke consumers and "Community Heroes" selected to carry the torch?

The opportunity to watch the Olympic Flame travel down the streets in your hometown was definitely **NEW**, something most consumers have never seen before and probably will never see again.

And the staging of the relay was choreographed to make an indelible impression on those 50 million consumers who lined the streets to watch the flame go by. Ahead of the flame, Coca-Cola employees worked the crowds, warming them up in cheering exercises, passing out miniature American flags, and giving everyone a sticker to wear proudly stating "I Saw The Olympic Flame". By the time the flame arrived, people were raucous, giddy, and filled with a sense of patriotism, meeting the criteria of The Big Bang Theory™ for **GIGGLE!**

Of course, just because Coke spent millions of this event doesn't mean you have to go broke to be a player. Creativity is often an effective substitute for cash. Using few dollars and a little imagination, Hawaiian Punch created a terrific stir at Miami's Calle Ocho event. Calle Ocho is an event like no other in the world. It is a two-day Cuban festival held each spring on 8th street in Miami, a straight, five-mile stretch of road. Vendors line the streets selling everything imaginable. Stages with live entertainment are positioned every few blocks, sponsored by different corporations or brands. Coke and Budweiser are everywhere, with their trucks parked in the road about every 300 yards. Over one million consumers pack onto 8th Street to enjoy the festival. It is wall-to-wall people for as far as the eye can see!

Hawaiian Punch realized it could not compete against the huge budgets of Coke and Budweiser and other sponsors to make a splash at this event, so it decided to focus their Calle Ocho efforts strictly against their target: kids. In a modest roadside tent, Hawaiian Punch managers passed out ice-cold cans of Hawaiian Punch to kids for sampling along with oversized helium-filled balloons tied on a 6-foot string. The balloons were Hawaiian Punch red and sported the brand's logo with the brand character "Punchy". Kid's loved them, and they reinforced the brand identity and the spirit of youthful fun. After about 2 hours of dispensing balloons, the Hawaiian punch team could look out at the sea of one million consumers and see Hawaiian Punch balloons floating above the crowd up and down the festival route. Hawaiian Punch was the only event sponsor passing out helium balloons, and the effect was stunning! Everyone saw the balloons, and every kid wanted one. The brand beat Coke at its own game for the price of a few tanks of helium and some big red balloons.

Grassroots Events

The NBA knows that its core audience is made up many who like to play pick up basketball games in playgrounds, churches, on driveways and in gymnasiums. To effectively reach these consumers through special events marketing, the NBA created a traveling event called "NBA Hoop It Up", a three-on-three basketball tournament that sets up on a city street with hundreds of participating teams.

To attract all skill levels, the teams are sorted into divisions:

Top Gun: College experience or better and those who can hang with 'em.

Competitive: Better than your average person, but not quite Top Gun.

Recreational: For those who play just for fun.

Couch Potato: Your usual basketball gear is drinks, pizza and the remote.

Young Guns: Kids with an average age between 11 and 17; play with kids your same age and height.

Up & Comers: All players on the team must be between 8 & 10 years old.

Older Than Dirt: Special division for teams with average ages of 40 or over.

The event is held over a two-day period, with dozens of basketball hoops set up in the street for simultaneous games. The event is sponsored nationally, regionally and locally, and each team pays an entry fee. NBA Hoop It Up is a terrific way that brand uses special events to relevantly reach its target audience and support the brand positioning of the NBA.

Ambush Marketing

Special events are magnets for immoral marketers to try and crash the party without paying for a sponsorship, an act known as "ambush marketing" or sometimes called "guerrilla marketing" or "stealth marketing". In all cases, companies who employ such tactics are wrong to do it. Sponsorship dollars paid to the event coordinators are necessary to stage the event and to make it worthwhile for consumers. Marketers who try to circumvent the system and crash the party without paying for the sponsorship rights to do so are no better than common thieves. I've seen marketing managers who have executed ambush tactics sit back, grin and brag about their so-called "brilliance". Ambush marketing is not brilliant marketing. If you haven't bought a ticket to attend a game, you shouldn't try to get in.

I don't want to dignify the efforts of those immoral companies that regularly use such tactics by describing any stories of their efforts. Suffice to say that companies that execute this type of marketing are not ones that I care to promote or discuss within this book.

Creating Your Own Special Events

Retailers often create their own special events to draw consumers to their store locations. Parking lot sales and carnivals, cheap food and beverages are the usual tactics. Some companies also opt to create their own special events for consumers. In an earlier chapter I talked about the rousing success Oscar Meyer has achieved with its touring Oscar Meyer Wienermobile. The brand effectively uses this tactic to drive home the key to their positioning strategy that kids love Oscar Meyer wieners. Movie studios regularly use "Premiere" events to launch new movies. Brands that sponsor NASCAR racing teams often use the cars as bait to lure consumers to retailer locations to see the cars. With all of these success stories to point at, one might wonder if it's worthwhile to create your own events.

Usually, the answer is no. Creating your own special event is a time consuming and expensive proposition. Unless you can dream up an idea that is truly brilliant (like the Wienermobile), or dead-on strategy (such as NBA Hoop It Up) chances are you'll regret having spent time, energy and money behind creating it.

I learned this lesson the hard way when I squandered nearly a quarter-million dollars on an idea I developed for Hawaiian Punch that took its inspiration from the Wienermobile. I created the "Hawaiian Punch Surfmaster", a hydraulic surfing machine mounted in the back of a pickup truck. The vision was that kids would climb on the surfboard, get strapped into the "life jacket", and the ride would begin. While surfer music blared, the board would rock from side to side. The rider would have to get into "surf" position in order to stay balanced on the board. If his foot slipped off the side or if he lost balance, the life jacket would snap into a locked position so that the child couldn't fall, and a stream of water would come gushing from the framework around the truck, soaking the rider while the music blared the 60's song "Wipe Out" and the voiceover "How Bout A Nice Hawaiian Punch". A fun, interactive concept, and right on brand strategy!

The grand plan was to take Surfmaster to two grocery stores each day for a 3-hour event. The store would simply agree to put up a display of Hawaiian Punch in order to earn a Surfmaster appearance. We built the machine, bought a brand new truck and customized it with a great "Hawaiian Punch" Surfmaster paint job, hired two surfer dude college-aged kids to drive the truck and "emcee" the events, and we were ready to go -- or so we thought. We soon discovered a few sharks in the promotional waters.

First, the Surfmaster had to endure extensive safety testing. Then the kids we'd hired to run it had to pass drug tests. Then the corporate insurance department had to decide whether or not to self-insure or buy event insurance. We had to develop custom point-of-sale materials to promote the events.

Finally, we had to schedule the stores for appearances. WIPE OUT. We had taken the word of our sales force that Surfmaster would be a "Big Idea", but nobody had actually checked with a few store managers to see if having the "Hawaiian Punch Surfmaster" was something they'd want at their locations. We began soliciting stores and came up empty. Store managers didn't want it taking up space in their parking lot. We offered Surfmaster to over 300 different stores in the Southern California market, and only six signed up to take it. As a backup plan, we tried touring it to elementary school's and junior high schools during lunch breaks, but school administrators would call police and have us shut down. After three months of operation, the Surfmaster went to its watery grave.

Local TV and Radio Special Event Promotions

The best way to get involved with special events is to link with existing events with a proven track record, like tailgate parties in the fall. Another great resource is local radio stations and TV stations. Most have long-standing annual events that they stage in their local communities with which you can easily tie-in.

The best thing about TV / Radio special events is that there is plenty of media weight to drive consumer awareness. The stations don't want to be embarrassed in their own hometowns, so they promote, promote and promote some more to make sure a big crowd will be there.

Marketing Truth

Holiday events such as the 4th of July Fireworks and Holiday light shows are terrific special events with built-in audience appeal.

Relevant Brand Linkage Is Key

The most important consideration when assessing special events opportunities is how your participation can relevantly link to the event in a unique, "own able" way that supports your brand positioning strategy and sells your product. The trick is to make it fun for consumers -- be imaginative and dream up something wonderful! Be like Captain Kirk and the crew of the Starship Enterprise and "Go where no man has gone before!"

Chapter Twenty

Licensing

Wouldn't it be great to own a business where people sent you money, and all you had to do was walk down to the mailbox in your pink fluffy slippers and collect the checks? Unless you look good in an orange jumpsuit and like the idea of long-term roommates, you'll have to rule out running a Mafia family or engineering illegal pyramid schemes. So what does that leave you with? The next best thing: licensing.

Licensing, as a business is lucrative, relatively easy to maintain, and best of all, legal. When you own a coveted trademark that other companies will pay for the right to use, you can receive checks in the mail on a regular basis for very little effort. A pretty cool gig if you can get it. But many marketers are intimidated by the world of licensing, which exists just outside the borders of conventional marketing. They haven't had much hands-on experience, and they don't understand the rules of the game. Their ignorance often leads to missed opportunities and lost profits.

How Licensing Works

In its most basic form, a *licensor* (someone who holds the trademarks to something) sells another party -- who is called a *licensee* -- the right to use the licensor's logos, brand names, characters or other proprietary words or images for a specific purpose. The licensee usually pays the licensor a minimum guarantee, plus royalties on every item they sell using the licensor's trademark. I know this sounds a bit confusing, so let's use an example to clear it all up.

Let's say that you own the World Clock Company. Your research has shown that there is an unmet consumer demand for office wall clocks featuring the logo of Apple. Since Apple owns its own trademark rights, you can't just slap their logo on a clock without getting hit with a lawsuit, so you contact the Apple licensing attorney to negotiate a licensing agreement that would allow your company to manufacture and sell a wall clock featuring the Apple logo. Apple is the licensor. World Clock is the licensee.

In a typical licensing agreement, the licensee pay a small up-front fee (which varies by category), plus a royalty (roughly 15% of sales, depending on the deal) to Apple for each Apple-logo clock that World Clock sells. In the contract, Apple imposes a minimum performance guarantee, which means that World Clock must guarantee to sell a minimum number of Apple clocks each year (the number is specified in the contract) in order to keep the license valid. If World Clock fails to sell the minimum number of clocks, the license becomes null and void, and the rights to sell and manufacture wall clocks bearing the Apple logo revert back to Apple, which they could then license to someone else. This minimum sales guarantee protects the interest of Apple to ensure that World Clock actively tries to sell its clocks once they are licensed to do so.

Apple also imposes a clause for "creative approval", meaning that it must approve the design of the clock before World Clock begins manufacturing and sale. This supervisory right ensures that the licensee uses the trademark correctly on the product and in all advertising. Apple not only checks for correct colors, images and copy, but also for proper context – you can't have the Apple logo swallowing a Microsoft logo, for example.

Protecting World Clock's interests, the agreement contains a "non-compete" clause, which means Apple cannot license their trademark to any other wall clock manufacturers. The agreement will probably also specify that Apple must agree to display and sell the clock in their Apple stores and through their web store at apple.com.

Of course, since lawyers are involved, the actual licensing contract is long, complicated and horribly detailed, but those are the basics of a typical licensing agreement.

Why License Your Trademarks?

As a licensor who owns a marketable trademark, each query from a potential licensee brings you to a fork in the road: to sell, or not to sell, that is the question. Keeping the trademark -- manufacturing and selling the goods yourself -- is much more lucrative than settling for a licensing fee, since you make 100% of the profits instead of a 15% royalty fee. Intuition and greed will lead you to think that unless you simply cannot make and sell the product yourself, you should never license away your trademarks. But your intuition may be wrong.

Let's look at the math to see how the financials stack up in a "make it myself" versus "license it away" scenario. Going back to the Apple clocks as the example, take the point of view of the Apple licensing attorney:

	Apple Makes It	World Clock License
Wholesale Price	$12.99	$12.99
Cost To Produce	$8.79	$7.79
Gross Profit	$4.20	$5.20
OVERHEAD:	$ 2.33*	$ N/A
NET PROFIT:	**$1.87**	**$ 1.94****

*Overhead calculated as 18% of sales

**Licensing royalty equals 15% of wholesale price

Whoa Nellie! There are two key issues to flag. One is the cost to produce the clocks. Since Apple isn't in the clock business, it will have to hire a contract manufacturer to make the clocks. The contract manufacturer must make a profit, so Apple will end up paying more to make the clock than World Clock will pay to produce it in-house.

The second key issue is OVERHEAD. If Apple chooses to manufacture and sell the clocks, it must incur the costs of having someone manage the process, act as a sales force, process orders and ship the clocks. Since it will have to manufacture a number of clocks at one time in order to hold down the unit manufacturing cost, Apple will have to invest money into inventory -- the cost of the clocks sitting in the warehouse waiting to be shipped. The Apple accountants will also charge "carrying costs", the interest cost of the money invested in the inventoried clocks.

After looking at the potential finances, the option of "make it myself" doesn't look too appealing for Apple compared with "licensing it away" and collecting royalty checks. This example illustrates why licensing is a big business! *Unless you own the retail channel of sale so that you can claim both the manufacturer's profit and the retailer profit, it is much easier and almost as lucrative to license a trademark away as it is to keep it and deal with the added burdens of manufacturing, sales, inventory, and carrying costs.*

Marketing Truth

It is better to license your trademarks away and collect royalty checks from others with expertise in selling within their category than attempt to conquer a new product category on your own.

Procter & Gamble learned this lesson the hard way several years ago after it acquired the soft drink brand Orange Crush. P&G didn't have any expertise in the soft drink category, which is a highly competitive category with Coca-Cola and Pepsi being the two large players.

Typically, the owners of smaller soft drink brands (such as Orange Crush), cobble together licensing deals with Coke or Pepsi bottlers across the USA and have them produce and distribute their product. But P&G decided that it would instead manufacture the soft drinks and use their own shipping methods to get the products to stores. Bad move. Within 6 months the brand lost virtually all its distribution, as Coke / Pepsi flexed their muscles with the trade and convinced retailers to drop Crush. Shortly thereafter, P&G tried to go back to the Coke / Pepsi bottlers to do licensing deals, but most refused out of spite. After nine years of getting beat up, P&G finally sold the brand to Cadbury Schweppes.

General Foods made the same mistake when it created the hugely popular Jell-O Pudding Pops. General Foods owned no brands in the frozen confection (ice cream) category. They didn't have any expertise in shipping frozen foods. But instead of licensing the brand to someone like Popsicle (who also makes Fudgecicles and Creamsicles, and had the expertise in manufacturing and delivery), they tried to do it on their own by contract manufacturing the products and contracting the shipping / local delivery of products to stores. With all the extra hands grabbing profits out of the product manufacturing and delivery chain, General Foods lost money on every Pudding Pop it sold. After growing the brand to over $350 million a year in annual sales, they finally killed it, dashing the dreams of millions of children in the process.

The Mickey Mouse Licensing Company

Disney is the king of licensing. The Consumer Products division of the Company earns over $40 billion dollars each year. The sales are generated between two different areas: <u>Disney owned properties</u> such as the theme parks and The Disney Stores, and non-Disney retail outlets, which in effect is <u>everywhere else</u>.

The way that Disney approaches its consumer products business is pure genius. With the retail channels of distribution that Disney owns -- such as the Disney theme parks, The Disney Stores and the Studio Store -- Disney contract manufactures and sells the products in these locations, capturing full profits. You will find very little licensed product in these "captive" locations. In retail distribution channels Disney does not own, nearly all Disney products get there via licensees, and Disney just collects a royalty check. This strategy allows the Mouse to maximize its profits.

To dimensionalize the opportunity, let's look again at the clock example, and pretend it's a Disney clock this time. The first column is a clock Disney makes and sells in its theme parks. The second column is a clock licensed and sold in all other non-Disney retailers:

	Disney Clocks	**Licensee Clocks**
Retail Price	$24.99	$19.99
Wholesale Price	N/A	$12.99
Cost To Produce	$8.79	$7.79
Gross Profit	$16.20	$5.20
OVERHEAD:	4.49	$ N/A
NET PROFIT:	**$11.71**	**$ 1.94****

*Overhead calculated as 18% of sales

**Licensing royalty equals 15% of wholesale price

Again there are nuances to the financials, notably the retail price. Disney theme parks can charge more for virtually the same item because it controls the sales environment in its retail establishments. Consumers expect to pay more for an item at Disneyland or inside The Disney Store, but the ambiance and impulse to buy is too strong to walk away, especially from an "exclusive" item.

Another key Disney strategy is product development. When you spot a particular item at The Disney Store or in a theme park, you won't find it anywhere else. Disney only produces products in its exclusive channels that are not available in any other non-Disney retail channel. This strategy prevents consumers from price comparison shopping or thinking that they can go buy the item cheaper at Target. If you spotted the item in a Disney-owned outlet, you won't see it at any other retailer.

In all non-Disney owned retail outlets, hundreds of different licensees do the actual manufacturing and selling of the Disney products. Disney licensed merchandise is sold in virtually every product category imaginable, from towels and sheets to toys and treats. And that's not just a U.S. phenomenon. In fact, 58% of Disney's consumer product sales come from international operations! There's all Beauty and no Beast in this business. Lots of money and no risk. The Mouse just sits back and collects the checks from the licensees who do all the work! The one-two punch in Disney's retail strategy makes it the strongest retail brand in the world.

When You Should Consider Licensing

There are right ways and wrong ways to get into the licensing business.

> ### *Marketing Truth*
>
> *Licensing makes the most sense when your company already manufactures and distributes products <u>and has excess manufacturing capacity</u>. Through licensing a new trademark, you can expand your business within your existing product category, increase manufacturing efficiency, and lower YOUR products overall costs. Licensing should not be used to try to break into new product categories in which you do not have manufacturing and distribution capability.*

Hallmark Cards has executed this strategy brilliantly. As the world's largest purveyor of greeting cards, it annually has to create thousands upon thousands of high-quality card designs to address all occasions in which a consumer might be in need of a greeting card. Hallmark was faced with a dilemma: just how many cards can you make using only flowers and generic illustrations? The answer: not enough to satisfy all consumers' needs. By shrewdly acquiring licenses -- Peanuts characters (Charlie Brown, Snoopy, Woodstock and pals), Winnie the Pooh, Garfield, and others -- Hallmark has used licensing to do exactly what it does best; creating new greeting card product lines that peacefully co-exist with their basic non-licensed greeting cards. This integrated strategy offers the consumer a breadth of selection that guarantees that there is a card available for nearly any sentiment or occasion.

When I worked at P&G, we had an incredible idea for a new licensed product line that unfortunately never made it off the ground, but the story is one worth recounting. Our idea focused on the Duncan Hines brand. Duncan Hines primary business is cake mixes, cookie mixes, and frosting. The brand has several manufacturing facilities dispersed nationwide and a retail distribution network that reaches nearly 90% of all grocers -- a perfect scenario for expanding the business through intelligent licensing.

We had nearly 30% excess capacity in the manufacturing facilities of the cookie mix business and looked for a way to expand beyond Duncan Hines branded sugar cookies, chocolate chip cookies and peanut butter cookies through licensing. In our consumer research, we discovered that consumers had a high regard for several fresh baked cookie brands such as Mrs. Field's Cookies. Most moms expressed a high interest and desire in baking a cookie at home that tasted the same as the "mall" cookie stores.

We met with Debbie Fields and the licensing attorneys for Mrs. Field's Cookies in Park City, Utah, with a concept to license the rights to her name to create a new co-branded premium line of cookie mixes. Duncan Hines would call the product line "Mrs. Field's Home Recipe Cookies". These mixes would bake into great tasting cookies similar to the ones you buy inside a Mrs. Field's store. Debbie loved the idea, and came up with another great idea for a kid's targeted line called "Mrs. Field's Kid's Cookies" by Duncan Hines. These would have all sorts of colorful decorations and ingredients such as M&M's and candies, so that moms and kids could spend quality time in the kitchen together making fun and colorful cookies. The meeting was a love-in, and everyone walked away feeling like this was a partnership made in heaven.

We immediately began making plans to develop the products and packaging and launch them into a test market. We anticipated that these new product lines could grow the Duncan Hines cookie mix business significantly. Unfortunately, we hit a bump in the road shortly thereafter that derailed our plans. Mrs. Field's attorney demanded a one million dollar up-front licensing fee from P&G in order for us to execute a test market. The dollars were completely unreasonable and couldn't be negotiated down, so the idea was tossed into the trashcan and we moved on. It is a crying shame that these products never made it to market. They would have been great.

We weren't completely stymied by the Mrs. Field's disaster; we simply rechanneled our efforts into a licensed line for Duncan Hines Cake Mix. The Procter & Gamble Invention Team developed a proprietary disposable paper-baking pan in which "shaped" cakes could be made at home without the use of expensive metal pans. The shapes could be anything we could imagine; a simple heart, a baseball field, a football or the face of a cartoon character. As the brand team developed the concept, we found that consumer demand increased significantly when the cakes featured popular licensed kids' characters and major league sports properties.

We went about putting together an array of licenses with several different licensors -- a fascinating process. We decided to make our first stop at The Muppet Mansion in New York City to meet with Jim Henson and discuss the opportunity to license Kermit Cakes and Miss Piggy Cakes. P&G had approached Henson a year before with the idea for licensing and creating a brand of kids soft drinks called Muppets Soda -- Kermit Lemon-Lime, Miss Piggy Pink Lemonade, Fozzie Bear Orange Soda, etc. Although Henson thought the idea was cute, he declined the offer, saying that he's always held the position that you don't eat the characters. He'd been approached in the past with licensing opportunities for everything from Muppet chewing gum, to Kermit Toothpaste, Miss Piggy Twinkies to Muppet Popsicles, but he'd turned down all comers. He admitted that he'd probably tossed millions of dollars of royalties aside by holding the line on his conviction, but that was just the way he felt. He didn't want people eating his characters.

With that knowledge and anticipating rejection, we baked up prototypes of a Kermit Cake and Miss Piggy Cake, loaded them onto a plane to New York, and marched into the mansion. We were shuffled upstairs into the conference room, a stately chamber with deep cherry wood bookcases and a long table extending down the center. Above the head of the table hung a six-foot tall by four foot wide oil painting of Kermit the Frog, and to the left side was a large chair that had appeared in "The Muppet Movie".

When Henson stepped into the room, my boss got right to the point. He said he knew Jim didn't want people to eat his characters, but this idea was such a phenomenal concept that we had to run it by him. His pitch was simple. "These cakes will make every kid's birthday party special," he said. And with that we lifted off the boxes covering the cake prototypes and waited for his reaction.

To our surprise and delight, Henson loved them! He thought the cakes were the coolest things he'd ever seen, and decided to wave his no-eat rule for the very first time. He agreed with our assessment that kids' birthday parties would be great fun with these cakes, and told his licensing folks to cut a deal. We had bagged our first licensor.

We next met with the various people who control the trademark licenses for Garfield, Major League Baseball and the NFL. All agreed to let us license their marks for a cake mix. The deal was simple. Whatever we negotiated with Henson, everyone else would get the identical deal. If at any time any new licensor received more, we'd up the ante for them all. What should have been a nasty and prolonged negotiation wrapped up in just a couple of weeks and we were able to move ahead with production and test marketing of the cakes.

As soon as the cake mixes hit store shelves in the test market, consumers started buying them by the armful. It was one of the most amazing things I've ever witnessed. I'd see a woman loading five or six packages into her cart and I'd ask why she was buying all these cake mixes. The typical response was that these cakes weren't being sold where her kids or grand kids lived, and so she was buying them for upcoming birthday parties for their extended families. The U.S. Postal Service was doing box office business shipping cake mixes around the country. In just three weeks, consumers cleaned off of the store shelves what should have been a six-month supply of mixes -- with absolutely no advertising other than a direct mail flyer to consumers supporting the product introduction.

Marketing Truth

The criteria for identifying and evaluating licensing possibilities are very straightforward. You only need to answer one question: "Will the use of the trademark with this product increase its value to the consumer more than it will cost me to acquire it? If the answer is yes, go for it!

Product Categories That Intelligently Use Licensing

T-shirt manufacturers do most of their business -- and its big business -- through licensing. Nobody wears a blank T-shirt anymore. I have a friend in Atlanta who owns a small T-shirt printing business that does several million dollars of business each year, printing shirts featuring everything from Hooter's Restaurants to NASCAR to Coca-Cola. And he's just a small player.

Hanes is savvy in maximizing the power of the Olympic trademark. Hanes is granted the license to produce all Olympic apparel through the Sara Lee worldwide sponsorship package (Hanes is a subsidiary of Sara Lee). Since Hanes only makes the basic garments and doesn't do any imprinting, it "sub-licenses" the rights to imprint apparel using the Olympic trademarks to different T-shirt imprinters (like my friend in Atlanta). Very smart, as it helps Hanes recoup the cost of its sponsorship through the fees it charges for the sub-licenses from the T-shirt imprinters!

Many video game manufacturers are heavy into licensing. Electronic Arts is one of the best. As the largest producer of sports games, they quickly realized that consumers have a much higher interest in purchasing NBA video games featuring star players and teams than a generic "Basketball" game that doesn't use the trademarks of the NBA or the marquee name players. The same is true of its popular Daytona 500 NASCAR racing game. The licensed trademark brings added consumer value that is much more valuable than the cost of the license. If Electronic Arts didn't acquire the licenses and instead offered just generic sports games, consumers wouldn't buy. They'd go get their games from some other manufacturer who did offer games with the "real" goods -- the official licensed products!

The Key Benefits of Licensing

Licensing offers three key benefits to both the licensor and the licensee:

-- Enhanced brand imagery

-- Increased brand awareness

-- New profit centers

Think of the NBA. By shrewdly licensing the NBA trademarks, team logos and star players to a variety of product categories, the league has created the most powerful licensing business in all of sports. Kids buy NBA apparel on every continent in the world. Most international consumers have never seen a live NBA game, but the imagery the league projects through all of its licensing efforts is that the league apparel is fashionable and desirable. NBA jerseys can be found on the back of some child in nearly every city or town in the world. The NBA licensing program keeps the league in front of consumers 365 days a year, not just during the season. Licensing has created an incredible revenue stream that the league didn't have 15 years ago and has built the NBA brand image.

Marketing Truth

Nearly any business can be grown through licensing. Sometimes it requires out-of-the-box thinking. Who would have imagined an entire section of Taco Bell Mexican foods in grocery stores? Why hasn't Wienerschnitzel licensed its trademark chili to grocers, and licensed its hot dogs to a hot dog manufacturer? Seems like a no-brainer to expand and grow the brand!

I have a DVD in my office created by a company called Creative Multimedia that is a complete guide to Hollywood movies and videos. It contains over 23,000 movie reviews encompassing 65 years, along with video clips, vintage photographs, and a variety of other features. A nice informative disk. Now it's quiz time. Which has a higher perceived value and more authenticity to you as a consumer -- "Creative Multimedia's Ultimate Guide To Movies & Videos", or "The Academy Awards Guide to Movies & Videos"? I hope you selected the latter. Since the Academy awards is synonymous with movies, it makes perfect sense to license their name to increase the perceived consumer value of the disk. That's the power of licensing.

I know it's tough to get moving when you are venturing into unknown territory such as the world of licensing. It's much more comfortable to sit around and procrastinate. It's kind of like your friends who didn't go to college who sit back and say "I know I would have been a doctor if I had been able to go", or "I was going to be a doctor but the professors didn't like me and gave me bad grades." My Mom has a favorite saying for folks like this: "If *ifs* and *buts* were candy and nuts, everyday would be Christmas." The moral is to stop thinking about what you could have done and start doing! Get off the dime and start hunting up licensing opportunities. They are all around you if you only look.

THE SMART MARKETER'S TOOLBOX

BONUS CHAPTER

★★★★★★★

Eric D Schulz

Chapter Twenty-One

Effective Job Interviewing Skills

Over the years, I have been asked regularly "How did a guy like you get all those cool jobs?" What they were really saying was "Look, you're not the sharpest tool in the shed. How the heck did you bluff you way through all those interviews to land those great gigs? What did you do to separate yourself from the pack?"

What I've found is that interviewing it is very simple. Do you remember Stuart Smalley, the "Daily Affirmation" character that Senator Al Franken (Minnesota) used to perform on Saturday Night Live? Stuart was a member of 7 twelve-step programs, and he had a lot of challenges in his life. But he kept a positive spirit and his head up, and he would begin each day by getting smartly dressed, looking at himself in the mirror, and saying "I'm good enough; I'm smart enough; and dog-gone it, people like me".

As it turns out, those three things are precisely what you need to communicate in a job interview, along with one more: I get things done. In every job interview, if you can communicate these four things, you are way ahead of the game:

> I'm good enough
>
> I'm smart enough
>
> Dog-gone it, people like me
>
> I get things done

So how do you manage an interview to ensure that you have the opportunity to communicate these things? You certainly can't leave it up to chance. You can't sit back and hope that the interviewer asks the right questions to let you put out your best answers. YOU have to manage the interview. And here's another insight: if you prepare correctly, it doesn't matter what questions they ask you, because you're going to have the right STORY prepared to respond correctly in any situation.

There are really only three true job interview questions. They can be ask in a whole variety of different ways. But in the end, the three questions are very simple:

1. **Can you do the job?** Do you have the intelligence, the skills and strengths to do this job effectively?

2. **Will you love the job?** Is this something that you'll want to get up every morning and get after it? Do you have the motivation?

3. **Can we tolerate working with you?** Are you going to fit well within our organization?

Interviewers will ask you a whole variety of questions, but at the end of the day, it all boils down to these three queries.

Interview Preparation Is the Key

In order for you to effectively manage an interview, communicate that you're good enough, smart enough, that people like you and you get things done; and that you have the skills to do the job, will love doing the job, and I'm a good person that will be an asset to your organization, you have to prepare for your interview the same way actors prepare for a Broadway show.

We've all been to the theatre. The actors speak their parts in a way that sound like the conversation is completely spontaneous; like it's the first time their lips have ever uttered these words. But the truth is that the actors have rehearsed these lines thousands upon thousands of times, and perfected their delivery of the lines in such a way that it sounds completely spontaneous.

In order to prepare for a job interview, you have to PREPARE just as a Broadway actor does. A job interview is not the place to be winging it. Every word out of your mouth needs to have been carefully thought through and practiced. You need to prepare STORIES from your life that communicates your key attributes WITHOUT you having to say them literally.

Common Interview Blunders

Most job seekers fail to properly prepare for interviews. They walk in and create their answers on the fly. Don't do that!

Have THREE STORIES prepared and rehearsed that communicate all the wonderful assets you bring to the table, the things that make you different, better and special. No matter what the interviewer asks, just start telling your stories, because if you have your stories built and rehearsed correctly, they will communicate whatever the interviewer asked.

First Impression is Key

They say that first impressions are made in the first three seconds, and that is absolutely true. The interviewer will have begun forming an opinion of you before a single word comes out of your mouth – which means APPEARANCE IS EVERYTHING! You need to be in your best threads, dressed to the nines, hair perfectly coifed. It doesn't matter if the place you are interviewing has a casual dress code. YOU need to dress as if this is the most important day of your life (and in some cases that may very well be true.)

Ladies, get your hair done. Men, get a haircut. Men, your shoes need to be spit-shined – and I'm not kidding. Your shoes will be scrutinized. Ladies, you need to be dressed appropriately for the workplace, (no revealing necklines or short skirts) and for both men and women - DO NOT WEAR PURFUME OR COLOGNE.

As you approach the interviewer, you need to look him or her straight in the eye, exude a sense of self-confidence in your voice and SMILE! Greet the interviewer introduce yourself, and offer a firm handshake. The handshake needs to be firm, not bone-crushing!

Smiling is KEY! You don't want your first impression to be that you're not friendly. And make sure your confidence doesn't come off as cocky. There's a difference.

Take A Seat

When you sit down, DO NOT MAKE YOURSELF COMFORTABLE! Do not sit back in the chair relaxed. Don't cross your legs. Sit on the forward edge of the chair, with both feet on the floor, directly facing the interviewer.

Big Opening Number

Every Broadway show begins with a big opening number. Your interview needs to do so as well. You want to come out with all your guns blazing, so you need to have your tongue warmed up and be ready to roll.

Often times the interviewer will start out with a question like,"Tell me a little about yourself." Go ahead and give a brief employment background, where you are from, and your education. For example:

> "I grew up in Utah, and have an MBA from Brigham Young University. I've had an interesting career, working in consumer-packaged goods for Procter & Gamble, The Walt Disney Company, and Coca-Cola. At Coke I was in charge of Worldwide Olympic marketing for the 1996 Summer Games in Atlanta, the biggest marketing program ever executed by Coke. Following the Olympics I shifted into entertainment marketing, serving as VP of Marketing for Ringling Bros. & Barnum and Bailey Circus, and in 2001 worked with NBC and Vince McMahon at World Wrestling Entertainment to develop and launch the XFL Football League. The XFL only existed for one season, and following that I moved back to Utah and started up a preschool with my wife, and began teaching marketing courses at both BYU and The University of Utah, both undergraduate and in their MBA programs. In 2005 the Utah Jazz contacted me about coming on board to head the marketing for the team and other entities in their sports and entertainment group, which I did until 2011. From there I moved into what is now my third career, teaching full-time at Utah State University in the Jon M. Huntsman School of Business."

Notice the tone. Factual. Not braggadocio. I offered a succinct review of my past. But what did I communicate without having to say a word?

- Guy has worked for some of the top companies in the world
- Has consumer product, entertainment, and sports marketing background, as well as entrepreneurial skills
- Global marketing experience
- He must be a pretty smart marketer if he has taught MBA-level marketing classes at three major universities
- Has launched new brands (XFL)
- Senior management experience
- Seems to have good communication skills

Now we're off and running. The chase has begun.

So then the interviewer often asks, "tell me about a time where.... you were innovative... you overcame a challenge... you developed a plan.... it can be any of these, it doesn't matter which. You have your first story cued up in your brain and get ready to start storytelling! If you have crafted the right kind of story, it will address whatever question the interviewer asks. Here's one story that I would always tell:

> My first real innovation challenge came to me in the final days of my MBA program. I was invited to visit Cincinnati and interview with P&G on the last day of final exams. I had two tests scheduled for that day, both taught ironically by the same professor.
>
> So I went to Dr. Schill and explained the situation: "I need to go to Cincinnati that day, and so what can I do to make up the finals?" Both were "Harvard case discussion" exams to be held in-class. "Could I do a write-up on each case? Could I come into your office and discuss the cases one-on-one?"
>
> Dr. Schill replied, "In order for you to get your final grade for the course, you must participate in the final case discussion." "But I have to go to Cincinnati," I replied. "Not my issue," he said. "In order for you to get your final grade for the course, you must participate in the final case discussion."
>
> I was stunned. I had a choice to make. I could try to reschedule with P&G, or blow off the finals and see what happens? How in

the world could I participate in a case discussion while interviewing in Cincinnati?

This seemed like a no-win situation, but I thought back to a story told in the Star Trek movies about how Captain Kirk overcame a similar problem.

There was a computer simulator program called the Kobayashi Maru that all Star-Fleet academy cadets had to complete. The test was considered a no-win scenario because it was impossible for the cadet to simultaneously save the *Kobayashi Maru*, avoid a fight with the Klingons and escape from the neutral zone with the starship intact. Kirk refused to believe in the 'no-win" scenario, so the night before his test, he reprogrammed the simulator to provide a path in which he could win.

So I put on my thinking cap and pondered "How can I create a win-win situation that would allow me to be in Cincinnati, yet simultaneously participate in the final case discussion in Utah."? Remember, this was long before the Internet and SKYPE or Facetime. There were no video conferencing alternatives. There were no phone connections inside the classrooms. There were no cell phones.

The solution I came up with? I rented a video camera and videotaped myself discussing a particular section of each Harvard case. Then I arranged with all of my classmates that when that particular part of the final exam discussion came around, all of them would raise their hands together and whoever was called upon would say "Eric would like to discuss that," and another classmate would plug a tape into the VCR and voila, I was in the classroom, discussing the case, while simultaneously going through my interviews in Cincinnati."

So, what did that story communicate to the interviewer?

- Innovative, creative thinker (Good enough)
- Problem solver (Good enough)
- Proactive (Good enough)

- Not afraid to take a calculated risk (Smart enough)
- Creates win-win situations out of no-win situations (Smart enough)
- Convinced classmates to assist (People like me)
- Conceived and executed the plan (Get's things done)

That my friends, is how you land great jobs. You tell great stories of what makes you different, better, and special.

Rehearse Your Stories HUNDREDS of Times

Over the years, I've probably interviewed 200 or so candidates for positions that I was hiring for. And I've seen so many mistakes made. But the first and most critical mistake is that they don't have stories prepared! They sit there and try to react on the fly (not a success strategy), and by doing so, they don't communicate their unique benefits very effectively.

The truth is, if you have done your homework, if you've got your stories right, you will have practiced the telling of that story hundreds of times BEFORE you told it to that interviewer. The story will sound completely spontaneous – just like a Broadway show. And you will have a HUGE advantage over the guy who's answering on the fly. You have to have THREE stories from your past that without you having to say it, communicate that you are good enough, I'm smart enough, people like me and I get things done.

Another question often asked is "Tell me about a time when you had a problem that you needed to solve quickly, and what did you do?" Here's the story I have for that question:

> When I was about to begin my position with the Jazz organization, one of the brands I was responsible for was the Salt Lake Bees, the Triple-A affiliate of the Los Angeles Angels, which the Jazz group also owned.
>
> I was going to start my job on Monday, but the day before I decided to go to the Bees game just to get a sense of what was going on at the ballpark and to maybe get some ideas. It was a beautiful Sunday afternoon in early May. Seventy-five degrees,

sunny, and not a cloud in the sky. And as I looked around the ballpark, there were about 500 fans in the entire stadium!

"How could this be? How could there only be five-hundred people here on a perfect day to watch baseball?" So I went home that night and started pondering ideas to jump-start attendance at the ballpark. I discovered the next morning that the team was only averaging about 1,000 fans per game, and that Sunday's were the worst day for attendance.

I thought back to my days at P&G and wondered "If we had low sales for a product, what would we do to try to get it in more people's hands?" The answer: conduct a sampling program. You put the product in people's hands, you let them try it and see how wonderful it really is, and then they'll come back and buy it.

But how do you sample a baseball game? I suppose you could just open the gates and invite everyone in for free. But that idea caused heartburn with the ticket sales teams who had season ticket holders and groups they had sold that would demand refunds if we opened up the gates, they claimed. There were 363 seats sold as season tickets. There were three groups sold for the upcoming home stand of seven games. "What if we write a letter to the season ticket holders, telling them what we are doing and why, and send them free tickets to hand out to their friends and family as well as a couple of free hot-dog and soft drink coupons", I proposed as a way to alleviate the season ticket holder concerns. "And what if we offer the groups that are coming another free group night later in the year as their make-good. Would that make everybody happy?" I asked. The ticket team agreed, and so I quickly developed a plan to create a "Free Family Fun" Home stand where any family could come enjoy a game for free.

To execute the plan, advertising was created with the team owner, Larry Miller (who also owned 29 car dealerships in Salt Lake City, in addition to the Utah Jazz, a movie theatre chain, a motorsports park, a TV station and radio station). Mr. Miller personally offered every family the chance to come to the park for free (giving him a "nice guy" halo effect for his other business entities). To get their free tickets, fans just had to go online to the team website and fill out a long form that captured family names, birthdays, ages, demographics, addresses, emails and phone numbers. By having the names and birthdays, I could then send little Sally a free ticket for her birthday, and how many tickets will I sell because I gave on to Sally? The rest of the family will have to buy a ticket. This built a fan database from zero names to over 75,000 families within a week, which we then were able to use for remarketing purposes for the next several years.

We executed the plan for a week, putting over 15,000 fans into the park for every game. Our projected attendance had we not done the promotion was about 18,000 people over the seven nights. Instead, we put 85,000 fans into the ballpark. We sold over a quarter-million dollars of food and concessions. But importantly, from that week on, attendance averaged over 5,000 fans per game and has continued to build for the past five seasons.

So when I tell that story, what did it communicate?

- Problem solver
- Cross-pollinates ideas from earlier marketing roots
- Looking out for betterment of the entire organization
- Creative
- Analytical
- Knows his math
- Strategic
- Cool under pressure

Advance the Storyline

If you have crafted your stories correctly, after you have told all three, you have communicated effectively over a dozen factors that demonstrate your abilities and how you have differentiated yourself from the sea-of-sameness.

The stories have to SELL YOU. They need to answer the fundamental fit questions – "Is this the kind of person that I could work with?" If you are aware of critical feedback that you've received in the past, are you ensuring that you've effectively neutralized the criticism? If you have these issues, use your third story to overcome these possible complaints.

Beware Trap Questions

Savvy interviewers often have a few trick questions up their sleeves that they use to catch candidates off-guard. "Tell Me About Yourself" could be a trap question if you are winging it, as you won't have any strategic rationale for what is coming out of your mouth, and likely will be unfocused blabber. "What are your weaknesses" is a huge trap question. I've had people tell me that they have a hard time getting up in the morning! Let's hire him! Another trap question is "What is your five-year plan?" Answer that wrong and you've just shot yourself in the foot. "I plan on working here for two years then going off to grad school" isn't going to land you any jobs. Sometimes when you answer one of these trap questions, you say the right thing but you give off a vibe with your body language or voice inflection that cast doubt on your sincerity.

"Tell me your weaknesses" is almost always asked. This question is a great opportunity to recast a supposed "weakness" into strength. They way I always answer this (and yes, you can steal it) is:

> My biggest weakness is that I think too much. I analyze everything. I'm always analyzing from a marketing perspective, from commercials I see on TV to brands I encounter in stores or on billboards, or online. When I see something crazy, it drives me nuts, and so my brains usually starts thinking of how to fix the marketing for this poor lost brand. Most of it happens at night. My brain never stops, and I've developed marketing plans for hundreds upon hundreds of brands through my lifetime that I've never worked on or consulted for, but just because that's the way I'm wired I guess.

Did I really just admit a weakness? No, not at all.

Don't Talk About Personal Issues

Leave your personal issues at the door. Don't bring up your divorce, or your home situation. They can't ask about it (it is illegal) but I've had dozens of candidates I've interviewed over the years crack open this can of worms all by themselves.

Example: "I'm a single mom and just getting back into the workforce. My ex husband...." NOOOO! Don't go there. I don't want to hear about your bitter divorce battle. You have just put a fork in yourself. You're done.

What Questions Do YOU Have?

Usually towards the end of the interview, you will be asked, "What questions do YOU have for me?" DO NOT say "Nothing". Have at least TWO good, smart questions prepared that demonstrate you are interested in the company and the position. You want to use those questions to "WOW" them.

Here's a tip: Once you know you are going to be interviewing with a company, go online and in Google, type "Google Alerts". Google Alerts is a free service offered by Google that most people have no idea exists. What it does is it allows you to load in a search term, in this case the "company name", and every time something new about that company pops up on the web, it will send you an email link to it. If you want to dazzle and amaze your interviewer, be up to speed on the latest developments from the company on the morning you interviewed, and ask a question about that. You'll get BIG brownie points!

Questions You DON'T ASK!

Do not ask about salary, compensation, benefits, or anything related to it! When do you talk about money? NOT NOW! It is completely irrelevant until they have offered you the position. You talk money AFTER you have been made an offer, and not until.

Sometimes they will open that door and ask you about where you are salary-wise. This is dangerous territory. Go too high and you can shoot yourself in the foot. Go too low and you hose yourself. One way to handle it is to say something like: "I would feel more comfortable if we could defer that question right now. If you like me and I like you, we'll find a way to make it work for both of us. So if you are OK with that, I'd rather put that off until we know that you and I are the right fit for each other. If they press you for a number, one resource you can use is Salary.com, which is a good place to find out average entry-level salaries for your job in your locale.

Be Nice To EVERYBODY!

You need to make sure that you are nice and interact with every single person that you come in contact with at their organization…from the driver to the door man to the administrative assistant along with everyone you interview with. Here's a big secret. Sometimes the tiebreakers are the little people. Sometimes the hiring manager is on the fence, and can't decide, and will go walking around and talk to everyone that had contact with the candidate. If you sat in the lobby and played with your mobile phone while you were waiting to see the hiring manager and didn't have a conversation with the administrative assistant instead, guess what their feedback will be. "He just sat and answered emails on his phone. I didn't really talk to him". Bad move. You want the answer to be "What a nice guy. We had a great conversation".

Be a Closer!

In sales, it's called closing the deal. How do you get a sale? You ask for it! The same goes with jobs. At the end of the interview, you need to be in closer mode. Here is where you conjure up the big finish! Here is where you really show your motivation for the job! One of the things you want to do for the big finish involves several verbal and non-verbal cues. Scoot up on the front edge of your chair, almost to the point of falling off. Start talking a little faster as you communicate that you really would love to have this job, that it's precisely what I want to do, and that I'd love doing it with your company. Use your hands to help communicate. Use facial expressions. Use tone inflection. Ramp up the excitement! Show enthusiasm and motivation!

After the Interview

After the interview, prepare a nice, hand-written note to every single person you touched while inside the offices – from the doorman to the president. Do not send emails! Hand-written notes only, expressing your thanks to them and again expressing your hope that you'll soon be working with them. Make sure the tone is enthusiastic and energetic.

Follow-Up

Usually at the end of the interview you can ask for a timeline. "When do you expect to make a decision?", or "When should I expect to hear back from you?" Ask if it's OK if you can follow-up with a phone call at some point if you haven't heard back. For example "Would it be OK if I followed up with you next Friday if I haven't heard back by then?"

Don't assume not hearing back as an automatic doomsday scenario. Sometimes people get busy and forget. Sometimes they are waiting for someone's approval in order to extend you the offer. Follow-up, with enthusiasm and energy. Sometimes that little nudge is what it takes to get the offer.

Use Every Interview as a Learning Experience

After every job interview, sit down and analyze what happened. What did you do really well? What didn't go so well? What could you have done differently? Effective job interviewing is an acquired skill. Only through practice and refinement can you improve performance. The good news is that learning to interview well can significantly accelerate your career path and earnings potential. Use these tips to define and refine your skills, and go get that dream job!

ABOUT THE AUTHOR

The Smart Marketer's Toolbox is written by Eric D. Schulz, a 25-year marketing veteran of Procter & Gamble, The Coca-Cola Company, The Walt Disney Company, consultant to several Fortune 500 corporations and now a marketing professor at the Jon M. Huntsman School of Business at Utah State University.

In preparing this book, Schulz has analyzed hundreds of brands in dozens of product categories to synthesize this learning into easy to follow principles and strategies. His conversation-like writing boils down the information into easy-to-execute, down-to-earth insights which can be understood and utilized by anyone. Schulz previously authored "*The Marketing Game, How The World's Best Companies Play to Win*", a marketing textbook that has been used in many of the top business schools around the world.

I hope you found some nuggets of wisdom that you can use to jump-start your marketing. Feel free to contact me with any questions or thoughts through my website – www.ericschulz.com. I love hearing from readers – especially success stories!

Cheers!

Eric Schulz

eric@ericschulz.com

(801) 369-8509 mobile

http://www.ericschulz.com

I am always accepting new consulting clients, large and small!

THE SMART MARKETER'S TOOLBOX

Made in the USA
Lexington, KY
21 January 2013